Community-Based Ethnography:
Breaking Traditional Boundaries
of Research, Teaching,
and Learning

Community-Based Ethnography: Breaking Traditional Boundaries of Research, Teaching, and Learning

Ernie Stringer
Mary Frances Agnello
Shelia Conant Baldwin
Lois McFayden Christensen
Deana Lee Philbrook Henry
Kenneth Ivan Henry
Terresa Payne Katt
Patricia Gathman Nason
Vicky Newman
Rhonda Petty
Patsy S. Tinsley-Batson

LEA LAWRENCE ERLBAUM ASSOCIATES, PUBLISHERS
1997 Mahwah, New Jersey   London

Lawrence Erlbaum Associates, Inc., Publishers
10 Industrial Avenue
Mahwah, New Jersey 07430

Library of Congress Cataloging-in-Publication-Data

Community-based ethnography : breaking traditional boundaries of research, teaching, and learning / Ernie Stringer . . . [et al.].
        p. cm.
    Includes bibliographic references and index.
    ISBN 0-8058-2290-9 (alk. paper). — ISBN 0-8058-2291-7 (pbk. : alk. paper)
    1. Ethnology—Methodology. 2. Ethnology—Research. 3. Community development. 4. Action research. I. Stringer, Ernest T.
    GN345.C643 1997
    305.8 dc21   97-9208
                                                          CIP

Books published by Lawrence Erlbaum Associates are printed on acid-free paper, and their bindings are chosen for strength and durability.

Printed in the United States of America
10 9 8 7 6 5 4 3 2 1

Contents

Preface

CONTEXT AND CONTENT

The genesis of this book is in a series of graduate courses I taught at Texas A&M University in 1993–1994. I was in the United States to study the theoretical underpinnings of the qualitative research methods that were an integral part of the community development practices my colleagues and I had formulated at the Centre for Aboriginal Studies at Curtin University in West Australia. The courses I taught in Texas stemmed from my experience in a wide range of Australian organizational and educational contexts and enacted community development as both pedagogical process and research method.

My first course, Community-Based Ethnography, was presented in the spring semester of 1993 to a class of 18 students; it was so well received that I was asked to teach a similar course, Qualitative Research for Educators, in the summer term of that year. Fifteen students, including some who had attended the first course, enrolled for the second. Each course was structured to teach qualitative research methods, contextualized as both community building and action research. The accounts presented by Shelia Baldwin, Lois Christensen, Deana Henry, Kenneth Henry, Terresa Katt, Vicky Newman, Rhonda Petty, and Patsy Tinsley-Batson relate to the first spring semester, class, although Vicky, Kenneth, and Deana also participated in the summer term class along with Mary Frances Agnello and Patricia Nason. Readers may find it fruitful to compare and contrast the various interpretations of these experiences, revealing as they do the ways that the same or similar events can be represented in such different ways.

The process of exploring the academic and practical dimensions of this approach to research was so productive that 12 students from the previous class attended an advanced methods class I offered in the fall semester of 1993. The major purpose of this class was to investigate further the methodological and philosophical issues related to "the writing of text" that had emerged in the previous classes. Most papers produced in that advanced methods class are included in this book. They are the outcome of our attempts to come to grips with fundamental issues about writing narrative accounts purporting to represent aspects of people's lives.

The fundamental project, around which our explorations in writing textual accounts turned, derived from my initial ethnographic question: "Tell me about the [previous] class we did together." This exercise proved to be particularly rich; it brought into the arena all of the problems related to choice of data, analysis of data, structure of the account, author's stance, tense, case, adequacy of the account, and so on.

As participants struggled to formulate their accounts they were constantly confronted with questions such as, "Does this account tell what the experience was really like?" "What was it like for me?" "What are the key features of the class that can enable readers to understand our experience?" "Is this a biography or an ethnography? And what is the difference?" As they shared versions of their accounts and struggled to analyze the wealth of data they had accumulated in the previous classes—products of in-class observations, interviews, and so on—they became aware of the ephemeral nature of narrative accounts. Reality as written in textual form cannot capture the depth, breadth, and complexity of an actual lived experience; it can be only an incomplete representation arising from the author's interpretive imagination.

The final chapter results from my discussions with the contributing authors, including a final visit in April 1996 during which each author briefly revisited the text, then, in dialogue with others and myself identified the elements for an overall framework to represent "the big message" of the book. In this way we attempted to provide a conceptual context that would indicate ways in which our private experiences could be seen to be relevant to the broader public arenas in which education and research are engaged.

The book can therefore be read in several ways. It may be read as a series of case studies of ethnographic writing that show different ways neophyte ethnographers write their experience of the world or, more specifically, their experience of a research methods class. Such a reading focuses on the techniques of ethnographic research revealed in each chapter.

The book may also be read as a description of pedagogical process or as an account of teaching research methods. In this reading readers focus on the instructional techniques, learning processes, or classroom activities revealed in each contribution. The accounts, however, should not be read as an illustration of best teaching practice, excellence, or exemplary practice; they depict approaches to pedagogy and research that resonate with the authors' perspectives or professional viewpoints. Although formal student evaluations provided exceptionally high scores for the instructor, the perspectives of people whose professional styles were intrinsically directive, or whose career paths in hierarchical institutions were not served by the inherently egalitarian ethos of community-based research do not feature in this book. As Vicky's account shows, there are inherent contradictions between a community-based approach to educational life and the common structures and processes of classroom life.

The book may also be read as a postmodern text, a collage or montage of ideas presented as a polyphonic account of the class. Because this approach is, indeed, one of the purposes of the volume, I have attempted to keep my editorial voice to a minimum and have desisted from impulses to "extend," "clarify," or add comment to "fill in the gaps" or to tell what "really" happened. Each contribution stands in its own right as a legitimate authentic account of one of the first two classes. Readers can select and interpret these accounts as they will.

Introductory comments in the first and last chapters move away from this editorial philosophy, as much because of the current geographical distance between the authors as from the desire to frame the accounts in a particular way. Although we formulated the first and last chapters dialogically and "member checked" their content on several occasions, they remain, ultimately, the editor's own creation. The ways in which the chapters have been edited and ordered are my ways of providing structure to our collaborative work.

In my editorial capacity, I framed the narrative in the broader context of the current ethos of social, educational, and academic life. In keeping with Wright Mills's dictum to link private and public, the book speaks to the context of a world where postmodern, critical and feminist writing have become key elements of the academic landscape. The introductory and final chapters, therefore, signify the links between the voices of the contributing authors and the broader social, educational, and academic arena.

METHODOLOGY

In its entirety the book presents an interpretive study of teaching and learning, a multivoice or polyphonic account that reveals how problematic, turning point experiences in a university class are perceived, organized, constructed, and given meaning by a group of interacting individuals. Technically, the accounts derive from steps to interpretation suggested by Denzin (1989) that include:

Framing, where "teaching and research" are located within the personal histories of the participants and interpreted in the educational, organizational, and community contexts that are the sites of their professional lives.

Deconstruction, in which previous conceptions, definitions, observations, and analyses of "teaching and learning" are laid bare and critically analyzed.

Capturing, in which "teaching and research" are situated in the natural world by securing multiple personal and self-stories that locate crises and epiphanies within the experiences of the subject-participants.

Bracketing, in which the participants' experiences of "teaching and research" are held up for serious inspection and are taken apart to reveal their key elements and essential structures or features.

Construction, in which the bracketed elements are classified, ordered, and reassembled in a coherent account that re-creates the way that participants experience and interpret "teaching and research."

Contextualization, in which the participants' interpretive accounts are located in the broader social world where "teaching and research" are enacted, so that the main themes are synthesized, compared, and contrasted with existing interpretations of teaching and research.

To some extent we have played creatively with Denzin's framework and have modified it to fit the demands of the teaching, learning, and research agendas of this complex, reflexive process of inquiry. Because of the poly-phonic nature of the text, for instance, the interpretive processes are not linear; each contributor enacts them distinctively and adds new lights or lenses that shade, nuance, and focus the emerging picture. We have also disrupted the accepted practice of "reviewing the literature" in the earlier stages of the study; we wished to guard against the possibility that predetermined views would work to pollute our considerations and turn them toward preconceived ideas in the literature.

STRUCTURE OF THE BOOK

The book's structure reflects its origin in research practice. Chapter 1 presents the social, professional, and academic contexts of teaching and research; shows how the focus of the book is relevant to a variety of teaching–learning contexts, and reveals the methods employed in the investigation from which the book was derived.

Chapter 2 presents the perspective of the instructor-research facilitator. It provides an account of the ways in which I enacted a collaborative, reflective approach to teaching as a means for modeling a community based approach to research.

Chapters 3–12 present perspectives on this process by focusing variously on the participant responses to this approach to teaching and research. Chapters by Deana Henry, Kenneth Henry, and Patricia Nason highlight the impact of the instructional processes. Vicky Newman wrestles with the contradictions inherent in these processes and shows how the history of institutional practice tends to reproduce itself through the responses of the actors in the setting. Mary Frances Agnello and Lois Christensen present their perspectives of the outcomes of their experiences; Terresa Katt shows how the experience is relevant in a biographical sense, in the way it fits into the movements of her life. Rhonda Petty, also in biographical mode, presents a vivid account of the pitfalls and possibilities of ethnographic work, and shows the revelatory and epiphanic possibilities inherent in research that actually touches real-life settings. Patsy Tinsley and Shelia Baldwin present accounts of how the research process they enacted in class spilled out into their work lives and became part of their professional experiences. Teaching and learning, they discovered, can easily become directly relevant to everyday life.

The final chapter is based on key elements that were nominated by each contributor and "analyzed" by me after extensive discussions that followed the authors' reading of the complete text. This chapter provides an interpretation of the accounts, which places them in the broader academic and philosophic context of our time.

ACKNOWLEDGMENTS

I gratefully acknowledge Jim Kracht who, as then head of the Department of Curriculum and Instruction, provided the opportunity for the class in community-based ethnography to be taught at Texas A&M University. I also wish to thank my friends and colleagues at the College of Education whose welcoming hospitality made my time there so enjoyable.

Acknowledgments are also due to my partner, Rosalie Dwyer, who was deprived of my company during the long months when I was absorbed in the demanding process of writing and editing. I also wish to acknowledge the work of Sari Hosie, whose editorial advice provided clarity and direction to the process of constructing a book from a disparate collection of accounts; and to Catherine Vann, for the hours of detailed work required to bring a rather patchy text up to publication standards.

Thanks are also due to the reviewers at Lawrence Erlbaum Associates, Walter Ullrich of St. Cloud State University, and John C. Stansell of Texas A&M University, whose meticulous work sharpened and refined the text. Their efforts in considerably raising the quality of our writing should be appreciated by readers.

Finally, I acknowledge the authors themselves, a living community who represent, in their professional lives, the spirit from which this book grew. Their collective minds fill these pages and infuse them with the energy and vitality that made our experiences of living and learning together so very special. I thank them all.

—Ernie Stringer

1

Reinterpreting Teaching

Ernie Stringer

Conventional instruction is based on the premise that knowledge can be transmitted and contrasts strikingly with Dewey's (1916/1966) description of an effective learning environment: "Any social arrangement that remains vitally social, or vitally shared, is educative to those who participate in it."
—Lois McFayden Christensen, chapter 4

Disciplined by the educational system, we internalize the concept of success and how success is often defined in the educational institution, i.e., connected with negative concepts of power such as domination, control, and competition, and with the subsequent encoded desire to reproduce these models.
—Vicky Newman, chapter 9

Our system of schooling perpetuates [the view of] teacher as transmitter of knowledge to students whose perspectives are rarely considered.
—Shelia Conant Baldwin, chapter 10

This university is too traditional, structured. It is like stuffed shirt city. ... I like helping people take action, empowerment, helping them help themselves.
—Lois McFayden Christensen, in Deana Lee Philbrook Henry, chapter 8

Older, authoritarian styles of leadership are being replaced by participatory, democratic processes ... so that there is more discussion about shared authority ... that complements a continuing debate in education about the efficacy or desirability of collaborative and constructivist approaches to research and learning.
—Deana Lee Philbrook Henry, chapter 8

The group research processes encountered in a graduate research class proved to be different from the sterile, text-bound and solitary experiences graduate students often encounter in their educational careers.
—Mary Francis Agnello, chapter 7

I [was] able to stand my ground when confronted by the bureaucrats who arrived at my classroom door with the truth carved in curriculum documents of stone. My professional life fluctuated between the incredible power and excitement in my classroom ... as I watched children learn in ways perceived to be blasphemous. [I also felt] incredible frustration and mounting anger at my

professional peers, who believed they had discovered the truth about ways to
teach children and were ordering me to be faithful to the canon.

—Terresa Payne Katt, chapter 12

Universities and schools in general teach the learner that collaboration is
cheating, unprofitable, unfair and unproductive.

—Patricia Gathman Nason, chapter 6

PERSPECTIVES ON TEACHING AND LEARNING

We commenced writing this book as part of a process of inquiry initiated in a
graduate research methods class. Although the initial focus of our investigation
was unclear, it became apparent that although each of us was talking about
different things, an area of commonality pervaded our reflections and our
writing. Some of us were talking about writing the text, the seemingly simple
process of narrative production that turns out to be a rather unwieldy
instrument for capturing human experience. Others were talking about research, a process of exploration and discovery that enables people to understand the problems they are experiencing. Yet others of us were directly
engaged with the problems of teaching and learning in classroom environments; still others explored the implications of our research experiences for
the corporate world or for community development work.

The eventual transition of this text to an exploration of teaching and
learning, therefore, takes into account our various perspectives. Although we
all have significantly transformed our thinking about the processes of teaching
and learning, we each apply the thinking in different ways, according to the
particular arenas in which we work. This book tends to focus on institutionalized educational contexts like schools and universities, but teaching is an
activity that must be broadly conceived as a process of facilitating learning, an
activity that occurs in a variety of ways in a variety of contexts. Parents can be
seen as teachers of their children, researchers as teachers of the research
audiences, organizational development consultants as teachers of their client
organizations, and community development workers as teachers of the communities in which they carry out their work.

Our focus on teaching, therefore, must be read with these contexts in mind,
for our explorations of teaching in a university research class led us to
understand it in a very different way. As dedicated professionals we now
experience teaching as something more akin to a calling. This notion refers to
an era when teaching was less subject to the intense, objective scrutiny of
positivistic science and was defined more broadly than is possible within the
strictures and processes of the contemporary approach to knowledge production. We do not wish to deny the utility of such an approach, but our writing
has been constructed through a rather different method of investigation. As
becomes clearer as the text progresses, the perspectives revealed in this book
are derived from thorough, rigorous, reflective processes of investigation,

which are themselves the product of teaching—a process of facilitating learning.

IS THERE A PROBLEM WITH TEACHING?

We write at a time when schools and other educational institutions are almost in a state of siege. Education systems in many parts of the world have been subject to a continuous series of attacks for several decades. In the United States education has been blamed for the nation's failure to place a satellite in space ahead of the Soviet Union, for national economic decline, rising crime rates, increasing poverty, teenage pregnancies, unemployment, drug abuse, the decline of the family, and a host of other ills that accompany modern social, economic, and political change. Political pressures to hold educational institutions accountable for these widespread changes in the social fabric of modern societies have led to an almost continuous procession of reports and papers on the organization and operation of schools, the structures of educational funding, the processes of teacher education, and so on.

As a central component of the educational process, teaching has been subject to intense scrutiny. The research literature on teaching is now voluminous and ranges from an extensive overview provided by the massive *Handbook of Research on Teaching*, through many volumes of academic texts about teaching, to a veritable mountain of journal articles that speak to various aspects of the profession. Most literature is drawn from experimental studies that, especially in recent decades, endeavor to determine which elusive qualities might reveal the "best" or "exemplary" teaching practices. The outcomes of the search for the "foundational assumptions" of teaching have been neither unequivocal nor fruitful, to judge from the conflicting outcomes of experimental literature or the public perceptions of schooling and teaching. Education today is perceived to be more problematic than ever, and academic investigations, legislative inquiries, and media reports continue to decry the quality of teaching.

In a social context that valorizes "accountability" and "performance targets," there are increasing pressures to specify the characteristics of the good teacher and, in some instances, to legislatively mandate that these characteristics be included in teacher education programs. Attempts to reduce teaching to a fixed set of testable competencies have been accompanied by an increasing tendency to monitor the outcomes of the teaching process through state and national tests that have the well-meant but misplaced intent to insure that all children get a "good education." In response to these pressures, many teachers tend to rely on mechanistic, repetitive, teach-to-the-test approaches to learning, which merely reinscribe the very real educational problems inherent in school life.

Part of the problem probably lies in unrealistic expectations about the outcomes of schooling. Schools cannot compensate for large-scale movements in redistribution of wealth or modes of production on national or international scales. Nor can schools be held totally responsible for the radical social and cultural changes that accompany economic and political changes related to technological production and ideological conflict, although all these processes are intimately related. Schools are sites where social, economic, and political movements are manifested, but they remain *educational* institutions. This book, therefore, focuses on the educational functions of teaching. All the authors have a commitment to schooling as a means to enhance people's social and economic prospects, and believe that this commitment is most readily accomplished in the ambit of a truly educational environment. What is wrong with schools and teaching might be revealed more effectively by closely examinating of the real-life experience of people in educational settings and by focusing on the quality of the teaching–learning activities therein.

We do not intend by these words to add our voices to the "ain't it horrible" genre of criticism that has recently targeted schools. Nor do we seek to denigrate the many dedicated, creative teachers, professors, and community educators who bring joy to the lives of their students and colleagues or the schools that actively enrich the lives of the communities they serve. Our assumption is not that schools are defective or that teachers are inadequate, but that they often fail to reach their full educational potential by remaining trapped within the boundaries of conventional or customary practice. Our accounts suggest that relatively minor modifications to the style, structure, and organization of school and classroom life might dramatically enhance students' educational experience and teachers' professional lives. A community-based, reflective approach to teaching promises to open people to their full human potential and to provide an education that enhances the quality of life in a truly democratic community.

We begin this book, then, with the proposition that people can enrich their understanding of teaching by reconceptualizing how they think about processes of learning. The interpretations in this book emerge from our own classroom experiences and are encompassed in narratives that describe how new ways of thinking about teaching emerged from processes of reflection and discovery incorporated into a community-based research class. The narratives reveal how we came to see as educationally problematic what we had previously experienced as ordinary and how we came to articulate a model of teaching that was not only rewarding in a personal sense, but also provided possibilities for renewing and revitalizing our own professional practice. These new ways of portraying teaching, we believe, are not only germane to educational institutions, but are significant in the broader contexts of community and corporate practice.

REVISITING THE EVERYDAY LIFE OF SCHOOLS

The everyday life of schools is such an ordinary part of social life that people tend to accept what goes on there unquestioningly. Problems are usually interpreted as personal problems relevant to individuals or their particular situations. What is rarely understood is that many problems arise from the inbuilt complexities of social life, are part of the very fabric of institutional life, and are rarely apprehended because they are so ordinary.

Teaching as a profession has evolved in response to the demands of modern societies to educate their citizenry. The modern school is so pervasive an institution that its basic forms are readily recognizable in almost any social context. From the Arctic to the tropics, on any continent, the traditional processes of schooling are a taken-for-granted part of modern social life. Not only do schools exist for the purposes of education, but the forms in which schooling is enacted are so insitutionalized, so heavily ritualized, that they pass without comment. Schools organize groups of like-aged children into classes meeting at specific times, under the direction of an adult teacher who arranges a curriculum and ensures that students learn its content. Education takes place, in other words, in specific, time-honored ways that were laid down when mass education, designed for small children, was instituted in the 18th and 19th centuries. Teachers control what is to be learned, how it is to be learned, by whom, when, and where. Students learn what is given to them and are tested and ranked according to their performance. Parents have a great deal of interest in this ranking procedure, which affects the future life chances of their progeny.

On the surface these processes of teaching and learning are relatively unproblematic and require teachers merely to organize sets of knowledge, plan learning processes that enable learners to acquire knowledge, and use assessment procedures to evaluate the learning. At one level, the problems of teaching focus on ways that individuals who do not learn may be led or made to learn. The apparent simplicity of these processes, however, masks an intricate and complex web of issues that are characteristic of any social activity. Not only must teachers deal with large numbers of students with diverse individual personalities and cultural characteristics, for instance, but the education they provide is enmeshed in the massively complex administrative machinery that makes up the education system.

To deal with this complexity, education, or more correctly, schooling, has become enshrined in a relatively simple set of teaching–learning procedures and fairly predictable patterns of organization. Administrators, teachers, parents, and children enact schooling in traditional ways generally accepted as right and proper. The organizational machinery of the school maintains the cycles of activity in forms that fit the ongoing demands of modern social life. Courses, classes, timetables, tests, examinations, grades, and graduation mesh with occupational credentials, child-care facilities, parental occupations, national holidays, state legislation, and so on. In these circumstances teachers often feel tightly bound to the ongoing conventions of school life and continue to arrange their classrooms accordingly, even when they experience discomfort and discontent. To the extent that they feel bound by the system, they experience stress and frustration and fail to realize the potential of their professional lives.

When schooling or education is described in the academic or professional literature it is usually embodied in terms that focus attention on social and technical functions—providing educational credentials, ranking students according to merit, preparing people for the occupational world, socialization, skills development. This emphasis tends to restrict the practice of education to its more functional, technical dimensions. Teaching can become achingly boring when there is an overemphasis on these features of educational life. Teachers spend many hours of mindless grading in order to "assess" student "performance" and rank students according to their "achievements." They can also engage in mind-numbingly repetitive presentations that cover the same material, class after class, year after year. Teaching can be a problematic activity.

REORIENTING THE WAY WE THINK
ABOUT TEACHING

As many experienced and dedicated teachers know, however, teaching is much more than a mechanical routine. Teaching can be a dynamic process that encompasses the broad dimensions of human experience related to community life and to the "whole person." In recent times some scholars have pointed to the need to reorient the way people think and write about teaching so that language and thought encompass this broader perspective.

Aoki (1992), for instance, questioned his own understanding of teaching: "I have become more sensitive to the seductive hold of the scientific, technological ethos that enframes education, and thereby our understandings of teaching ... [and] to seek a way to be more properly attuned, not only to see but also to hear more deeply and fully the silent call of our vocation, teaching (p. 17)."

Aoki wrote of the need to move past layers of understanding that identifies teaching solely in terms of its outcomes or that engages theoretic and scientific views focused solely on teaching techniques, strategies, and skills. He discussed of the need to reflect on the profession in different ways, so that "[we] may awaken to the truer sense of teaching that likely stirs within each of us," and to seek new visions that not only offer new orientations to teaching, but draw people to a deeper level of understanding of its purposes.

His own work is instructive. Through explorations of narrative he focused on themes markedly different from those in most literature. He talked of "pedagogical watchfulness," for instance, as "a mindful watching overflowing from the good in the situation that the good teacher sees." This watchfulness is "filled with a teacher's hope that wherever his students may be, wherever they may wander on this earth ... they are well and no harm will visit them." He also talked of "pedagogical thoughtfulness ... that way of thinking that is an embodied doing and being—thought and soul embodied in the oneness of the lived moment." Such themes represent Aoki's attempt to refocus attention not only on what he terms "disciplined abstractions" but also on the ways that teachers and students actually experience the educational contexts in which they are engaged.

Van Manen also conceptualized teaching in very different ways from those in much technically oriented literature. He suggested, for instance, the need for "pedagogical tact"—a sensitivity that enables a teacher to do the right pedagogical thing for a learner. Such tactfulness is not found in a body of knowledge, but in "a knowing body"—a way of being with students that incorporates an "improvisational thoughtfulness" and recognizes pedagogical actions appropriate in a given moment with a given learner; a way of being with students that knows when to exert influence and when to hold it, that strengthens what is good and enhances what is unique in the learner, and that has "an ability to 'read' and interpret the social context enveloping the relationship between the child and the teacher (Brown, 1992)."

The perspectives provided by Van Manen and Aoki should not be interpreted as being in opposition to technical or functional viewpoints. They are complementary perspectives that enable people to enrich their understanding by placing the technical or functional aspects of education alongside other perspectives. By describing, analyzing, interpreting, and investigating experience from multiple viewpoints, people become attuned to its multidimensional nature and enact a holistic approach to education which captures these many dimensions.

It is necessary to understand the limits of scientific modes of inquiry that have dominated thinking about education in recent decades. Although scientific investigation can enhance the understanding of many aspects of schooling, it is limited in its ability to speak meaningfully to many issues of value and culture, which are an inherent part of attempts to understand teaching and education. The concepts investigated by science are themselves functions of a particular way of viewing education and are embedded with social messages that cannot be adjudicated by scientific processes.

Education, for instance, is not just about achievement or grades which often merely tap into an emphasis on competitive values and mask the fact that students' knowledge can be irrelevant or meaningless outside the test, essay, or project that produced the grade. Science cannot reveal the possibility that grades and credentials may be interpreted as mere social byproducts of a process that, when viewed holistically, concerns learning in a fundamental, human way. It cannot reveal whether education in this age of masses—mass education, mass media—has become mechanized, sanitized, and technicized to the extent that is counterproductive in human terms. Forms of investigation that complement positivistic science and enable people to understand education not only functionally and technically, but also in ways that bring new meaning, purpose, and vitality into educational lives are necessary.

The visions that Aoki and Van Manen presented may differ dramatically from the everyday world of classrooms and schools described in most literature on schooling. Certainly their ideas bear little relation to the way that education is represented in most official "texts" of the educational world—research reports, official documents, curricula, university texts, school newspapers and bulletins, and media reports. These documents usually refer to education in prosaic, technical, or competitive terms that are concerned with social, economic, and political purposes and outcomes. In reality, social, economic, and political purposes are not in conflict with other visions of teaching; all could readily be encompassed in a compassionate, humane curriculum. The understanding of schooling and education should, however, not become too focused on these agendas at the expense of multidimensional approaches to teaching and learning.

Teaching can be presented not in an idealized "objective" form, but in terms that reflect the actual experiences of teachers and learners in everyday classrooms and community contexts. Teaching must not be constrained by official stereotypes but enriched by understandings that describe the way it actually is, from the perspective of the participants in educational contexts. Teachers, for instance, know how demanding everyday classroom life can be as they engage the learning needs of 20 or more students, hour after hour, day after day, throughout the school year. This fundamental condition taxes the personal resources of the most dedicated teachers, and in its worst moments, leads to teaching that is dully repetitive, energy-sapping, and stressful, teaching that is often made all the more unpalatable by unrealistic demands of legislators, administrators, parents, and other community interests. Teaching can become an even greater burden for teachers when students approach adulthood and push to assert their adult independence, or when students' home experiences are characterized by problems like poverty or parental disharmony. In these circumstances, teachers are confronted daily with the products of stressful social and family environments.

In his book *Life In Schools*, Peter McClaren (1989) presented vivid images of his experiences teaching in an inner-city school in Toronto. In just one of many heart-rending incidents, he told of an interaction with a boy who, one moment happy and cheerful, suddenly fell to the ground, weeping uncontrollably:

"I miss my mom! My REAL mom!" he cried out to me.

"Your real mom? Where is she?" I asked, as I picked him up in my arms to comfort him.

"She's in New Brunswick," he whimpered. "My dad's sendin' me on the train to see her in July, and they're gettn' a divorce!"

I tried to cheer him up by saying, "Why that's only a few weeks away, all you have to do is wait a while."

But he continued to sob. "But my dad's getting divorced now from my other mom so that means I'm gonna have three moms!" (p. 147)

As he reflected on this and many similarly injurious incidents, McClaren (1989) pondered the social context in which these children live:

> The incidents of violence and brutality in this book are undeniably part of the working-class experience. (I suspect there are subtler, but equally as debilitating, forms of violence in middle-class communities.) But before we judge too quickly the casualties of societal oppression, we would do well to examine the inhumane conditions in which the poor are permitted to become entrapped. We need only to witness the growth of "instant cities" springing up in the suburbs—high density apartment living with few, if any, social or recreational services—to realize the extent of our "benign" neglect. Family violence cannot be considered solely as individual action outside the context of social forces that position the poor within asymmetrical relations of power. (p. 152)

McClaren (1989) sought, therefore, to focus on these negative aspects of schooling as a means to identify the social processes, structures, and issues linked to teachers' and students' experiences of schooling. The literature that points to the need to change the structures and practices of everyday school life is now voluminous and stretches back at least to the 1960s. Less common, however, is literature that speaks to the practical ways and means to institute changes that make sense to teachers in their everyday classroom life, or to administrators responsible for intricate organizational strands of school life. Many people recognize the problem, but few have been able to supply a solution that works at the blackboard.

INVESTIGATING TEACHING

How, then, can people extend their understanding of teaching? How can they reconceptualize the processes of facilitating learning to make education more productive and energizing, and less stressful? Learning occurs in many ways: Sometimes it evolves slowly as people grasp new meanings and change the way they think as a result of the impact of pressures in everyday experiences. Sometimes learning results from the gradual accumulation of knowledge within a program of formal education or professional development. Sometimes it emerges relatively quickly from rigorous, structured processes of inquiry, which are the hallmark of good education or academic research.

The ideas from which this book emerged arose from a combination of factors. Not only were the authors also students in a class, but they also applied the rigorous research processes that were the subject of the course to their own teaching–learning processes. Thereby they unconsciously enacted transformative processes that have been mentioned by various scholars in recent decades.

Feminist writing, for instance, has recorded the need to change professional life so that it takes account of recent changes in gender roles and of the increasing participation of women in professional and public life. These changes, feminist writers have proposed, require modifications to professional practice that mirror needs other than those of a male-oriented society. In *Women of Academe* Aisenberg and Harrington (1988) suggested that women and their male colleagues need to work in ways that allow them to integrate the full expression of their intellectual and creative capacities with their professional lives. Respondents in their study indicated a desire for a different system of professional organization to oppose excessive hierarchy, incorporate diversity, spread authority through processes of cooperation, resist centralized political and intellectual authority to define truth and value, and protect individuality by legitimizing the personal components of professional life.

These views are consonant with postmodern perspectives obvious in the literature on teaching and education. A postmodern view, however, does not come with a readily identifiable set of practices or a predetermined program that can be implemented at an organizational or institutional level. Postmodernism implies that important knowledge about teaching must be derived in local contexts: totalizing, generalized knowledge of scientific texts cannot speak in detail of the reality of any particular setting. Therefore, people must seek to understand teaching and learning through local investigations of real life experiences, rather than by relying solely on generalizable studies that are broadly relevant to large populations.

This perspective on inquiry, or research, echoes the work of Aisenberg and Harrington (1988). The key to transforming the ideas about professional life, they suggested, lies in the transformational process itself. People develop other dimensions of personhood and professional and social identity through approaches to learning that increase their intellectual capabilities and through methodological tools that enable them to acquire and assess new knowledge. This viewpoint is reflected in the rise of such developments as teacher-as-researcher and practitioner research (e.g., Anderson, Herr, & Nihlen, 1994; Kincheloe, 1991; McKernan, 1991). Despite the continuing ascendency of positivistic approaches to scientific inquiry, recent trends toward diverse forms of inquiry enable educators and other professional and community practitioners to enrich their understanding of the work in which they are engaged.

The current study used processes of interpretive inquiry suggested by Denzin (1989). Based on an extensive scheme of reflection, description, and interpretation, Denzin's processes examined turning-point experiences of an educational context that transformed the way we conceptualized teaching, learning, and professional life. We have provided narrative accounts to try to make our lived experiences directly available to readers, with the intent that they develop an empathetic understanding of these events and realize how we now experience teaching and learning. We have attempted to portray how these interpretations and understandings were formulated, implemented, and given meaning through reflective, interactive, and collaborative processes of investigation. By illuminating our own experiences we hope to contribute to the development of solid, effective programs and policies that enhance the potential of educational systems and other areas of community and organizational life.

Several authors talked of epiphanies—interactional moments that leave marks on people's lives and can transform their views of the world. These turning-point moments not only reveal significant aspects of the situation but expose its problematic features. They uncover what critical theorists refer to as hegemonic practices and ideologies—ideas and practices that are accepted as ordinary, and are often actively maintained and promoted, despite the inherent problems associated with them. The interpretive, interactional research processes on which this book is based not only exploit the revelationary potential of the epiphanic experiences, but reveal problems and the underlying ideology that drives these experiences.

Like the research procedures used by Garfinkel (1967) these processes of inquiry acted phenomenologically to reveal new ways of reading the authors' everyday words. They served to disrupt the taken-for-granted order of things and to expose the underlying assumptions that were an intrinsic part of the context. From this perspective, therefore, the teaching–learning processes described in the following chapters may be interpreted as examples of critical pedagogy.

The accounts also reveal the multiplicity of events, perspectives, possibilities, agendas, and interactions that are an inherent part of social life's complexities. These, in turn relate to the biography, emotionality, history, and interactional styles of each person involved. The narratives thus reveal the complexity and diversity of the participants' lived experience as they struggled to accommodate their individual perspectives to the ongoing demands of institutional life.

CHANGING OLD HABITS AND PATTERNS: THE BIOGRAPHICAL GENESIS OF A COMMUNITY-BASED PEDAGOGY

The events captured in the following narratives have their genesis in my own history. As instructor of the classes described in chapters 2–12 I enacted an approach to teaching that evolved from my educational experiences in disparate community contexts on three continents. To understand where I was coming from, therefore, and to "declare myself," as people might ask, I provide some relevant history.

I have been a teacher, in one form or another, for most of my life. For 10 years I was classroom teacher in a variety of urban and remote rural settings; I followed the prescribed routines for classroom teachers and was subject to these apparently sacred imperatives: "Cover the Content of the Curriculum," and, "Keep the Kids Quiet."

To accomplish these objectives, I had to prepare all lessons thoroughly, and I had to control the classes I taught. Thus I would carefully plan all aspects of my classroom life: what was to be taught, when, where, how, to whom, and for what purposes. I would determine class goals and objectives and the way student "performance" was to be evaluated. As I enacted my carefully defined curriculum I used procedures and processes that were part of a professional repertoire I had learned in teachers' college and from my schoolteacher colleagues. I monitored the behavior and performance of children in my classroom to ensure that they were behaving "correctly," were carrying out the activities that I had prescribed, and were performing at a level adequate to their varying abilities.

When things went well, the clockwork routines of my classroom proceeded smoothly and efficiently and, at the best of times, produced learning outcomes that were most fulfilling. I can still remember the pride of children who were able, under my tutelage, to master the complex reading material with which they were working. I can also vividly picture the look of accomplishment on the face of Jim, a boy whom I had rated as having limited academic ability, when he presented a project on the Antarctic that was not only fascinating for its detail and complexity of information, but was enhanced by the carefully illustrated booklet that he displayed to the class.

These experiences, however, were balanced by the memory of other times when, weary and with frayed nerves, I sought to control bored or fractious students; when my creative imagination failed me and the constant demands of keeping children engaged or in check threatened to overwhelm me. These experiences, in turn, contrasted with the occasions when I encountered children whose cultures and lifestyles were so dramatically different from my own that I could not imagine how the material in my carefully prepared syllabus could possibly be made relevant to their lives.

I have taught in schools in remote Aboriginal communities where the state-prescribed curriculum was almost laughably inappropriate to the educational needs of children from these communities. I have taught as an English master in a London school, where the curriculum was so old, worn, and dog-eared that it was almost unreadable. Yet in these circumstances, because of my youth and naivete, as well as my ignorance of curriculum development processes, I struggled through the required syllabi.

I clearly recognized the insanity of my predicament during a social studies lesson in a remote Aboriginal community. I found myself reading out a question from the social studies text: "Who discovered Australia?" I was given, without comment or question, the answer, "The English navigator, Captain Cook." When I think of this situation now, I can see that this was but one small drop of nonsense in an ocean of irrelevancy for children in this community. To suggest to children whose people had lived in the country for at least 40,000 years that it was "discovered" two centuries ago by an English sailor would be less remarkable, I am sure, than much of the rest of the curriculum.

There is little doubt that the Aboriginal children required formal education, if only to help them deal with the modern world imposed on their lives, but the context and the forms of knowledge of the education were inadequate according to the most benign interpretation. Fundamentally, however, these forms of education were probably culturally damaging because of the vision they presented and the consciousness of everyday life that they imposed. I can now see this curriculum and these forms of knowledge as part of a continuing process of colonizing indigenous people. Their world views were ignored as irrelevant and their own visions of social life overwhelmed, in the school context, by those like myself who controlled the texts of their educational experience: the curricula, the school texts and materials, the day-to-day forms and processes of activity and interaction that make up the organized schedule of activity.

This experience continues to dominate my thinking about education; it has made me increasingly sensitive to the extent to which educators' mind-sets, worldviews, and perspectives continue to dominate the lives of the people they teach. Because teachers and administrators control the curriculum, organization, and operation of schools, they enact a form of education largely drawn from their own experience and life history; they formulate educational contents and processes according to what makes sense to their experiences and perspectives.

I once wrote in a report based on my observation of several classrooms taught by non-Aboriginal teachers in remote schools in Western Australia: "It is not just that Aboriginal people are presented as unimportant: It is as if they do not exist!" Teachers do not just teach the set curriculum; teachers teach what they are. And what they are, in many instances, is foreign to their students' experiences. The educational ends teachers wish to accomplish in any school or classroom setting cannot be attained because of the extent to which curriculum content and activity fail to resonate with the experience, perspective, and history of the students they teach.

In my own recent educational history, this fact has been brought to my attention in direct and forceful ways. In the last decade, much of my work has entailed active participation in training and community development projects with Aboriginal community groups. Many are alienated from mainstream Australian social life, either because of a disastrous history of oppression or because of the dramatic cultural differences that still characterize the social life of many Aboriginal groups. In these situations my familiar classroom routines proved to be not only inadequate, but often counterproductive. Aboriginal adults, in many situations, do not countenance a non-Aboriginal authority figure who dictates the course of events or presents "expert" information.

I can still remember the responses of Aboriginal people when, in the early days of my community-based work, I went into well-oiled teaching routines that, in effect, presented them with the *truth* and then formulated activity on this basis. In concert with a person of authority, I defined the problem, the context of the problem, and the solution to the problem. The real *problem*, in these circumstances, was that the problems, contexts, and solutions were defined from my or from official representations and interpretations of the situation.

In one situation a member of my audience gave me a thorough dressing down. "You come here telling us what we are doing wrong and tell us how to go about our business," he intoned angrily, and the workshop I was facilitating basically fell to ruins at this point. These angry responses, however, were less numerous than the times when people either failed to appear at all or attended the first session and never returned. Without a captive audience, my schoolteacher routines proved inadequate; I was forced by these circumstances to learn a new approach. From several colleagues I learned of a community-oriented approach to developmental work, which not only respected people's perspectives, interests, and agendas, but actively sought them as the basis for describing the situation, problem, and context and used them to formulate actions, activities, and solutions. When circumstances dictated that I was unable to exercise high degrees of control of the "texts" that made up my work, I learned how to organize activities that accommodated the varying experiences, perspectives, and agendas of the people in the context (Stringer, 1996).

Over the past decade or more, therefore, I have had to unlearn many of my teacher habits and to develop new approaches to learning and development, which are not only acceptable to Aboriginal people, but effective, insofar as they have actual, pragmatic outcomes. I have learned to engage in learning and developmental processes not evaluated by a grade or a number, but assessed by their capacity to accomplish desirable objectives. The outcomes of this process have been immeasurably rewarding both personally and professionally. I have participated in the development of highly successful training programs, helped initiate educational programs that boasted high student retention and graduation rates, helped establish new organizations that effectively served the needs of special client groups, and facilitated the successful redevelopment of community organizations.

As I learned these new approaches to education and development, I was forced to rethink the underlying, usually implicit, assumptions that formed the basis for my practice. In doing so I have been fortunate to have had opportunities to withdraw from my work for extended periods, to read, reflect, discuss, and write about the complex issues embedded in the social arenas in which I work. I became conscious that Aboriginal people, with their different worldviews and life orientations, challenged many assumptions of the university system itself. The theories and assumptions about educational life, learning, and, indeed, social life itself were now presented to me in ways that not only questioned the basis for much that went on in educational institutions, but challenged the very forms of knowledge on which schools and all other facets of social life are based.

This, then, was the genesis of this book: the changes in thinking and professional practice forced on me by my interaction with people whose culture was distinctively different from my own; the justification of these changes through my readings of postmodern, feminist, and critical social theory. These readings made sense and spoke to my social and cultural experiences; they provided academic and theoretical legitimacy for the forms of practice that I had developed as I had worked with Aboriginal people.

REFERENCES

Aisenberg, N., & Harrington, M. (1988). *Women of academe: Outsiders in the sacred grove.* Amherst: University of Massachusetts Press.

Anderson, G., Herr, K., & Nihlen, A. (1994). *Studying your own school: An educator's guide to practitioners' qualitative research.* Thousand Oaks, CA: Corwin.

Aoki, T. (1992). In W. Pinar & W. Reynolds (Eds.), *Understanding curriculum as phenomenological and deconstructed text* (pp. 17–27). New York: Teachers College Press.

Brown, R. (1992). Max Van Manen and pedagogical human science research. In W. Pinar & W. Reynolds (Eds.), *Understanding curriculum as phenomenological and deconstructed text* (pp. 44–63). New York: Teachers College Press.

Denzin, N. (1989). *Interpretive interactionism.* Newbury Park, CA: Sage.

Garfinkel, H. (1967). *Studies in ethnomethodology.* Englewood Cliffs, NJ: Prentice-Hall.

Kincheloe, J. (1991). *Teachers as researchers: Qualitative inquiry as a path to empowerment.* Philadelphia: Falmer Press.

McClaren, P. (1989) *Life in schools: An introduction to critical pedagogy in the foundations of education.* New York: Longman.

McKernan, J. (1991). *Curriculum Action Research: A handbook of methods and resources for the reflective practitioner.* New York: St. Martin's Press.

Stringer, E. (1996). *Action research: A handbook for practitioners.* Thousand Oaks, CA: Sage.

AT THE START OF OUR FINAL CLASS, ERNIE SAID, "WE NEED TO TELL THE STORY OF THE CLASS THAT WE DID TOGETHER."

THIS IS WHAT WE WROTE:

2

Teaching Community-Based Ethnography

Ernie Stringer

THE CONTEXT

Community-based ethnography is a form of qualitative research that is both academically rigorous and socially responsive. Its intent is to extend the potential of formal research by providing those who work in professional and community contexts with tools of knowledge production normally perceived as the province of academic researchers. A fundamental premise of community-based research is that it enables ordinary people to extend their understanding of their situations and to devise effective solutions to problems confronting them.

Community-based research is implicit in much of the literature on action research (Kemmis & McTaggart, 1988; Reason & Rowan, 1981; Van Willigen, 1993; Whyte, 1991) and on a socially responsive approach to research (Stringer 1993a, 1993b). In the educational context, such inquiry provides a means for making research responsive to the realities of schools and the communities they serve. Community-based research relates to an increasing body of literature that includes to teacher-as-researcher (Kincheloe, 1991), practitioner research (Anderson, Herr, & Nihlen, 1994), constructivist approaches to evaluation (Guba & Lincoln, 1989), and constructivist curriculum development (Stringer, 1993a).

Community-based research is intrinsically participatory; its products are not outsider accounts, portrayals, or reports, but collaborative accounts written from the emic—or insider—perspective of the group. Such accounts, grounded in hermeneutic, meaning-making processes of dialogue, negotiation, and consensus, provide the basis for group, community, or organization action. People can review their activities, develop plans, resolve problems, initiate projects, or restructure an organization. In education, community-based research can be applied to a wide range of problems and issues at classroom, school, or system levels.

Community-based research not only signals the intent to work with a group identified by common purposes, but also provides group members with a sense of community. It is, in essence, a community-building or team-building activity as much as it is an approach to the production of knowledge.

The task of teaching community-based ethnography to students in an educational context is problematic. Schools and universities usually operate within an organizational model that is essentially bureaucratic, based on hierarchic structures of authority, and philosophically tied to notions of the expert knower. Teachers and professors, as experts in their respective fields, control the nature of the knowledge and the mode of its transmission. In most settings this control is an essentially authoritarian process whereby the teacher-professor-expert defines the curriculum's content and processes. Typically, students expect instructors to clearly define the content of the course, the nature of the learning activities, and the products of learning (course "requirements") before classes begin. Instructors therefore both expect and are expected to control all aspects of a course's operation.

The culture of an educational institution is not, therefore, conducive to social and educational activities that are essentially democratic, participatory, and emergent. The well-rehearsed and comfortable formats of traditional classrooms militate against an approach to teaching that seeks to deconstruct familiar processes of knowledge acquisition and empower participants to redefine the official texts governing their educational lives. Community-based research, emphasizing as it does the definition and resolution of problems according to locally derived interpretive schema, is at odds with the ideology of centralized control inherent in most classroom settings.

Teaching community-based research, therefore, requires a pedagogy to enable learners to acquire necessary knowledge and skills in ways that reflect the philosophical principles of this approach to research. In this chapter, I discuss the way in which a graduate class in community-based ethnography was planned and taught according to a framework of values that entailed empowering, participatory, and collaborative approaches to teaching-learning. The results suggest that carefully structured knowledge and skills acquisition processes, allied to participatory decision-making procedures and collaborative learning processes, provide a powerful context for learning and an approach to professional practice that can be effectively applied in various educational, organizational, and community arenas.

CAPTURING A LIVED EXPERIENCE: METHODOLOGY

This book presents an interpretive study of a university graduate class in qualitative research methods. It uses a methodology proposed by Denzin (1989b) and it portrays the events of the class through the interpretive lenses of the professor; therefore, it is partially autoethnographic (Denzin 1989a). In providing an account of the class, as author I placed myself in the text, provided an account of events in which I was a central participant, and relinquished the stance of objectivity. I consciously took steps, however, through reference to multiple accounts of the same events and through reiteration of member checks, to present a portrayal that made sense to and had a veracity affirmed by the students who participated.

I recorded notes of class events continuously and used them as the basis for an initial account a few weeks after they occurred. Detailed documentation was available through my own lesson notes, class syllabi, teaching charts, personal journal notes, formal interviews, and three forms of class evaluation—individual written accounts, formal university evaluation forms, and group collaborative evaluations. As suggested by Denzin's methodology, key elements of the class were derived from a content analysis of these data—a process of bracketing—and used as a framework for formulating descriptive and interpretive elements of the text. Contextualizing commentary derives from theorizing that places private events in the class in the public context of postmodern social theory.

I have revised this account according to the experience of participants in a similar class given later the same year and based on the commentary of members of both classes during the production of the text. The veracity—or believability—of the portrayal may be checked by reading the sister narratives accompanying this account. Together they provide a polyphonic narrative that represents the lived reality of the class from many perspectives.

TEACHING COMMUNITY-BASED ETHNOGRAPHY: PERSPECTIVE AND PREPARATION

In the spring semester of 1993, I was scheduled to teach a graduate course in community-based ethnography in the College of Education at Texas A&M University. I had eagerly grasped this opportunity as it provided not only the prospect of working closely with scholars eminent in the field of qualitative research, but also offered opportunities to teach a form of ethnographic inquiry derived from the community-based research processes that had been part of my professional experience for the previous decade.

Two major issues influenced the preparation and implementation of this course. First, my experience with Aboriginal community groups in Western Australia had left me suspicious of traditional ethnographic accounts, which frequently represented perspectives and interpretations grounded in an historicity (life-world) removed from that of the subjects of "investigation." This suspicion was reinforced by the often negative impact of outsider authoritative accounts of Aboriginal people's lives and was increased by many ethnographic accounts that "slide fleetingly past" the subjects' lived realities and perceptual universes to engage the interpretive frameworks and academic agendas of the authors. These accounts were rarely relevant to the lives of the people studied, but nevertheless often spoke authoritatively on behalf of these people.

The second influence on my thinking derives from my readings of postmodern social theory. Huyssens (1986), for instance, urged people to take seriously the perspectives of those they study and to listen to the voices of those who have been silenced. In similar vein, West (1989) suggested the need for intellectuals to: "[reconceptualize] philosophy as a form of cultural criticism that attempts to transform linguistic, social, cultural and political traditions for the purpose of increasing the scope of individual development and democratic operations" (p. 23). West asked for "philosophy"—which I interpret as academic activity—to be used directly for social transformation; to exchange the search for the elusive "foundations" of knowledge for pragmatic or socially productive activity.

In centering the course on community-based research, I attempted to provide participants with an approach to ethnographic work that was less "colonial" and more action oriented. The philosophical stance that provides the orientation to the course was stated in the syllabus rationale as follows:

> Ethnography has traditionally been the realm of the scholar, an approach to research which provides accounts of human settings which extend our understanding of social life.
>
> Recent scholarship in social theory, however, has heightened our awareness of the political and social nature of research work, including ethnographic study. We are more aware of the broad range of meaning which can be derived from any human activity and inscribed in any text which presents an account of those activities. We need to question the right of scholars to produce definitive accounts or interpretive narratives of people's lives and to question the authority of authors to use those accounts for their own purposes.
>
> Philosophically, this course will seek to extend the possibilities for description and interpretation of social life by exploring the production of ethnographic accounts which are not solely tied to the privileged position of the scholar. It will explore the potential of ethnographic work as a tool or resource which may be used internally by institutions, organizations, social agencies or community groups.

Although not discounted for use in academic work, the course focused on ethnographic study as a tool for research, review or evaluation relevant to the life of any community, operationally defined in the course as any group that identified itself as a "we."

ENACTING A PHILOSOPHY: COMMUNITY-BASED
APPROACHES TO TEACHING AND RESEARCH

It was 5:30 PM on the first day of spring semester in the College of Education at Texas A&M University. The large, well-lit classroom in the Harrington Building, obviously an early childhood lab, was spacious and homely, well equipped by the standards of university classrooms and pleasantly decorated. As visiting professor, I stood before a class of 18 postgraduate students, all but one doctoral candidates according to the list before me, and prepared to commence class. I felt a little nervous: this was my first class in the university, and I was far from home. Although I had lived in the United States a number of times, including the 3 years in which I had acquired a PhD at the University of Illinois, I was in strange territory, far from the familiar environs of Curtin University in Perth, Western Australia, which was my natural and academic home.

"My name is Ernie Stringer," I commenced, "and this is EDCI 690—Community-Based Ethnography."

All attention was centered on me, and there was an obvious stirring of interest. Not only were the participants in this class eager to hear the details of the course, but many were obviously intrigued by the novel sound of an Australian voice in the heartland of Texas.

I continued my introduction by providing a brief autobiographical sketch that highlighted what I considered to be the salient points in my academic and educational history—classroom teacher, teacher in Aboriginal community school, Illinois doctorate, teacher education, community development work. I then asked members of the class to introduce themselves and listened as each in turn, in halting tones that echoed in the silent room and served only to underline the awkwardness of opening day, provided the brief, stilted synopses that masqueraded as an introduction in these circumstances.

"I am Shelia Baldwin. I am a doctoral candidate and I teach at Conroe High School."

"My name is Jack Fields, and I am from Illinois."

As the litany continued a thumbnail sketch of the class emerged. Most were educators, mainly Texans with a few from out of state, including a man from Singapore. Between them they exhibited a wide range of experience and interests, including early childhood, primary and secondary education, teacher education, adult education, community college, community development, and technologically based distance education.

I presented a brief synopsis that placed ethnography in the realm of qualitative research and explained the community-based orientation of the course. "It derives", I explained, "from my work with Aboriginal people." I then presented an extended narrative that described some of my experiences in schools and community contexts in outback Australia. The level of interest rose and enthusiastic comments and questions indicated that the class was beginning to "work."

Then came *crunch time*, the event that as I knew from previous experience, would spark a mixed bag of responses.

"We need to start thinking about what we will do in this course," I said. "What would you like to learn?" I asked evenly, "And how would you like to learn it? I would like you to help me formulate a syllabus for the course."

My intent was to model a community-based approach to educational activity from the beginning by providing opportunities for class members to participate in course-planning processes. I wished to show them how I, an outsider, could ensure that the objectives of the class were appropriate to their academic and professional needs, that the content and strategies suited these objectives and were encompassed in course requirements that their schedules could accommodate. As I reflected later on these hidden purposes, I realized that I should have signaled these agendas, although I suspected that the responses would not have varied much. The silence that followed was underlined by the emotions in the eyes of the class members, the worry lines that furrowed their brows and wrinkled their eyes. Some kept still. Others stirred restlessly, moving cautiously in their seats and quietly shuffling their feet under the desks.

"Wait time," I said to myself. "Let it sink in. Give them time to think."

Eventually someone provided a suggestion. "I would like to learn how to do observations in the real world."

"Real world observations," I wrote on the board.

"How to do ethnographic studies," a thick Texan drawl suggested.

"Applying research across the community," came another response.

As the list emerged, I continued to fan the spark of interest with affirmative grunts. As we reviewed the completed list, I commented on the variety of interests and agendas and indicated that these items would provide the basis for the syllabus. I asked for suggestions about how the syllabus could be organized, what learning activities might be relevant, what projects might be appropriate to provide them with opportunities to practice what was learned, how they might evaluate these projects, and so on.

As we explored these issues, some people became excited as the range of possibilities emerged—presentations, debates, practice sessions, "fish bowls," group projects, discussions, ethnographic studies, journals. For many, however, the levels of discomfort became increasingly evident, and some asked, at first obliquely, then more pointedly, when they would get the syllabus, when they would know the class requirements and the dates for assignments and projects to be handed in.

By the end of class the energy levels, both positive and negative, were high; some students talked excitedly about the emerging possibilities, while others huddled in small groups exchanging obviously worried comments. Although I had provided, as required by university regulation, a syllabus that I had labeled preliminary, it was too obviously a loose framework that gave only an indication of the content and requirements of the class and provided none of the meat that students expected. By the end of the class they knew in more detail what they were going to learn, but had no indication of what would be required of them, in terms of "work to be done," or "course requirements," or due dates.

Their body language spoke to me more clearly than their voices. "What are we going to do?" their worried frowns asked. "Where am I going? When will I have to do my assigned work? How can I prepare a study schedule? How will I fit my classwork with my work requirements?"

Some were unperturbed, and their voices expressed excitement and interest; others, although intrigued by the process and interested in the content of the course as it had emerged, exhibited responses that ranged from consternation and concern through annoyance and doubt to disquiet and anxiety. The bubble of voices at the end of class told me of the energy that had been generated, but also warned me that many class participants needed the safety of the structures and routines with which they were familiar. They would need, I thought, a relatively fixed syllabus the following week to provide the feelings of security that would enable them to enter the mind-set of inquiry and exploration that I wished to generate.

By next class I had prepared a more detailed supplementary syllabus, written on chart paper and taped to the board, and asked for comment and suggestions. I explained that I had crafted it, as far as possible, to fit the inputs they had provided the previous week. I sought their approval of the syllabus and asked whether they would suggest additions or amendments. There was some discussion and debate about the projects I had assigned and we were able to make several modifications and amendments, including the times when work was due, so that by the end of the first hour the syllabus had been ratified by all members of the class. Once again, the range of emotions was evident in the participants' responses as excitement and energy competed with relief.

These opening classes were harbingers of a teaching experience that was, for me, epiphanic. From the energy that emerged from the interest, excitement, doubt, and disquiet of these classes, I was able to fashion an ongoing process of inquiry and discovery that I marked as one of the most exciting classes I have taught in over 30 years. Now, some years later, I am still in contact with most members of the class, and many of them have joined me in the project that is the focal point of this book—an exploration of teaching. "What was it," we asked in the semesters that followed, "that made this experience of teaching and learning so special? What can we learn from that class that will inform us about teaching that might be relevant to our future professional lives? And how can we describe it in ways that will allow others to understand the experience and to learn something that will enrich or enhance their professional lives?"

The text that follows emerges from these questions. It presents a reinterpretation of teaching derived from the attempts of participants in the class to reflect on their experiences and to formulate accounts that can provide other educators with a new way of envisioning their educational roles.

TEACHING-LEARNING

Teaching is often described in technical terms that prescribe particular flows of activity—a step-by-step approach to instruction that ensures that learners acquire the knowledge or skills stipulated in the syllabus, curriculum, or lesson notes. As my analysis of class ethnographies revealed, however, participants in the community-based ethnography class consistently identified features of the teaching–learning environment—the nature of the relationships in the class, participatory learning processes, structured learning frameworks, skills development processes, and collaborative work—which, according to the participants, greatly enhanced the quality of their experience. Their responses suggested that teaching and learning need to be envisaged as more than a set of mechanistic steps.

Relationships

From the outset, the processes of teaching and learning in this class diverged from standard formats of graduate study. Participatory, collaborative approaches to learning were constantly emphasized and enacted in a context where all aspects of the class were open to negotiation.

As instructor I suggested that participants—not students—should view me as their educational consultant and that they should therefore feel free to approach me if they were not satisfied with my services—if they felt, in other words, that their learning needs were not being met. In this way I attempted to place class participants in a relationship to me that mirrored the consultant role that had been part of my previous professional life. As consultant to community groups, business corporations, and government agencies, I had been expected to deliver effective services, to achieve clearly designated learning or developmental outcomes for those who participated in the programs for which I had been contracted. In view of these situations, it had been imperative to develop a climate of cooperation and trust for the participants to feel free to reveal the issues and problems that were the focus of the program and to work carefully through these problems to achieve resolution. The knowledge and skills learned by participants in these activities had very real and immediate applications.

This contractual approach to teaching has some elements of risk for all participants. It requires learners to take active responsibility for their own learning, and it transfers decision-making power from the instructor to the students. There is no captive audience, and the sanctioning potential of the grading system is considerably diminished. As became evident, however, the educational benefits of this change in teacher–learner relationships far outweighed the negative effects. Orientation changed dramatically: People focused on the knowledge and skills required to engage in productive ethnographic activity rather than on merely "doing what the professor wanted."

Participatory Processes: Building a Learning Community

The principle of participation was applied from the very start of the course when I asked participants to tell me why they had taken this class and what they hoped to gain from it. The responses were listed and used as the basis for framing needs and objectives from which I formulated a syllabus. The following week I presented the syllabus to the class and suggested that we discuss it with the intention of modifying those parts with which people were dissatisfied. Although few changes were suggested, participants were obviously surprised and, in some instances, somewhat discomforted that a professor should take class time to devise a syllabus. What had previously been a taken-for-granted, unproblematic feature of their courses suddenly became a phenomenon to be studied and discussed.

In addition to developing a syllabus, I instituted activities and projects that encouraged people to overtly observe and reflect on the nature and processes of the class itself. In the first days of class each person interviewed another participant, then constructed a brief life story that was presented verbally in one of the small work groups that made up the class. In this way people began to know each other at a deeper level, while they extended their interview skills and obtained data that were used as part of the first major project—a collaborative ethnography of the class itself. One project included a description that clearly illuminates the effect of this process:

> Although we were still unclear about the eventual outcome of the class, even though we had our printed syllabus, it began to dawn on us that this was part of the emergent design that we were all participating in ... Ernie was modeling a more "facilitative" teaching model. The atmosphere seemed loose and spontaneous. We were able to extend, clarify, or extrapolate each other's ideas to make them more complete. Our class was a tremendous potential of resources because we came from diverse backgrounds and a wide variety of experiences that we learned as we shared our respective stories.

Because the class was not only open to negotiation but also was one of the subjects of inquiry, a reflective and questioning ethos was gradually established that enabled participants to express their ideas relatively freely. Basic ground rules devised by the class produced a climate that encouraged people to speak with a minimum of fear or embarrassment. The rules highlighted the participatory and collaborative nature of the class and encouraged interaction and debate in a context emphasizing relationships of equality and "respect for the dignity of others."

Because of the formal university context, however, the professor–student relationship was initially strong, and participants voiced their misgivings rather hesitantly. Some sotto voce grumblings and questions, together with more overtly expressed anxieties, enabled me to demonstrate my desire to be responsive to the expressed needs of the participants. One group report noted:

"Our group has found this semester ... to be both incredibly frustrating and immeasurably satisfying. Particularly at the beginning of the semester, we longed for the structure that is the trademark of higher education—a syllabus, teacher, "top-down" decisions, specific dates when specific assignments were due, etc."

Another group portrayed the first weeks in this way: "We also have evidence of one of the first signs of any significant paradigmatic change—tension and stress. Once the change begins to occur actors do not have a frame of reference for acting. We have, in effect, lost our recipe for learning and the ground-rules for typical student/professor behaviors. In the new paradigm ... we are working through the process of building new frameworks for acting."

Over time, participants began to accept the reality of their power to question how the class ran and to take increasing control of their own learning processes. By the end of the semester each group was an active learning community, with members engaging in constant questioning, dialogue and demonstration as they grappled with the myriad concepts, issues, and problems inherent in ethnographic work.

Learning Frameworks

The notion of negotiated curriculum, although a common tool for community and organizational consultants, was foreign to the experience of most students. In the context of a class that focused as much on learning processes as on products or requirements, students were initially perplexed about the apparent looseness of the course. This flexibility, however, was anchored in a series of basic frameworks that gave substance, order, and constancy to the processes of learning. Several participants noted the efficiency and clarity of the instructor's planning and one group commented that the professor had organized the class, "Almost too well [*chuckle, chuckle*]. We often commented on how *organized* our spontaneous sessions were."

Many frameworks were listed on charts and taped to the wall of the classroom. Some charts provided sequences of activity, such as one suggested by Denzin (1989b), Steps to Interpretation:

Framing
Deconstruction
Capture
Bracketing
Construction
Contextualization

Other charts listed elements of ethnographic process, skills development, and community development that were relevant to the work of the class. They provided an admirable backdrop for the teaching–learning processes that I, as consultant, facilitated, and provided participants with ongoing reminders of the nature of the learning in which they were engaged. The charts not only emphasized the stages and details of these processes, but highlighted the integrated nature of the learning activities in which participants were engaged. The charts were the subject of considerable comment, both during the class and in the evaluations at the end of the semester, with participants appreciating their constant availability and their consequent contribution to the processes of learning.

In time the other participants and I came to appreciate the safe harbor provided by these frameworks. As learning activities became increasingly complex, recursive, and reiterative, the charts provided a compass with which to plot a course to clarity and understanding. When the focus and purpose of our activity became fuzzy, I would draw attention to a chart and ask, "Where are we in this process?" A brief review of the framework usually clarified the purposes and directions of activities and allowed us to formulate our next steps. Learning was accomplished, therefore, not just as a conglomeration of discrete skills, but as an integrated set of learning activities tied to frameworks of understanding that gave substance and coherence to the course.

Skills Development: Walking the Walk

Academics are sometimes criticized because they can talk the talk, but can not walk the walk. In the community-based ethnography class, participants not only gained a comprehensive *understanding* of the nature of ethnographic activity, but also acquired the *competencies* to enable them to become skilled practitioners. A skills development process, labeled learning framework, provided guidance for our activities and was charted as:

> Explanation
> Demonstration
> Trial
> Feedback
> Practice

This process was applied to all skills required in ethnographic work. The structure and purpose of Spradley's (1979a) framework for descriptive questioning, for instance, was described carefully and an example of each type of question presented to the class, which then split into pairs to practice formulating questions related to a particular research focus. Paired students provided each other with immediate feedback, then returned to the class group where I provided comment and, where necessary, further explanation and demonstration. These continuously reiterated processes provided a rich field of activity that, according to comments from many members of the class, greatly enhanced the learning of ethnographic skills. As one group reported:

Using the interview with Dr. Stringer as a model, we interviewed one of our group members. This approach allowed us to practice Spradley's elements of the ethnographic interview, to pose his kinds of descriptive questions and then to discuss the quality of our follow-up questions. Together, we began to get a feel for which questions were "open enough" and which questions suggested an inherent value judgment.

The skills development sessions provided the impetus for considerable discussion about the problems and potentials of ethnographic work. Practice and evaluation of each aspect of interviewing, for instance, provided opportunities for people to feel firsthand the impact of ethnographic questioning on both the questioner and the questioned. Feedback sessions extended beyond the initial focus on the technical aspects of ethnographic work to the inherent personal and ethical issues involved. As subjects of study, participants in the class were able to gain an empathic understanding of the impact of an interviewing process.

It would be wrong to assume, however, that only the demonstration of specific skills was implied by the skills development framework. Throughout all aspects of the class, an attitude of acceptance and equality was actively encouraged, and I purposely took a nonauthoritative stance to teaching to model a participatory approach to ethnographic work. People in the course frequently expressed their appreciation of the fact that I exercised in my teaching what I was advocating for ethnographic practice. One student commented: "I think it's neat that Ernie turns the class over to us. The end product we know, but how to accomplish it is all up to us. This causes more frustration than if we are told step-by-step how to do it. Also, a lot more learning is taking place because we are having to grow through it on our own to make decisions and think critically."

As the class worked through the program of study, the texts reinforced and provided substance to learning activities. Spradley's (1979a) *The Ethnographic Interview* and its companion volume *Participant Observation* (1979b) provided resources to guide the development of data-gathering skills. Denzin's (1989b) *Interpretive Interaction* likewise helped us to learn how to formulate interpretive narrative accounts. Issues related to subjectivity-objectivity, validity, and reliability were explored with the assistance of Eisner and Peshkin's (1990) book *Qualitative Inquiry* in education and other readings garnered from a variety of academic journals. The complex learning processes gained further substance and clarity through the frameworks contained in these books and readings.

Evaluation was oriented toward competency-based assessment. Class members nominated the grade they wished to attain for the semester, and all their work was evaluated at this level. If the work did not meet the required level of understanding or skill, it would be returned with appropriate comments, which noted the deficiencies and explained how they could be remedied. Students were then free to resubmit their work to demonstrate the acquisition of the desired level of competence. This approach proved very popular, as students were able to get direct and specific feedback on the quality of their work and to eliminate specifically identified deficiencies. This aspect of the course was applauded in student assessments of the course.

Collaborative and Community Work: The Ties That Bind

Writing a collaborative ethnographic account of the class caused much perplexity and consternation among participants. Despite the variety of problems that surfaced as group members struggled to achieve a text representing their diverse viewpoints, the project proved extremely productive. The reiterative nature of activities and the need for a constant exchange of ideas resulted in extraordinarily rich understandings about the pragmatics and epistemology of ethnographic work.

In the first weeks of the class each group had acquired a large body of data from practice interviews, classroom observations, and a range of pertinent documentation in the form of syllabi, class notes, texts, and readings. From the outset the problematic features of ethnographic work became highlighted. The processes became increasingly complex as the groups with their multiple perspectives, formulated the focus of the study, selected the methods for data collection and analysis, and constructed a text that provided an account of the corporate experience of the class.

One issue that continued to haunt those who worked through this exercise was the question of voice. In trying to capture the lives of the people in this class, to reflect their lived experience in ways that would enable readers to experience the class vicariously, they struggled to find a stance from which to present their experience. Questions of I-we-they problematized the writing of participants' ethnographic accounts. Once a person became a participant in a true sense, he or she ceased to be an outsider and wrote as one of the community. Questions of authority and power—who has or appropriates the right to define the text—became pre-eminent as group members confronted the divergence between their various perceptions about events and their interpretations of events. The power struggles that evolved in the writing of the text and consequently the power of the text writer became issues that, far from being inscribed in a reading, became part of their personal experiences. The power of the author to control texts, the assumptions built into the text, and the effects that the text can have on the lives of people who are the subjects of the accounts became immediate, personal issues. One participant noted: "Because I assumed the task of textualizing the information, I placed the experiences back into my life more than into the lives of [those] who actually narrated their experiences." (Newman, p. 124)

For some this became a significant experience when they realized the power they appropriated each time they wrote about people's lives. For one class member the experience became an epiphanic changing point as the realization of the relativistic nature of meaning-making, acknowledged intellectually, become an emotional experience. She wrote of the experience in this way:

> I write less sure of answers than I have ever been, while simultaneously growing more confident about what constitutes the questions ... Is everything we hear, see, experience, etc. merely an interpretation through our frameworks? If so, does truth exist? Is there reality? Should we discount our interpretation or be acutely aware of the implications of our interpretations for ourselves and others? Can we truly understand another person's reality if we translate their reality through our framework? Can we resist imposing our agenda on others if we perceive our agenda to be the moral thing to do? ... If truth is separately constructed, can I claim to possess truth for others? By what right do I impose my construction? Do I use the rationalist base of supporting data and research to substantiate my claim and in so doing undermine my philosophical base? Or do I simply share my constructions with others recognizing their right to accept or reject those constructions for their own brand of truth?

The recursive nature of this activity created some confusion. Students sought first to distance themselves from the events to develop a third-person account as is deemed appropriate for most academic research; then they confronted the reality that they were developing a narrative account of a group that included themselves. Some tried referring to themselves as *we* to distinguish the part of their narrative referring to their own group from the part referring to *they*, the larger class. Whether the accounts were defined as etic (outsider) or emic (insider) became problematic as they sought to develop styles that would enable readers to understand classroom events and, by inference, to extend their ideas about graduate qualitative methodology classes.

Many teaching–learning processes in this class were therefore based on collective activity that made the processes of ethnographic research problematic by enacting them directly as tools of applied or action research. This orientation was applied to the requirements for the final project in which individual members of the class conducted an ethnographic study that was to be useful to the people who were subjects of their study.

People chose a wide range of projects and generally found the action-oriented approach to research refreshing and exciting. They developed accounts that provided the participants in their studies with information that would extend their understanding of their own situation and would be of some use to them. In these contexts they learned the value of working from the insider perspective to develop accounts that assisted the community-building processes that are an essential part of any productive group activity.

RESPONSES AND OUTCOMES

The outcomes of this course from my perspective were most gratifying. Ultimately even those students for whom the course had been most problematic indicated satisfaction with the outcomes. Almost all students stated that the class had been highly effective in its desired learning outcomes; they also found that they had exceeded their expectations in acquiring or increasing competence in ethnographic research processes. More important, perhaps, were the types of learning that students indicated were important. Their comments suggested not only complex and deep levels of understanding, but reflected a degree of commitment to professional and academic goals not always encountered in formal study.

Overall, the response of participants in the class can be summed up in two enthusiastic comments that seem to typify the outcomes of the class: "This class has been an eye-opening experience and well worth all the uneasiness I felt during the course. I think I'll actually *use* the information from this class in "real life." "This course is by far the best course I have ever taken. The professor helped me challenge my thinking and the thinking of others. It was a joyous sort of struggle to grow and learn."

In the final class session, I asked students to define the key elements they would use to describe their experiences of the class. All participants commented positively on the methods used in teaching-learning, including the active engagement in experientially based activities such as interviews, observations, document analysis, and planning sessions. Further, most student evaluations noted the close connection between theory and practice as a particular strength of the course, and many commented on the direct impact of this association on their professional and academic lives.

More important than the technical features of teaching-learning were the participants' responses to the collaborative context of learning consciously structured into the class environment. Community building, in each group and in the class as a whole, was mentioned as a key characteristic of the course by almost all participants. Students appreciated the extent to which this aspect gave them multiple sources of information, extensive feedback for their work, and support and enrichment that come from close collegial relationships. As Mary Frances noted:

> What surfaced as the most salient issue was that the more we looked at the class's experiences, the more we understood ourselves. The work we completed became secondary to our understandings of ourselves as graduate students. By reading and rereading the data, we saw reflections of ourselves in transition. We were becoming people other than we knew ourselves to be; these changing definitions of ourselves afforded us a better understanding of where we were, where we were going, and the dangers that we needed to avoid as we journeyed. (Agnello, chap. 7, p. 96)

Community building, therefore, as an aspect of community-based ethnography, provided a fruitful context for learning in this situation. It extended the possibilities for analysis and interpretation through a consciously introspective assessment of work in progress.

The recursive nature of the descriptive and interpretive work also highlighted many issues involved in developing accounts. As insider subjects of their own studies, people became increasingly sensitive to the ways in which memory, selection, and interpretation of events are colored and shaped by the processes of learning and development. Several student evaluations mentioned the extent to which the collaborative and dialogic nature of classroom activity heightened their awareness of the multiple realities at work in the class, of their perceptions of themselves, the class, and the teacher's methods. Others spoke of the sense of responsibility and commitment that came with being able to prove themselves adequate in a risk-free environment where they believed they could learn complex skills and ideas.

It should not be anticipated, however, that the course was an overwhelmingly positive experience for all participants. Some students experienced high levels of anxiety, especially in the early stages. In an environment in which students have historically had all details of a class presented to them within the first hours, an emergent curriculum was a cause of concern to many. Some noted that in the first stages of the course the process was too vague and they would have appreciated more guidance. There is little doubt that the processes of a negotiated curriculum, together with the diffuse outcomes of ethnographic activity, created some concern for students who were most comfortable in highly structured learning environments. For others, community-based research seemed antithetical to the existing structures of the real world of schools and was therefore deemed by them to be of little relevance to educational practitioners.

The overall outcomes of the course in educational terms, however, were highly satisfying from both the students perspectives and from my viewpoint because of the abundance and complexity of learning detailed in the participants' accounts of the class. In framing their differing perspectives for a follow up project that attempted to build a polyphonic account of the class, participants provided portrayals indicative of the depth and strength of their understanding of ethnographic work (see the chapters that follow).

As class consultant, I wrote of outcomes that included "high levels of student satisfaction, well-developed technical skills, and rich understandings of the epistemological and ideological issues related to qualitative research." These ideas were translated by Lois (Christensen, 1993) in the following terms:

> Philosophic development powerfully reinforced the ability to understand others' perspectives. The myriad collaborative processes challenged or enhanced individual belief systems resulting in a mutual shaping of individual philosophies through dialectic processes. The implications ... are that effective philosophical

development is accomplished through authentic experiences of situated learning; that modeling processes provide a constructive apprenticeship for novice
ethnographers; and that heuristic experiences provide occasion for personal and
group development of philosophies which undergird pedagogy.

Vicky (Newman, 1993), sensitive to the issues of authority and power
relations involved in the writing of ethnographic text, described how:

> The group dynamic functions to deconstruct the central authority of meaning-
> making and interpretation by providing an ongoing shift in the power focus. It
> allows the play of other possibilities of meanings, other claims and positions,
> within the process of writing one text. It provides a setting for resistance and
> opposing strategy (Foucault, 1979). ... Given these multiple perspectives,
> monological power is undermined, providing the possibility of polyphonic voices
> within the texts. It invites an exploration of multiple forms demonstrated by
> Derrida's (1974) use of marginal texts that disrupt, merge and reemerge, in
> order to accommodate the deconstructive and polyphonic.

The outcomes of the class, however, were not merely textual or philosophical. Individual projects enacted at a community or institutional level provided
a clear indication of the ways in which this approach to ethnographic research
could be effectively applied in a variety of contexts. Shelia described how the
ethnographic methods suggested by community-based ethnography were used
by a group of African American, Hispanic, and White students to explore
cultural diversity in their school and community (Baldwin, 1993). Another
participant successfully applied these processes in teacher preparation as she
supervised a group of student teachers doing field work (Ellis, 1993). Yet
another demonstrated the effectiveness of the conceptual framework and
processes of community-based ethnography as a tool for management when
applied to a broader, extended community in the corporate world (Tinsley,
1993). These projects demonstrated that it was possible to design and implement effective action research projects even in the limited time constraints of
a semester course. They also demonstrated the efficacy of approaches to
teaching-learning based on the application of qualitative research processes to
real-life problems in school, organizational, and community settings.

SOCIAL AND EDUCATIONAL CONTEXTS
OF TEACHING AND LEARNING

I have presented this account of a class that focused on the problem of ensuring
a concomitance between the philosophical principles and pedagogical processes required for an action-oriented, community-based approach to ethnographic research. As instructor of the course, I have endeavored to provide an
empathic understanding of a graduate class in community-based ethnography

by portraying the activities and responses of those involved and attempting to capture the energy, excitement, frustration, and fulfillment that characterized the experience of the participants.

Although the narrative relates to the professional lives of educational practitioners in a university setting, the events portrayed are set in a context that encourages me to look past the particular events portrayed to explore the broader contexts to which these events are relevant. The processes of teaching and learning that characterized the class were encompassed in the institutional life of a large university that, although somewhat conservative, embodied many attributes characteristic of other universities in the United States and other industrialized nations.

The intuitive leap from the particular to the general is accomplished with considerable hesitation, however; such leaps of faith often encompass theoretical formulations that are poorly linked with the perceptual universes of those who are subjects of study. In aspiring to connect this private account to the public context of other educational institutions, therefore, I am enjoined to emphasize that my attempt to extrapolate reflects the understandings that were at work in the cultural system of the group about which the story has been told. I am not, therefore, attempting to generalize, in any direct sense, but merely to make perceptual links that make more or less sense according to their fit to the other contexts to which I refer.

Fortuitously, the analytic nature of much of the class work has enabled member checks that add to the credibility of my formulations. The multiple texts that follow this chapter collectively form a polyphonic account that adds substance to my desire to extend my analysis past the immediate events in the course. The participants' theorizing helps me to extend my understanding of the processes in which we were engaged, and the consciously reflective and reflexive processes contained in their accounts push back the frontiers of their everyday, taken-for-granted, lived experience and fashion new ways of seeing and interpreting the events depicted.

These reflective processes highlight the deconstructive potential of ethnographic work, as participants relive and re-create their lives and constantly interrupt their taken for granted worldviews to formulate different, more satisfying accounts and representations of their experience. People pondered questions such as, "How do we account for a particular phenomenon? What actually happened? How can we describe it? What meaning do we ascribe to or inscribe in these events?" Their life-worlds changed; events and their meanings took on new forms and new significance as they explored, described, and discussed them. By sharing their lives, people came to know themselves and their situations in new, different, potentially life-enhancing ways.

Reflection on class and group processes, for instance, enabled participants to see firsthand the mechanics of power and authority that go into the production of a text; to become conscious of the processes of meaning-making; to be aware of philosophic development as it occurred; and to explore the potential uses of ethnographic research. Yet they focused not merely on the internal workings of the microsetting; their dialogic, hermeneutic engagement enabled them to explore the larger schematics that impinged on the teaching–learning processes.

The emerging interpretations also reinforced conceptions of teaching and learning as integral features of the social context in which they are enacted. As social theorists have revealed, education does not occur in a socially or culturally neutral context; the outcomes of educational processes themselves have social, cultural, political and economic consequences apart from the *learning* that is the ostensible object of educational processes. The English sociologist Giddens (1993) proposed that the production of society, which includes the knowledge base of any social group: "is brought about by the active constituting skills of its members, but draws upon resources and depends upon conditions, of which they are unaware or which they perceive only dimly (p. 165)." These conditions, he suggested, include meaning, morality, and relations of power, cultural elements that, although the basis for social action in any group, are taken-for-granted elements of day-to-day interactions. In education, therefore, many assumptions embedded in the sociohistorical ethos remain not only unseen but unquestioned. The time-honored traditions, emanating from 19th-century educational structures designed for young children, continue as the modus operandi for teaching and learning at all levels. Epistemological and educational considerations of the educative enterprise receive scant attention from most people who teach in schools, colleges, and universities. Tradition, in the form of lectures, essays, tests, and texts related to a predetermined body of content, predominates.

This situation results, according to Bruffee (1993), in students who are authority dependent, passive, irresponsible, overly competitive, and suspicious. These negative outcomes of traditional approaches to teaching and learning tend to sustain authoritarian relationships and an epistemology that reinforces the authoritarianism. Knowledge tends to be viewed in purely cognitive, realist terms rather than recognized as the product of consensus-making activity among the members of a community.

The experiences of those in the course in community-based ethnography spoke directly to these issues. Their responses, emanating from a long history of experience with traditional classroom methods as both students and teachers and fraught with the frustrations, anxieties, and demeaning experiences therein, enthusiastically described the possibilities of collaborative and community-based modes of pedagogy. They have become more attuned to the political-power dimensions of the teaching–learning act, so that the intimate relation between the systems of knowledge—discourses—that codify techniques and practices for the exercise of social control and domination in particular localized contexts (Foucault, 1979) has become immediately relevant to their experience. They have also seen the relevance of Foucault's suggestion that the only way to eliminate the fascism in our heads is to explore and build on the open qualities of human discourse and thereby to intervene in the way knowledge is produced and constituted at the particular sites where a localized power-discourse prevails.

As a key feature of the teaching–learning situation inherent in the community-based ethnography class, the class enacted collaborative, empowering teaching–learning processes that were implicitly democratic and humane and resisted the repressive techniques common to institutionalized education discourses. The approach was inherently pragmatic as it focused on both the educational activities themselves and the texts that they produced. In learning and doing of community-based ethnography, we became subjects of our own inquiries, and the chapters that follow re-present the world revealed to us in the process. These chapters are not the potentially exploitative texts of outsiders or the authoritative rendering of our lives by another, but an account from within that serves the purposes of the group as it collectively explores and shares its members' interpretations of events and extends the collective understanding of the lived reality of teaching and research.

REFERENCES

Anderson, G., Herr, K., & Nihlen, A. (1994). *Studying your own school: An educator's guide to qualitative, practitioner research.* Thousand Oaks, CA: Corwin.

Baldwin, S. (1993). *High school students' participation in action research: An ongoing learning process.* Unpublished paper, College Station, Texas A&M University.

Bruffee, K. (1993). *Collaborative learning: Higher education, interdependence, and the authority of knowledge.* Baltimore: Johns Hopkins University Press.

Christensen, L. (1993). *Pedagogical and philosophical development: An ethnographic process.* Unpublished Paper, College Station, Texas A&M University.

Denzin, N. (1989a). *Interpretive biography.* Newbury Park, CA: Sage.

Denzin, N. (1989b). *Interpretive interactionism.* Newbury Park, CA: Sage.

Eisner, E., & Peshkin, A. (1990). *Qualitative inquiry in education: The continuing debate.* New York: Teachers College Press.

Ellis, L. (1993). *A study to examine the effects of two teacher preparation programs.* Unpublished paper, College Station, Texas A&M University.

Foucault, M. (1979). *Discipline and punish: The birth of the prison.* New York: Vintage Books.

Giddens, A. (1993). *New rules of sociological method: A positive critique of interpretive sociologies.* (2nd ed.). Stanford, CA: Stanford University Press.

Guba, E., & Lincoln, Y. (1989). *Fourth generation evaluation.* Newbury Park, CA: Sage.

Huyssens, A. (1986). *After the great divide: Modernism, mass culture, postmodernism.* Bloomington: Indiana University Press.

Kemmis, S., & McTaggart, R. (1988). *The action research planner.* Geelong, Australia: Deakin University Press.

Kincheloe, J. (1991). *Teachers as researchers: Qualitative inquiry as a path to empowerment.* Philadelphia: Falmer Press.

Newman, V. (1993). *Writing the collaborative text: Reproduction and resistance.* Unpublished paper, College Station, Texas A&M University.

Reason, P., & Rowan, J. (Eds.) (1981). *Human inquiry: A sourcebook of new paradigm research.* New York: Wiley.

Spradley, J. P. (1979a). *The ethnographic interview.* New York: Holt, Rinehart & Winston.

Spradley, J. P. (1979b). *Participant observation.* New York: Holt, Rinehart & Winston.

Stringer, E. (1993a, April). *Postmodern theory and constructivist curriculum processes: The next generation.* Paper presented at American Educational Research Association National Conference, Atlanta, GA.

Stringer, E. (1993b). Socially responsive educational research. In D. Flinders & G. Mills (Eds.), *Theory and concepts in qualitative research: Perspectives from the field* (pp. 141–162). New York: Teachers College Press.

Tinsley, P. (1993). *Digital distance education: Qualitative research in a corporate context.* Unpublished paper, College Station, Texas A&M University.

Van Willigen, J. (1993). *Applied anthropology.* Westport, CT: Bergin & Garvey.

West, C. (1989). *The American evasion of philosophy.* Madison: University of Wisconsin Press.

Whyte, W. F. (1991). *Participatory action research.* London: Sage.

3

Community Building
in Small Groups

Kenneth Ivan Henry

A COMMUNITY VISION

A central question in group work is how to enable people to work effectively together to accomplish a set of goals or to achieve a vision. Developing a sense of community is an important part of the process of effective group work. How is it possible for disparate groups with mixes of old friends, strangers, and enemies to work together productively? This chapter tells the story of the experience of graduate students in an advanced qualitative research methods class entitled Community-Based Ethnography and illustrates ways to build a sense of community with a diverse group in an educational setting. A comment by the professor-facilitator, Dr. Ernest Stringer (Ernie), made during a class interview, sets the stage:

> Ethnography is the process of working with a group of people ... to tell a story or produce a narrative about some aspects of their lives. Most ethnographic work is performed by an outsider who comes to that setting, observes it, interacts with the people and goes away to write the story. Community-based ethnography focuses the work by working with a group of people to assist them to write stories which enable them, in some way, to accomplish purposes they have together.

This chapter focuses on four main categories that emerged from analysis of the data about building a sense of community. The categories include: shared experiences; power sharing between class members and facilitator; intentional use of space; and a facilitating paradigm of community building.

METHODS

This chapter relates to my own interest in community development and community building. The data were collected from written documents produced by class members, who included 17 doctoral candidates and 1 masters degree student. Teams of 4 or 5 members wrote ethnographic accounts of the class itself, accounts compiled from information drawn from individual journals of reflections and observations and from interviews between class participants. Each class member kept a journal of reflections and observations of class meetings. In some cases Spradley's (1980) Descriptive Question Matrix was used by class members to increase the scope of their journal entries.

Data from team ethnographies and individual journals were analyzed using a modified form of Denzin's (1989) six steps to interpretation: framing, deconstruction, capturing, bracketing, construction, and contextualization. In this study, capturing and bracketing occurred before deconstruction, according to a process described by Glaser and Strauss (1967). These authors suggested the need to let theory emerge from the data before reading relevant literature.

Bracketing was accomplished by reviewing all the accounts in the documents to reveal people's perspectives on community building. Comments about community building were then categorized and used as themes discussed with other class members to check whether the categories represented their experiences of the course. This chapter is therefore limited to what class members thought about community formation at the time of the course. It should be noted that I was a member of the class and an active participant observer.

COMMUNITY BUILDING:
THE FACILITATOR'S PARADIGM

As participants talked and wrote of the class, many told of shared experiences such as eating together, creating a story of themselves as a community, working in groups, and gradually changing from individuals to a community. Ernie's teaching–facilitating paradigm was that of a community builder. He treated each of the class members as if he or she was a member of a community that had hired him as a consultant to assist it to solve a problem. His style was informal and from the start he expected us to refer to him as Ernie. We seldom called him Dr. Stringer. He used space as a tool to change the way class members related to him and to each other and moved the center of power in the class from himself to a more equitable place that included both the class members and himself. In numerous ways he presented a new paradigm of education.

Ernie revealed his perspective on teaching and learning not only by the way he facilitated the activities of our class but also by the way he talked of education. The following excerpt from a class interview with Ernie during our first social event-class meeting in a class member's home reveals some important elements of his approach to education:

Student: You used a term that I'm not familiar with, teacher-centered interaction, how would you define it?

Ernie: In most classrooms most interaction goes through the teacher, so that I will talk to person 'A' who will respond to me and I will then talk to person 'B.' The response will be … from student to teacher all the time so [that] there is an enormous amount of activity going on with the poor teacher [and little with any one student]. So that's the problem with teacher-centered classrooms. In less-teacher-centered classrooms there is much more interaction and direction that comes from the participants themselves. It is one of the things I am trying to gradually work towards in this class. A process whereby the people themselves, the participants in the class, take over the processes of the class, so that I listen [more and talk less] and less of the attention is focused on me. The class members can start taking corporate responsibility for the structure of the situation in the ways that are most constructive for them.

In this exchange Ernie was obviously speaking about a paradigm of teaching in which the role of the teacher changes from the teacher-as-expert to the teacher-as-facilitator-of-the-learning-process. Here is how one group ethnography describes this change: "On the theoretical level, this represents a shift in classroom experience, from one in which knowledge is transmitted via an expert—the professor—to one in which learning is constructed collectively."

A member of that group put it thus: "As a group we're attempting to construct our own framework of what community-based ethnography can be. The way we are attempting to do that is dialoguing and negotiating objectives, purpose, and projects so that we build this course as we go."

Ernie's paradigm for teaching, therefore, was a significant feature of this class. Although it was not part of the syllabus, strictly speaking, his approach to instruction permeated the class. Throughout the semester the multitude of activities we engaged in as part of the process of learning qualitative research could only be understood by reference to his paradigm, which enabled us to make sense of these activities and ultimately helped us understand his focus on community building.

Ernie's teaching facilitating paradigm was also apparent in his writing about educational research. Our class structures were built from a set of values that he defined as the basis for socially responsive research. These values included processes that are:

Democratic: Enabling participation of people.
Equitable: Acknowledging people's equality of worth.
Liberating: Providing freedom from oppression and debilitating conditions.
Enhancing: Enabling the expression of people's full human potential.

Ernie believed that "participant well-being is best defined locally, according to the perceptions and values of the people at hand" (Stringer 1993).

Dr. Stringer's educational paradigm was thus revealed in a number of ways. The following sections of this chapter present an account of the ways in which his perspective was enacted in practice, for one of the most remarked features of his educational practice was his ability to practice what he preached; to model what he advocated through his teaching.

SHARED EXPERIENCES

Our class shared many experiences: common remembrances, snacks and meals, social events, and decision making. All this seemed particularly important to Ernie who suggested the need for everyone to know each other by more than just name, for everyone to understand each other. Shared experiences provided the context for developing this understanding.

Common Remembrances

The first class began with brief self introductions. Most of us introduced ourselves by giving our names and two or three sentences about our educational directions and history. Little information is shared in such presentations so that our introductions were flat: "My name is Kenneth. I received my undergraduate degree from the University of Illinois in Chicago in accounting and my masters from the University of Missouri in community development. I am currently in the PhD program for urban and regional science in the College of Architecture."

This introduction was obviously insufficient for Ernie's purposes. He asked class members to pair off, interview each other, and then introduce the partner to a group formed of three or four pairs. The 20 minutes allowed for these interviews provided the opportunity to share a great deal of information about ourselves. In my group we found that one of our members was the fifth of seven children and that another had taught in a bilingual kindergarten in Glendale, Arizona, for 6 years. Still another classmate had been a school administrator in Elgin, Illinois, near Chicago, and was bilingual in English and Spanish. These interviews gave us a better feeling for our classmates as each of us added a personal story to the tapestry that would eventually become the class story. Several of the groups later wrote that this exercise had a resounding affect on their overall experience of the course. One of the group ethnographic accounts reported:

> In order to enhance the sense of togetherness in the class, Ernie asked us to interview a member of the class that first night. One member recalls, "By being introduced to each other in that unique manner, we have learned [an important] lesson—that a community is really about the people within it." Knowledge of each other is the main ingredient of a shared culture. The culture of individual community members is the basic component of their collective identity.

Following this activity Ernie began to introduce himself to the class, and then realized that some of us had heard his story in an earlier class and asked if someone would introduce him. In doing so he acted in a way that we would become accustomed to; he shifted the focus to the class away from himself and toward the students. A class extrovert quickly jumped at the chance and related what he could remember from an earlier class.

Other means Ernie used to help us get to know each other were various name games, as we came to call them. One student wrote in response to one of these games: "We continue to build the community by playing 'Name Recall,' remembering the name of each person introduced before you around the class circle. My initial reaction was 'no way,' but by the beginning of the third class, I knew each person's name, which is amazing considering how very bad I am at remembering names."

Ernie continued to demonstrate the importance of the community in a variety of ways. He showed how the class could remember the events of the previous meeting without notes, an activity that, in a quiet way, brought us closer together. At the beginning of class meetings, we participated in an activity during which we recalled what happened the previous week. One group ethnography stated: "We related what had happened last week. Ernie's rule was that no one could use their [sic] notes, so we all had to remember what had happened. By combining our efforts we were fairly successful in recounting the events of that class. This was to become a routine in almost every class."

Eating Together

Our experience in this class suggested that sharing food may be a critical part of community formation. Ernie's strategy certainly featured eating together. When one student asked about coffee breaks, Ernie suggested we bring food to the meetings and have a light supper (the class met from 5 to 8 PM). He further suggested we not sign up to bring food in advance, but organize only for the following week. Ernie said we all should bring what we could, just like a community meeting, and that no one should feel obliged to participate. A group narrative related:

> Ernie solicited volunteers to bring food for our next class and two people volunteered ... One student brought a lovely tray and some dip to accompany the delicacies to share with our class. There were bananas and pears, apples and oranges. The other student brought *chili con queso* dip, a chili dip with meat and tortilla chips for dipping. ... As people arrived, they did not seem as quick to settle into a seat but rather chatted with each other and helped themselves to the food.

Food thus became a focal point for facilitating communication and for further developing our growing sense of community, as people talked with each other around the snacks table before class or during breaks.

Social Events

The class met twice at students' homes for potluck suppers. The change of location added a new dimension, and although we engaged in class activities, we experienced them differently. The home environment enhanced our learning situation and facilitated the development of a sense of community.

The class also had two other voluntary social events. One evening as class was ending, someone asked whether anyone wanted to go to a local hang out. Part of the class went to the Dixie Chicken to drink beer and coke and to tell stories and jokes. Another evening our class was invited to Ernie's apartment for a cocktail party with others of his friends, an event that turned out, to our surprise, to be Ernie's birthday party.

These social occasions were an integral part of the class experience. Not only did they serve to develop positive relationships and enhance communications between class members, but they also heightened our sense of being part of a community. By offering us opportunities to share experiences such as these, Ernie provided an environment that enhanced the learning potentials of the class.

POWER SHARING

When a professor decides that power should be shared with other participants in the classroom and not be monopolized by the teacher, he or she creates a context that few students have experienced in educational settings. This class was composed of people who were successful products of traditional educational settings, to the extent that they had advanced to graduate school. They were well imbued with the common approach to the exercise of power in classrooms.

The experience of the change in power relationships inherent in Dr. Stringer's class, however, had a dramatic impact on many members of the class. Some reported that the experience inspired major changes in their lives. They were impressed by the shift in decision-making power that emerged in the first class session and the sharing of power, which was an essential feature of consensus formation in many class activities.

Student Decision-Making: Consensus Formation and Ownership

Ernie's instructional approach was characterized by a shift from a teacher-centered to a student-centered classroom. The most startling manifestation of this shift related to a change in decision-making processes: Class members found themselves responsible for details related to the operation of the course. The following comments from a group ethnography illustrate this change in focus:

In most graduate classes the professor hands out the syllabus that will define what the class will be doing for the balance of the semester. One student was looking for the syllabus that is given in the first class of every university course she had attended. Time was winding down quickly. It was drawing closer to seven-thirty. Still no syllabus. Next, we were asked to list our needs, wants and expectations for the class. Ernie wrote them on the board and Francis recorded them on a legal pad at Ernie's request.

Our combined list filled the board. Class members were amazed and pleasantly impressed that their wishes about course content were treated as significant, to the extent they were asked to elaborate on these issues they wanted to include. Ernie said, "I will include each of these goals listed on the board in the framework of [the syllabus I prepare for] this class ... I have agendas [that] I will negotiate [together] with the group's agenda." As a class, we were designing the curriculum with the professor.

From the start, Ernie was interested in bringing the class into the decision-making process by building a consensus about the syllabus. All groups documented this opening session in great detail and noted that the syllabus was not merely the work of the professor but was formulated in collaboration with the students. We were taking responsibility for the course at a much deeper level than was possible in most classes.

Ernie was telling us that we would not only have opportunities to make decisions but would be required to assume responsibility for the operation of the class. He continued to shift power to the students in ways that not only built a feeling of community but also allowed participants to form a sense of ownership as they sought consensus about details of the course. A group report stated, "He [Ernie] always seems to want to get the class involved in the decision-making so we could have ownership over the decisions we make."

Another student's journal entry at the time was:

We all knew something that we wanted out of this course. Ernie helped us to create a syllabus. However, I feel this exercise is helping "us" to form a better community since it is now clear what is everyone's agenda. Some of our class members had firm ideas about what a course of this type should include. I was relieved to see how this class was unfolding. I believe that unless there is ownership in the process—any process—that [sic] learning can't be maximized. Constructing a framework for learning can be a painful process for some people. We are steeped in tradition and have learned that someone—the expert—is telling us what we should know. ... We are used to it.

Another student wrote about these events in this way:

Unlike the routine process of the professor walking in with a set of pre-developed agendas and establishing the power structure by giving direction, this time the professor was providing us the opportunity for input. The professor's actions in asking for contributions from the students in developing the agenda for the course has [sic] been a liberating and frustrating experience. I have always practiced this method of teaching in my training programs, but have never thought it would be as effective in a formal academic setting. This style of presentation has given the course a new flavor. Many years of teacher-centered instruction have trained most of us to expect something different from our teachers. Dr Stringer's style of instruction is another way of teaching us the basics of ethnography!

Competition, Frustration, Compromise, and Excitement

One group wrote of the competition that emerged in the apparent void created by the lack of an authority figure to strictly define the activities of the class. One class member suggested that a competitive ethos emerged when students had the freedom to define their own goals and agendas—that some members promoted their own agendas and forced others to voice their own ideas to ensure that their agendas became part of the class. Having seemingly created a power vacuum as facilitator instead of an expert authority figure, Dr. Stringer seemed to invite our class to examine the nature of power and compromise as part of the learning process itself. There was some initial frustration as we set about learning how to negotiate.

Many class participants mentioned that, at one time or another, they felt frustrated at not knowing in advance precisely what they were expected to do. They found it more difficult to decide for themselves than to be told what to do. One group's ethnography included the following: "It's difficult for me to know where we're supposed to be in this course. I've always been in an area (dance or gymnastics) where someone is telling you what to do. I'm a good instruction-taker and he [Ernie] doesn't have many instructions." This student felt that she was always "flailing about" in the class and that too much time was spent making decisions about details. Frustration with the slow pace of community building and group decision making is best seen in this excerpt from a student journal:

> Dr Stringer begins by asking us to sit in a circle away from our books. We begin by talking about what we thought of class, our projects, what we want to do in class that night. In my opinion, that usually takes longer than is necessary. Everyone wants to get [their] two cents in about what we are doing. I enjoy small group discussion more because there is not so much rivalry among speakers.

This class member was only one of several who expressed some degree of frustration. Many experienced unpleasant feelings at the beginning of the course, but most of these reactions changed as we enjoyed the results of our endeavors. One group narrative reported:

> One student said that it was chaos in the beginning. She thought this constructivist approach a bit unsettling, like having the cart before the horse. She perceived discordance between her expectations and those of Ernie, but decided

that chaos has to do with living with ambiguity. Another student's metaphor in dealing initially with this class was one of giving birth, struggling with the issues.

Although most students experienced frustration at one time or another, most also grew to enjoy the overall approach and to see how they could incorporate these methods in their future work. Some members had reservations early in the course, but evaluations taken at the end of the course reflected little of this initial frustration. The benefits obtained from investing in student decision-making processes paid large educational dividends at the end.

USE OF SPACE

Another feature of Dr. Stringer's class was his use of space, which had an impact on the processes of teaching and learning. He arranged the environment to bring class members face to face with each other to remove barriers to communication and help engender a sense of community. Three categories that reflect this use of space were the arrangement of class space, informal uses of space, and the impact of space design on group interaction.

Configuring Classroom Furniture

A common barrier to the formation of a sense of community in classrooms and workshops is the arrangement of desks and chairs. All tend to face the front where the teacher stands, a configuration that not only focuses attention exclusively on the teacher, but serves to inhibit communication among class members.

The first session of Ernie's class set the trend for classes to come in the arrangement of the physical setting. Dr. Stringer had us move the tables and chairs to form a U shape. Those of us who sat in the center of the U quickly ascertained we were in the wrong place and rearranged ourselves accordingly. This arrangement obviously met with approval, for a small group started moving tables and chairs as soon as they arrived for the second class. At other times Ernie set chairs in a circle without tables to bring us closer together and to remove the barriers to communication created by intervening tables.

One student made the following observation in her journal.

> Ernie believes space and the learning energy of individuals in the group setting are in inverse relationship to each other. In other words, the closer to each other the group members are seated, the more energy for learning they will generate. Based on this belief, he changed the physical arrangement of the room upon his arrival in the class at the very first meeting.

As a result of these changes in configurations of space, the class was able to engage in dialogue, debate, and, sometimes, lively discussion. This new way of arranging seating met with mixed reviews from some students. Although most appreciated the interaction that became possible, some felt discomfort when they were asked to work without a desk. Dr. Stringer soon acceded to student requests and allowed people to work at their desks for most activities. The ultimate impact of the change in arrangement of desks, however, was to break down the rigidity of the formal classroom setting and to promote ongoing interaction between class members. The use of space facilitated the formation of a sense of community and enhanced our ability to learn.

Informal Space

Informal space came in two forms: the coffee snack center in the classroom and other locations such as homes and bars where we gathered for informal meetings. The first has already been mentioned in the section on food. Class members frequently gathered during breaks around the bench where food and coffee were laid out, to chat and have coffee and a snack. This practice brought a relaxed sense to the class and helped enhance our sense of community.

The sense of community was also facilitated in these occasional times we met for class in student homes. The relaxed atmosphere and comfortable environment enabled people to talk freely. There were some differences of opinion, however, about the educational value of these meetings. A journal account of a home meeting noted:

> Ernie has also attempted to get people to build a [sense of] community in the class by having events in places other than the classroom. One night he invited all of us to go have a drink after class. ... Then he instigated a pot luck at _____'s house. There was a lot of food, beer and some wonderful chocolate cake for dessert. We talked [and] ate, then Ernie attempted to start class while we were still eating. This was also a good way to build community, but it was difficult to accomplish much educationally. I think it almost has to be one or the other at a time.

The use of informal space was yet another means by which Ernie attempted to develop an effective learning environment. This attempt had a continuing impact on the ability of students to communicate and interact with each other and assisted in the development of a sense of community that was a central feature of this class. The impact on interaction was, in particular, most apparent. A group ethnographic narrative reported: "When we reflected on the importance of the different types of seating arrangements, we became convinced that this was deliberately done to initiate different types of group interaction."

CONTEXTUALIZATION: LEARNING
AND COMMUNITY BUILDING

The approach to teaching and learning recounted in this chapter derived from the instructor's definition of community and his experience in the field of community development. The concept of community building derived from this context came to frame many events and activities within the community-based ethnography class. In a class interview Ernie commented: "When I talk about community, I am not necessarily talking about a geographical location. … I am talking more about a group of people who have an identity, some common purpose which enables them to talk about each other as 'we,' a collective."

Examples from the literature helped us extend our understanding of this emphasis on community and helped broaden our understanding of the relevance of community building to classroom life.

Community as a Concept

Christenson, Fendley, and Robinson (1989) used four main components to define community. A community, they suggested, concerns involvement of people; an element of place or territory; social interaction; identification.

Agreement with these characteristics is by no means universal, and other writers have provided different formulations. Some have insisted that place can be replaced by "communities of interest" where people join together to form a network not related to geography. Social interaction can refer to various of phenomena including associational networks such as businesses, schools, police and fire departments, industries, banks, and units of local government. Social interaction can also include reference to common norms, customs, and means for obtaining desired ends.

Freidman (1993), in her article "Concepts of Community," extended the definition of community. She suggested "Today, we belong to communities of experience: groups of people who have undergone a common experience." She also talked about communities of interest, values, location, fear, age, and time.

These concepts helped us to understand some of the dynamics at work in the community ethnography class and to make sense of the instructor's approach to teaching. Ernie chose to develop a learning community that, in many respects, reflected the characteristics of a community just described. Ernie's idea contrasted in many respects to the forms of individually oriented organizations common in the classrooms of our educational institutions.

Community Building

Community building was a central term in the operation of our class. Dictionary definitions are not adequate to describe the sense in which these words were used in this context. The sense of community building in Dr. Stringer's class derived from the enactment of a particular set of values. These values, in turn, provided a different set of criteria for evaluating activities and events in the class. These included:

Pride: Feelings of self-worth.
Dignity: Feelings of autonomy, independence, and competence.
Identity: Affirmations of people's social identity.
Control: Local people's control of resources, decisions, actions, events, and activities.
Responsibility: People's ability to be accountable for their own actions.
Solidarity: Coherent groups of people.
Place and Space: Work in places chosen by the people, in spaces where they are comfortable (Stringer 1993).

Ernie's practice of community formation in our graduate course might be judged by any of these criteria. Dignity, for instance, derived from the practice of establishing a collegial atmosphere in the classroom: We began to work as equals. Ernie's use of classroom interviews helped deepen our awareness of individual identities, and the corporate recounting of our weekly remembrances was instrumental in creating of a community identity. The concepts of control and responsibility were manifest in Ernie's approach to developing a syllabus and in the way he had class members act as class facilitators. Solidarity evolved in the class as small groups worked together on reports, reading assignments, individual ethnographies, and group accounts. It was noticeable that class members worked cooperatively and spoke of themselves using the communal *we*. The special setup of the classroom and the use of homes for class meetings also gave this course a unique sense of sharing space and contributed to the formation of a sense of community. According to his own criteria, therefore, Dr. Stringer was successful in his efforts to define classroom life in terms of community.

Coe (1990) identified three elements of a successful approach to implementing community projects. These elements are: communication that links participants in a network and supports their goals and interests; leadership that encourages widespread and active leadership by other project participants; and collaboration that allows the development and refinement of a shared vision to guide the community.

Although all three of Coe's elements are illustrated in this narrative, leadership in our class was particularly significant. Leadership was structured as a sharing of power between the professor and the class members, a practice followed even when it might have been easier to follow old practices. The unwillingness of the professor, in this instance, to exercise his power to decrease the feelings of frustration and uncertainty felt by many during initial class meetings enabled participants to struggle toward new definitions and new roles in the educational process.

Sense of Community

According to one definition, a community development process stimulates opportunities for membership, influence, mutual needs satisfaction, shared emotional ties, and support (Chavis & Wandersman, 1990). Chavis and Wandersman suggested that a sense of community is characterized by "the relationship between the individual and the social structure." They elaborated three components: perception of the environment, social relations, and perceived control and empowerment in the community. The experience of people in the community-based ethnography class certainly seemed to illustrate the ways in which these qualities may be present in a university class. The class exemplified shared power, expanded forms of interpersonal relations, sharing, empowerment, and enhanced control. Although the sense of empowerment was slow to emerge for some class members the overall impact of Dr. Stringer's class was to build a strong sense of community and to enable members to form interpersonal links and to achieve their learning goals.

Shared Power

An underlying principle in Ernie's class was the sharing of power and responsibility. This sharing of power was not unlike the partnerships Eisler described in her book *The Chalice and the Blade* (1987). The following table provides a sense of the contrast between what she called the dominator model and the partnership model (Eisler and Loye, 1990).

TABLE 3.1
Dominator Model Versus Partnership Model

Dominator Model	Partnership Model
Fear	Trust
Win–lose orientation	Win–win orientation
Power over	Power to and with
Male dominance	Gender partnership
Sadomasochism	Mutual pleasure
Control	Nurture
Ranking	Linking
One-sided benefit	Mutual benefit
Manipulation	Open communications
Destruction	Actualization
Hoarding	Sharing
Co-dependency	Interdependency
Left-brain thinking	Whole-brain thinking
Negative conditioning	Positive conditioning

The traditional teaching–learning paradigm is based on the dominator model, no matter how gently it is carried out. The teacher or professor is the dominator who usually demands that everyone learn the same concepts and compete for a grade. Ernie's model, based on open communications and shared decision making, redistributed power among all class participants.

Facilitating

Another concept that Eisler and Loye (1990) used in working with groups is *facilitating*. They suggested that *facilitator* is a better word than *leader* in terminology more appropriate to a partnership model. Ernie's teaching style derives from a teaching–learning paradigm that is made visible, in part, by his fundamental assumptions about empowerment. Not only did he provide an environment where Eisler and Loye's idea of partnership could flourish but he clearly stated the fundamental premises of empowerment (Stringer, 1993) whereby people have: control of their own situation and feelings of control; decision-making opportunities that enable them to define their priorities and determine their directions; and the means to affect the events and activities that have an impact on their lives.

A COMMUNITY OF LEARNERS

Small groups are often depicted as sites for people to work to accomplish individual goals. The competitive ethos embedded in the social processes of many group contexts pits members against each other and works against the goals of the group. When small groups decide to honor individual differences; and to share power, they begin to experience a sense of community.

The experiences recounted here illustrate the ways in which members of a class group participated in a program of learning and, in the process, became a community of learners. As this account demonstrates, some people accept this approach more quickly or easily than others, but the power of community building to enhance the potential of educational institutions has yet to be realized.

The people depicted in this chapter were not novices to education: they were all graduate students with years of experience as classroom teachers or in community settings. Almost all reported a heightened sense of community by the end of the class, a phenomenon highlighted by the fact that eight of us are still working together to present workshops and to write and publish this book.

This story illustrates how we built a sense of community by sharing memories, decisions, food, and many activities. When the power in the class was shifted from being traditionally teacher centered, something happened.

Space was used to change the dynamics of the class and to provide the possibility of a new set of interactions while a process called community building was enacted. As a fundamental tool for education, community building provides the possibility for developing an approach to education that facilitates learning and enacts a set of principles reflecting human and democratic values.

REFERENCES

Chavis, D. M., & Wandersman, A. (1990). Sense of community in the urban environment: A catalyst for participation and community development. *American Journal of Community Psychology, 18*(1), 55–81.

Christenson, J. A., Fendley, K., & Robinson, J. W., Jr. (1989). Community development. In J. A. Christenson & J. W. Robinson, Jr. (Eds.), *Community development in perspective* (pp. 3–25). Ames, IA: Iowa State University Press.

Coe, B. C. (1990). Open focus: A model of community development. *Journal of Community Development Society, 21*(2), 18–35.

Denzin, N. K. (1989). *Interpretive interactionism.* Newbury Park, CA: Sage.

Eisler, R. (1987). *The chalice and the blade: Our history, our future.* San Francisco: Harper & Row.

Eisler, R., & Loye D. (1990). *The partnership way.* San Francisco: HarperCollins.

Freidman, E. (1993). Concepts of community. *Healthcare Forum Journal, 3,* 11–17.

Glaser, B. G., & Strauss, A. L. (1967). *The discovery of grounded theory: Strategies for qualitative research.* New York: Aldine De Gruyter.

Spradley, J. P. (1980). *Participant observer.* Fort Worth, TX: Harcourt Brace Jovanovich.

Stringer, E. T. (1993). Socially responsive educational research: Linking theory and practice. In D. J. Flinders & J. E. Mills (Eds.), *Theory and concepts in qualitative research: Perspective from the field* (pp. 221–242). New York: Teachers College Press.

4

Philosophical and Pedagogical Development: An Ethnographic Process

Lois McFadyen Christensen

> As we entered the classroom that evening, Dr. Stringer was sitting inside with about five students. The tables and chairs were arranged so the whole class could gather together and face each other. This classroom is cluttered and in need of a dust rag, but the atmosphere is more welcoming than most of the other austere alternatives, some with chairs bolted to the floor.

Conventional instruction is based on the premise that knowledge can be transmitted, but this premise strikingly contrasts to Dewey's (1916/1966) description of an effective learning environment: "Any social arrangement that remains vitally social, or vitally shared, is educative to those who participated in it." Traditional instruction, including graduate level course work, systematically elicits the lower-order thinking skills of comprehension and knowledge regurgitation, the exception an application phase generally in the form of a final paper. Analyzing, processing and debriefing through reflection are characteristically absent from the sanctioned approach; a product is the focus of traditional direct instruction (Ornstein, 1989; Unks, 1986). Instructors commonly use scantron sheets for multiple-choice tests to assess graduate student knowledge acquisition. Passive learning versus active participation in the learning process is another indicator of differences between traditional instruction and a constructivist approach that emphasis interaction, reflection, and analysis. A transmission rather than a constructed model persists in the halls of higher education.

By comparison, holistic, critically constructed learning is accomplished through interacting in learning environments where collaborative processes and reflection prevail (Gardner, 1991; McCarty, 1991). Likewise, Pintrich, Marx, and Boyle (1993) advocated a constructivist approach to learning, with the premise that conceptual change occurs through personal, motivational, social, and historical processes. Although educators know that learners con-

53

struct knowledge and make sense of the world by processing experiences holistically, the educational system traditionally reproduces an organizational structure that is not holistic, interactive, collaborative, or reflective (DeVries & Kohlberg, 1990).

This narrative account portrays the ways that powerful learning experiences of graduate students in a class in community-based ethnography shaped philosophical and pedagogical development for participants. The account describes voices that "chorally" shifted, molded, and redefined individual philosophical and pedagogical belief systems because of the transactive processes operating in the course. Development occurred more profoundly for some participants than for others, but the actual engagement in the context of situated, collaborative learning initiated cognitive transformation for many course participants.

Do traditional versus nontraditional educational approaches present a quagmire in the educational system? Specifically, how did an atypical framework and the dynamics of this graduate course trigger development of philosophical and pedagogical belief systems? Is it possible that a particular framework fostered thorough and critical knowledge construction beyond that of a traditional lecture method?

HOLISTIC PROCESSES

The model used to interpret, analyze, and report data in this chapter is a modified form of Denzin's (1989) suggested interpretive qualitative methodology. The account is derived from data that were the processes, products, and outcomes of a graduate course in community-based ethnography. The material quoted in this chapter includes portions of graduate students' life stories, personal histories, recorded during and following the class facilitated by Dr. Ernie Stringer and excerpts of interviews and written documents.

Data were gathered from individual interviews conducted during spring semester 1993 and from follow-up interviews conducted in fall 1993. Reflective journals kept by class members, group ethnographic accounts written about class proceedings, class members' notes, and final projects, both individual and group, were also used as data. Quotes were assembled from class members' notes and journals, collaboratively written group ethnographies, in-class interviews, and follow-up interviews. Interviews and subsequent drafts of this chapter were member checked and triangulated with the quoted participants in an effort to represent their voices as authentically as possible (Lincoln & Guba, 1985).

Data were interpreted and analyzed to illuminate the essential processes of the class. This analysis revealed the key elements that provided the substance for this study, including the group and individual processes that made up the learning activities in the course.

References to *processes* throughout this chapter are those learning activities that the course facilitator designed and in which graduate students participated. These processes were inherently holistic, interactive, collaborative, and reflective. The processes are outlined in detail in the catalytic events section of this account.

This narrative recounts class members' oral histories and reviews epiphanic experiences that made a marked difference in the lives of fledgling ethnographers, be they positive or negative (Denzin, 1989). The interpretive voice is mine as I seek to give readers a multigraphic account of this profound experience.

This chapter is written with my comments in italics in an effort to come to grips with telling the others' story and to keep my own autoethnographic commentary as separate as possible. Because I was a member of the class, a participant observer in a strong sense, it is impossible to totally silence my voice. My comments are written in the following form:

I heavily referred to my work–study group's collaboratively written ethnography, my class notes, and my reflexive journal.

SETTING THE STAGE

This odyssey is set in the context of a community-based ethnographic research methodology course in spring semester 1993, facilitated by Dr. Ernest Stringer, visiting professor from Australia. From the onset, it was apparent he was not a traditional direct-instruction professor and that the traditional textbook and lecture model would not be perpetuated in this course. "Ernie is tall with broad shoulders, a salt-and-pepper beard, with dark straight hair styled longer than the majority of professors at our institution."

On the first Tuesday night class, in a large room with an elementary classroom decor, a few class members observed the following:

Bulletin boards demonstrate attempts at warmth, an appreciation for history and even the aesthetic: a collage of Miro, Klee and Chagall, its figures challenged by another display of the presidents of the United States (Clinton was noticeably absent).

The professor, Ernie Stringer, had an ideological compass for the voyage; the student-crew brought their [sic] cognitive baggage ready for unpacking and repacking with inquiring souls.

At Texas A&M, a traditional system of education predominates. Most students are accustomed to and expect the conventional lecture approach to graduate course content, methodology and teaching, a system perpetuated by graduate teaching assistants who tend to reproduce this practice and sustain this pedagogy.

Almost immediately, however, Ernie modeled a decisively different philosophical approach to learning, an approach characterized by participation, collaboration, and discourse. This approach was maintained throughout the course and persists in his advanced ethnographic methods courses.

For 18 apprentice ethnographers and the facilitator, the theoretical frameworks and ethnographic processes provided heuristic tools that acted as catalysts to participants' philosophical and pedagogical development (Denzin, 1989; Spradley, 1980; Stringer, 1993). Overarching components integral to Ernie's pedagogy were: emergent flow (relates to allowing a process to emerge); negotiation; and critical reflection. Our development was often latent, hidden in the context of conflict, and obstacles; but as we collaboratively constructed meaning about community-based ethnography, philosophical and pedagogical patterns emerged. Class members recollected:

> Ernie talked about the definition of culture as being the sum total of the group's experiences and knowledge they have learned consciously or unconsciously and that it permeated everything in the group. With this definition, we felt that our class was evolving into a unique culture of its own. All of us were in some way simultaneously shaping each other and though the results may not be apparent yet, things were beginning to gel.

> The professor helped me to challenge my thinking and the thinking of others. It was a joyous sort of struggle to grow and learn.

A group reflected: "We have not just read and studied how others have done community-based ethnography, we have learned by doing it." Another classmate recollected the process of constructing knowledge out of dissonance: "This class has been an eye-opening experience and well worth all the uneasiness I felt during the course."

Some, however, saw the process conversely: "I found the collaborative writing difficult, not supportive ... trying to do something with a group that wasn't a group yet. I never felt good about it."

In still another perspective: "Some groups lost sight of the general purpose of the group tasks which was to experience different facets of working together in ethnographic activity. Instead, some had a tendency to take on assignments as merely another task that had to go from A to Z."

It is as if 18 graduate students and a visiting professor set sail exploring uncharted waters on an odyssey to the emic, the inside analysis, interlaced with reflection, of connections from theory to practice, to form a heuristic model. Storms that arose caused disequilibrium, but all members eventually achieved personal growth. I saw it, too, as if graduate participants became like apprentice potters observing technique at the wheel of the master potter. We moved in and out of observation and implementation in order to create elaborate, ever emergent pieces of pottery. Each piece was a particular culmination of a mutually shaped experience not to be replicated. Critical evaluation and reflection on the opus being sculpted were constant. Often there was dysfunction around the wheel. Centering the clay on the wheel became problematic, and obstacles and issues produced some asymmetrically shaped sculpting pots. The skills and knowledge gained and practiced alongside the artisan, however, intricate, resulted in distinctive, and useful vessels for doing and ethnography.

As we participated in the learning processes and reflected on our experiences, we realized that we collectively constructed meaning about community-based ethnography. Within our learning community, we began to understand that community-based research is also a participatory, collaborative process.

CATALYTIC EVENTS AND CLASS DYNAMICS

The catalytic events that nurtured philosophical and pedagogical development for most class members were the group and individual learning processes designed by Ernie. The group processes were inherently collaborative and included interviews, study groups, role playing, retelling the events of previous class meetings, community-building activities, a collaboratively written class ethnography, facilitating two class session agendas, and, for some, a collaborative community ethnographic final project. Collaboration was interlaced throughout all the transactive processes, group and individual.

The individual processes, strategies that were primarily individual accomplishments, consisted of keeping a reflexive journal, taking class notes, writing thickly described accounts of the course to be drawn upon for collaborative writing purposes, accumulating portfolio and, in some cases, carrying out an individual final project. Class members often discussed their development of these individual processes, and progress was also cultivated by the dynamics that occurred during and as a result of the learning processes. Transactive, spontaneous, collegial interaction in a social community of learners only partially characterizes the dynamics that resulted from participants' engagement in the learning processes.

Interviews were an important part of initial learning processes. During the first class meeting, members interviewed one another, first in pairs, then in groups of 4. Ernie asked us to delve to the depths of interviewees, not just in life's benchmarks. When we finished our interviews, we introduced our interviewees to the entire group. We continued the interviewing exercise through the third week of class. This was our initial rehearsal in telling another's story and "getting it right," in doing ethnography through discourse. "When we came together in our group of six, we spoke more smoothly, fluently. We had more confidence in what we were saying because we had a chance to correct and review our information, too, because we were better acquainted. There was a lot of laughter and sharing. We instinctively felt the dynamics of community building activated."

Work–study groups that we formed about 4 weeks into the semester became the context for much of our learning. We had sufficient time to know our colleagues through the interviewing process, and some work–study groups seemed to naturally emerge. Groups had 4 or 5 members. Group work, which revolved around course processes, involved discussing assigned readings, writing corporate ethnographies, collaborating on community projects, and organizing and facilitating two class sessions. A few class members recalled:

> I felt that Ernie deliberately had us organize [sic] into groups so that we could work with each other in a collaborative manner.

> These collaborative groups seemed to materialize before our very eyes.

> I think there are a lot of factors that were pretty unique in our situation. First the choice; we came together of our own free will.

Some groups functioned smoothly; others struggled to gain consensus, equally distribute power and establish harmony. A member of one group commented in a postclass interview:

"Other groups worked as teams. We were a bad group." This group found collaboration particularly problematic because of out-of-class responsibilities as well as for reasons mentioned earlier.

Role playing was another technique Ernie implemented as a learning process. In the "fishbowl," a type of role playing, he divided the class into two groups. The tables and chairs were in a U shape. He faced the 9 members involved in the discussion. The other class members sat behind Ernie in a backward L formation and took notes on what they saw and heard. The fishbowl activity was laced with content and demonstrated facilitative and direct teaching methods.

Another kind of role playing was part of the agenda in a class session that took place at a class member's home. Four class members, one from each work–study group, interviewed Ernie with the use of Spradley's (1990) elements of an interview process. During this process, Ernie symbolically exited occasionally from the interview to clarify or point out weak and strong interview techniques.

For the first 5 or 6 weeks, each class session began with a collective recollection of the events of the past class, told through collaborative reminiscing. "Bit by bit, piece by piece, class members put the puzzle together [so] that our collective memories recalled [sic] from the previous week. By consensus, our common story was built from our multiple realities."

The class processes inherently built community. Additional activities were specifically implemented to further this community-building dimension. A potluck supper was one such occasion. Other examples include socializing activities and the "name game." Beginning each of the first four class meetings with the strategy of the name game, enabled us to master each other's names quickly. All of us, including Ernie, sat at tables arranged in the customary U shape, gave our names in turn, and added them to those previously mentioned.

Class members were all responsible for bringing food to at least one class session. Each Thursday, class members placed their offerings on a ledge that bordered the south end of the room. Ernie sometimes invited class members to his apartment for a "sundowner," an Australian cocktail party, or to a local hangout following class. These social activities served to build a sense of togetherness and to contribute to forming a community of learners. We learned ethnography in a community that was scholastically, cognitively, emotionally, socially, and physically holistic.

Each of the four work–study groups wrote a collaborative ethnography. Many used an individual thick description assignment with raw data field notes to write their ethnographies. Class members commented on the process: "It is the consensus of our group that the process of ethnographic research, as we have seen modelled in the classroom, is more important than even the content." "We have learned [ethnography] by doing it."

During the last few months of class, each work–study group organized and facilitated at least one class session. Class sessions included group time to discuss readings and projects, a presentation by Ernie on the most salient topic in the readings, and a whole-class activity. This process enabled us to be literally responsible for community-based praxis.

Each class member conducted community-based research and wrote an ethnographic report. Class members negotiated their community-based projects with Ernie before beginning research. Some conducted research in pairs; others pursued research individually. As they progressed, the projects were reported on and discussed in the work–study group setting. This conferencing facilitated collegial input to each project. Final projects were the result of total immersion in the ethnographic processes of the class. The entire class discussed some community-based projects.

Throughout the course, we kept journals to record evolving reflections about the class. The journals served as raw data for our collaborative ethnographies and as field notes for projects. We submitted our journals at midterm, and Ernie returned them with extensive commentaries. The journals were submitted again at the end of the semester as a part of a class portfolio.

Members kept notes on reading summaries done for work–study group discussions; these notes were part of our field notes used as raw data for writing class ethnographies. Each class member wrote extensive notes, approximately 20 single-spaced pages, that thickly described our class interactions. The Spradley and Denzin (1989) texts were references, along with Geertz's (1973) methodology of thickly describing particular contexts.

Each class member completed a cumulative portfolio that included such work as a journal, class notes, summaries of readings, outside readings, and field notes. The portfolio served as a comprehensive compilation of accomplished course products.

The holistic, interactive, collaborative nature of these learning processes fostered development of class members' philosophical and pedagogical belief systems. The learning processes were the particular course activities that established the conditions in which philosophical and pedagogical growth flourished.

OUTCOMES OF CLASS PROCESSES

The frameworks and processes of this course, the discourse and transactions among class members, individual and group community projects, corporate writing, assigned and suggested readings, and reflection on the total experience created an intricately woven fabric that catalyzed philosophical development in several class participants.

Personal philosophy is dynamic and emergent. It assists people to define reality as it gives meaning to decisions and actions. For some class members, the cognitive dissonance and disequilibrium, the mental discrepancies and conflicts preceded philosophical development as people struggled to reconceptualize their experiences. As class members' philosophies shifted, however, the tenets of ethnographic work and its underlying assumptions spawned new meaning-making and behaviors associated with it. The new mental constructs enabled class participants to understand the problems that seemed to emerge naturally in the learning context. Class members provided evidence of philosophical development in the following areas:

Greater tolerance for others' views and acceptance of multiple realities.
Development of new, sophisticated mental constructs including increased understanding of the concepts of *interdependence, collaboration,* and *consensus.*
Realizations about emergent selves.
Examination of personal philosophies.

Tolerating Others' Views: Multiple Realities

Embedded in traditional teacher-centered instruction is an authoritative power system. A constructivist learning framework, on the other hand, diminishes authoritative power structures. Through negotiation, collaboration, and active student–teacher transaction in a constructivist learning environment, learners' ideas are valued, the learners are empowered. During the first night of class, Ernie asked for contributions from class members toward development of a course syllabus. The experience was both liberating and frustrating for some class members:

Unlike the routine process of the professor walking in with a set of pre-developed agendas and establishing the power structure by giving directions, this time the professor was providing us the opportunity for input.

Ernie asked the group to share goals and expectations they had for the course ... the majority of students who wanted to learn more about ethnographic studies became the victors in setting the goals for the course.

Fear and uncertainty about the emergent nature of the course surfaced early, even for Ernie, the course facilitator:

The development of the syllabus was not, however, without problems. Feeling the panic rising in some of the students, I presented them with a fully formulated program of study the following week, which, though it spoke to most of their concerns, did not in any way resemble the issues which they had presented to me. Had I been less fearful of their fear I would have spent the time to show them precisely how their issues and needs had been included in the program which was formulated.

The syllabus indeed materialized and reflected the issues stated by class members.

Most concerns, contrary to Ernie's account, did appear to be met in his compilation of the issues, in my estimation.

Through other processes such as group writing, study groups for processing assigned readings, and group responsibility for planning and facilitating two class sessions, class members developed tolerance for others' views: "We realize [sic] that we are undergoing a new paradigm in community-based research as Ernie is guiding us to become more self-autonomous in our search for community living and what it means for us who come from diverse backgrounds to be together and share and discover our common vision."

The idea of accepting others' reality marked almost all of the four collaboratively written ethnographies. Through the course learning processes, class members wrote that they had realized multiple realities existed in their work–study groups. Whole-class activities collectively recalling previous class sessions revealed a variety of participants' realities about the same event. The following example focused on the acceptance of multiple realities: "I grew, [insofar as the class] gave me a chance to look at other folks and what they thought about topics ... the importance of reconfirming that what we think was heard was what was said."

New Mental Constructs

Reconceptualization took place on many fronts. One class member reflected in a follow-up interview about the power relations in her work–study group. Speaking during our interview, she was still obviously deconstructing her philosophical position: "I am not sure where I went with that class. I did a lot of thinking about power relations. It came out of my group. Most of it came out of my frustration."

Enculturation to an approach to learning creates a learning environment. If the environment authentically focuses on collaborative work, then learners socially construct collaborative practice. The environment serves as a medium for cognitive apprenticeship (Brown, Collins, & Duguid, 1989) and for relevant social and contextual learning. Competition is an outgrowth of traditional educational settings; collaboration is a coordinate in a constructivist learning framework. Our class members deconstructed their situated experience in collaboration:

> To work in harmony with and to let the final product be larger than the sum of the parts.

> As a group, we are attempting to construct our own framework of what community-based ethnography can be. The way we are attempting to do that is dialoguing and negotiating objectives, purposes and projects so we can build this course as we go.

> All of us were in some way simultaneously shaping others.

> *I had a stake in it [the class format]. It was a collaborative effort and the methods were varied and student-centered.*

Ernie observed the dissonance: "However, the very act of compromising caused anxiety, insecurity, and even hostility, and the students reached back for the comfort of the old paradigm, while trying to grapple with the process of the new." Interdependence and collaboration were foreign elements in their formal education of some class members. Ultimately, struggling through the atypical approach to learning, some participants nevertheless gained philosophical growth.

REALIZATIONS: EMERGENT SELVES

The learning processes caused class members to confront and reconceptualize earlier beliefs. Philosophical systems were examined and redefined. "Ernie brought hand printed frameworks on chart paper to class on our third meeting. 'Journal writing' was neatly printed on a brightly colored marker on the poster bearing the framework heading 'Products'."

The experience of keeping a journal evoked reflections and realizations about the emergent self. On the basis of re-examination of her personal philosophy, one class member stretched her boundaries of previous self-conceptions: "I used a process where I sat down with my journal and started with description of what happened in the class. Then, I would write about what that made me think and what that made me feel. I started to ask myself questions. I would write a paragraph then read it and ask myself, 'So, why do I think that and why do I feel that way?' I actually journaled [sic] with myself."

This class member explained that journalizing allowed her long-buried questions to surface. She re-evaluated her position in life:

> The question was, who am I, anyway? What makes me who I am? What are the beliefs that guide my actions that make me who I am? Rather than fitting in the mould [sic], I started to ask myself and see why I wanted to fit in the mould. Do I want to be this person? Do others fit in the mould? Do others question themselves? Am I the only one who doesn't have a firm handle? Why do I feel this inner struggle to be free of a box? My thinking had boundaries and the process made me comfortable with pushing on those boundaries.

Another class member recalled his ruminations about the impact of the class processes in a follow-up interview: "This class was a stepping stone to higher realizations [sic] of who I am and what I am about in this world. It gave me affirmation of where my future will be and the type of work I will be doing which will be building community."

An experience was the result of this individual's final project: "I have learned what it is like to be on the giving and receiving end of suspicion associated with race ... the task of interviewing a community, then writing about that community ... looking back, my ignorance and naiveté in choosing a community, and my thoughts going into the project, are astounding."

Reflection, a component interlaced through the courses learning processes, evoked examination of existing philosophies. With cognitive accommodation of enlightened realizations, the boundaries of some class members' self-conceptions were stretched.

EXAMINING PERSONAL PHILOSOPHIES

The learning processes caused some class members to examine family and social learning. Through examination, deconstruction, and restructuring, philosophical growth occurred. One class member initiated research with some African American middle-school students who were somewhat disruptive in a classroom where she volunteered. Before conducting interviews, she called to ask for parents' permission. Two were quite congenial but one mother was adamantly against her son's participation in the research. This scenario led the class member to examine her unconscious prejudices and expectations in light of another's reality:

We, the dominant white culture are still more suspicious of people with skin color different from our own, but as I learned the hard way, the change in attitudes and perceptions must stem from something other than pity. The change must be about friendship and relating to people in their own realities, not about what we believe their reality to be and how we can alter it.

Reflecting on the experience caused her to rethink her personal philosophy and to alter her belief system. "Coming from a white, middle class background, I am used to feeling or believing one way, but behaving publicly and living another way. The public behavior usually being [sic] what makes the most people happy and comfortable and it made me happy to make others happy, but left me feeling morally uncomfortable."

Many of these quotations can be interchanged in each area of philosophical development. The quotes indicate critical reflection that produced understanding and tolerance for others' realities. In the process of attempting to understand the role of ethnographer, many class members grew better able to understand others' perspectives.

On the assumption that philosophy undergirds pedagogy, change in individual philosophies precipitated pedagogical restructuring for many class participants. Because of profound experiences, some class members wanted to practice this constructivist pedagogy, others desired to adopt only particular processes, and still others were more accepting of their students' mental constructions than they had been. Praxis was an outcome of our immersion experience in ethnographic processes:

I think more about the [group] dynamics. And it carries over into my teaching because of the way Ernie facilitated the class, the pedagogical technique.

Stringer did it in a more personal way, ethnography. People are people, not data. It was more humanistic. I feel being a graduate student made me feel as a practitioner there are meaningful methods to know and to learn that we really haven't used in the past.

Other class members recollected.

I am not very hopeful about higher education, but people like Ernie give me hope because they are interested in people and process.

Being able to apply it while I was actually in the course set the stage for what I am doing now. When doing staff development, I began with Ernie's model. They [teachers] set the stage. They began with what they wanted to learn. The whole idea of letting teachers having the ownership, and letting teachers collaborate and respond, studying the process of how their questions change, this whole community-based framework and providing whole language staff development fits [sic] together. It [sic] is connected.

IMPLICATIONS

A powerful learning experience in a community-based ethnographic course induced philosophical and pedagogical development for many class participants. An atypical, constructivist framework triggered examination of belief systems and promoted cognitive restructuring to accommodate new concepts. This phenomenon flourished in our constructivist learning setting and was without a doubt context specific. In previous traditional educational settings, class members had not experienced such marked philosophical and pedagogical development. A constructivist approach to learning is rooted in Dewey's (1930) experientialist curriculum. According to Dewey, the logical place to start the educative process is with the learners' interests. Dewey thought that learning should be approached in an integrated and participatory fashion to enable learners to construct and continually reconstruct meaning from authentic experiences. Dewey focused on an holistic learning experience rather than on discrete bits of memorized knowledge.

Collaboration in U.S. education, too, began with Dewey's philosophy (1916). Collaboration is the active participation that catalyzes learners to construct meaning from learning experiences (Calwetir, 1993). Collaboration adds another dimension that enculturates learning as it facilitates accommodation (Brown, Collins, & Duguid, 1989). Moreover, Brown, Collins, and Duguid pointed out that graduate students in most advanced fields become apprentices to the experts in particular fields; they learn through collaboration in social and cultural dimensions.

Johnson and Johnson (1991) asserted that working collaboratively can have profound effects. The method is clearly more comprehensive for conceptual learning and problem-solving tasks than are other methods (Johnson & Johnson, 1991). Group work places responsibility for learning on learners and it is empowering and liberating.

In liberating environments, networks of relationships are interconnected, and integrity is developed and maintained (Shrewsbury, 1987). In these environments, power is shared and participants empowered. A zone of transformation, akin to Vygotsky's (Vygotsky, 1986) zone of proximal development, is inherently part of a liberating learning environment.

Modeling and enacting ethnographic processes provide constructive apprenticeships for novice ethnographers. Heuristic frameworks, learning processes, and experiences are means for novice ethnographers to personally develop philosophies that are underpinnings for their pedagogy.

Dewey's account (1916/1966) accurately described the educative nature and conditions of this graduate course in community-based ethnography (as the quotation shows on p. 53). A collaborative and community-based approach, for the voices represented in this narrative, was holistically enlightening. Ernie created a learning framework that produced a particular social arrangement. It was an authentic context, a learning community with a viable culture that was vitally social and shared. This context enabled class members to reflect on and to analyze the learning processes that lead to authentic ethnographic products and understandings. This reflection shaped participants' philosophy and augmented their understanding of pedagogy. When participants enacted their newly constructed pedagogical understanding in their teaching contexts, dramatic philosophical and pedagogical changes occurred because class members were engaged in socially structured ethnographic learning processes. These changes represented a shift from traditional teaching methods to a constructivist learning philosophy.

As many teacher education colleges rethink pedagogical purpose and programs, constructivist methodology rather than traditional teacher-centered pedagogy should be strongly considered. A collaborative approach appears to be more effective than is a competitive one. Shared meaning, purpose, and process seem to establish a community of learners and allow them to reap collegiality and authentic ethnographic research. Related constructivist literature validates the philosophical and pedagogical learning won from our participatory apprenticeship in community-based ethnography.

Placing the focus on constructing rather than transmitting knowledge produces learning from, as well as about, practice (Lieberman, 1992). Connections between theory and practice were particularly salient in our class. Participants learned ethnography as they modeled, practiced, accomplished, and diffused it in other teaching and learning settings. Learning ethnography through immersion in a learning community with an emergent culture whereby ethnographic assumptions were enacted enabled class members to develop philosophically and pedagogically. This account suggests that it is time to inquire about the epistemology of traditional education and instruction, especially in graduate school settings.

REFERENCES

Brown, J., Collins, A., & Duguid, P. (1989). Situated cognitiona nd the culture of learning. *Educational Researcher, 18*(1), 32–42.

Calweti, G. (Ed.). (1993). *Challenges and achievements of American education: 1993 Yearbook of the Association for Supervision and Curriculum Development*. Alexandria, VA: ASCD.

Denzin, N. (1989). *Interpretive interactionism*. Newbury Park, CA: Sage.

DeVries, R., & Kohlberg, L. (1990). *Constructivist early education: Overview and comparison with other programs*. Washington, DC: National Association for the Education of Young Children.

Dewey, J. (1916/1966). *Democracy in education*. New York: Macmillan.

Dewey, J. (1930). From absolutism to experimenatlism. In G. P. Adams & W. P. Montgomery (Eds.), *Contemporary American philosophy* (pp.13–27). New York: Macmillan.

Gardner, H. (1991). *The unschooled mind: How children think and how schools should teach*. New York: Basic Books.

Geertz, C. (1973). *The interpretation of cultures*. New York: Basic Books.

Johnson, D. W., & Johnson, R. T. (1991). Classroom instruction and cooperative learning. In H. C. Waxman & H. J. Walberg (Eds.), *Effective teaching: Current research* (pp. 277–295). Berkeley, CA: McCutchan.

Lieberman, A. (1992). The meaning of scholarly activity and the building of community. *Educational Researcher, 21*(6), 5–12.

Lincoln, Y. S., & Guba, E. G. (1985). *Naturalistic inquiry.* Newbury Park, CA: Sage.

McCarty, B. J. (1991). Whole language: From philosophy to practice. *Clearing House, 65*(2), 73–76.

Ornstein, A. C. (1989). Theoretical issues related to teaching. *Education and Urban Society, 22,* 95–104.

Pintrich, P. R., Marx, R. W., & Boyle, R. A. (1993). Beyond cold conceptual change: The role of motivational beliefs and classroom contextual factors in the process of conceptual change. *Review of Educational Research, 63*(2), 167–199.

Shrewsbury, C. M. (1987). What is feminist pedagogy? *Women's Studies Quarterly, 15* (3 & 4), 6–13.

Spradley, J. (1980). *The ethnographic interview.* New York: Holt, Rinehart & Winston.

Stringer, E. (1993). Socially responsive educational research: Linking theory and practice. In D. Flinders & J. Mills (Eds.), *Theory and concepts in qualitative research: Perspectives from the field* (pp. 221–242). New York: Teachers College Press.

Unks, G., (1986). Product-oriented teaching. *Education and Urban Society, 18,* 242–254.

Vygotsky, L. (1986). Thought and language. In A. Kozulin (Ed.), *Thought and language.* Cambridge, MA: MIT Press.

5

Everything Is Different Now: Surviving Ethnographic Research

Rhonda Petty

Ethical neutrality is a veneer for irresponsibility.
—(Sydney Willhelm cited in Berreman, 1968)

The only thing necessary for the triumph of evil is for good men (and, I might add, informed men) to do nothing.
—(Edmund Burke cited in Berreman, 1968)

In our present-day world it is not enough to be scholarly; one must be concerned and angry enough to shout. It is not enough to understand the world; one must seek to change it.
—(Kenneth Winetrout cited in Berreman, 1968)

If today we concern ourselves exclusively with the technical proficiency of our students and reject all responsibility for their moral sense, or lack of it, then we may someday be compelled to accept responsibility for having trained a generation willing to serve in a future Auschwitz.
—(Alvin Gouldner cited in Berreman, 1968)

The most admirable thinkers within the scholarly community ... do not split their work from their lives. ... What this means is that you must learn to use your life experiences in your intellectual work.
—(C. Wright Mills cited in Denzin, 1989b)

These ideas reflect many facets of my personal philosophy. At times I have been forced to keep silent about many of these beliefs which did not match those of my family, friends, or both. It was therefore with a feeling of relief that I discovered these ideas in the readings assigned for my community-based ethnography class.[1] I had previously considered this way of thinking as weak,

---

[1] This chapter would not have been written without the unending patience and support given by Dr. Ernie Stringer, who not only listened to my story but provided invaluable guidance in writing and editing it.

or as a "liberal" response to the world's social problems. Liberalness and weakness were two characteristics not encouraged in the household where I was raised. I did not grow up with cold or distant parents, but they were firm believers in the philosophy that everyone in the United States had an equal opportunity to succeed and that giving people who were in straitened circumstances possessions or jobs they had not earned was no help. Giving people things only made them expect to receive more things.

I was never comfortable with this approach. I perceived my childhood Hispanic friends as less well off than I, but not as people who would take advantage of me if I somehow assisted them. I knew that they lived on the "wrong side of the tracks" and that not all their family members had jobs. I knew my friends had cultural beliefs and customs different from mine, but I did not see them as lazy or as "takers." In school they were often top students and athletes, involved in all aspects of academic life and lacking the negative attributes I had so often heard associated with their ethnic group.

I was elated, then, when I discovered through my course readings that there were people who believed as I did and could express themselves in ways that made sense to me. It helped relieve the stress I felt in my everyday work as a teacher of children who came from people I perceived as "takers." Course work legitimated my emerging perceptions, but did not provide experiences that showed me the practical consequences of my new insights. These opportunities soon presented themselves.

When I was assigned the task of selecting, interviewing, and writing about a community group for a university ethnography course, I chose to interview a group of African American boys. This chapter describes some problems in my interaction with these five boys and their mothers, and some resulting changes in my worldview. In contextualizing my story, I explain how I came to understand myself and my place in society differently. I also touch on some revelations about the broader implications of my experience. Through my encounter with these young men, I discovered that large issues can be explored on the basis of what is learned in a very small arena.

LIVED EXPERIENCE

This account derives from events that occurred during a project in a university ethnography course in spring semester 1993. The major sources of data were my own journals and reflections, the latter enhanced by written responses to stimulus questions given to me by the course professor and by constant dialogue with him over many weeks. Journal entries have been analyzed by bracketing the key elements according to an approach suggested by Denzin (1989b).

The account is autoethnographic in that it provides a portrayal of my own lived experience. According to Denzin (1989a), "The meanings of ... experiences are best given by the persons who experience them. A preoccupation with method, with the validity, reliability, generality and theoretical relevance of the biographical method must be set aside in favor of a concern for meaning and interpretation (p. 25)." Denzin also states: "There can be no firm dividing line between inner and outer experience. The biographical method recognizes this aspect of human existence, for its hallmark is the joining and recording of these two structures of experience in a personal document (p. 25)." With the biographical method advocated by Denzin (1989a), the reader receives my personal interpretation of events rather than one provided by an outside author.

DOING ETHNOGRAPHIC STUDY:
A WAKE-UP CALL

Setting Myself Up

For the major project of my ethnography class I was required to select a community or group, interview some of its members, and write an account derived from these interviews. As I contemplated the project, I decided to do something "meaningful"; to conduct a project that served a purpose larger than simply writing another paper, for a grade, to fulfill a course requirement. The desire for a meaningful project set me on a disaster course because, from the very start, I worked from the perspective of an "expert" and did not even define the audience for whom my project was to have meaning or purpose.

Because they fit our working definition of community—thinking and acting as *we*—I chose five fifth-grade African American boys from the classroom in which I did voluntary work once a week. "*We* means trouble," I thought after observing them together a few times. They were often disruptive in class; their teacher spent much of her time correcting their behavior. *Trouble* seemed to me to be somehow associated with a meaningful project.

The boys attended what is perceived by some as one of the worst elementary schools in the district. It is located in an "undesirable" neighborhood near a recently shut-down crack house; most of its students came from low socioeconomic minority families. I had previously been substitute teacher for the same class and had experienced an unnerving day. The students had been undisciplined, belligerent, apathetic about their work, and at one point violent. After lunch, one boy threw another face first into a desk because the victim had allegedly bumped the aggressor's forehead with the door. There was trouble everywhere I looked, and I was certain these kids needed me. At the inception of my project, this history added up to "meaningful," although I was to discover that by trying to find a meaningful community I had unknowingly sabotaged my project and would never write a study of a community.

Even before I approached the group of boys, many stereotypes about young black males rushed to mind: They were poor; their parents did not care about them; their grades were poor; they were mean and rough. Although most of these notions were dispelled as I became better acquainted with the boys, these stereotypes initially oriented me to my project and set me up for what was to follow.

Perhaps the most significant stumbling block, though, was my ego. On reflection, I was not totally honest with myself about who I was or what I was hoping to accomplish with this project. I wanted to believe that I viewed these five boys and their families as my equals and that I intended to interview the boys only for my assignment. I did not see the contradiction between my beliefs and my criteria for a meaningful project. How could I believe that we were all equals when I had chosen them for reasons that placed them in the position of needing my help? I had already dug a chasm between us, but was soon to receive a wake-up call from three mothers of the boys chosen.

"Is This a Minority Study?": Suspicion and Resistance

I did not expect much resistance from the boys' parents when I asked permission to interview their sons. My past teaching and work experience with Hispanic children in my hometown had been positive; their parents had trusted and welcomed me when I dropped by their homes unannounced. I had grown up with many of the children, and they had known my family for years. Unfortunately, I never considered this fact when I decided to work with children in a town where very few people knew me. I assumed that the parents of the five boys would somehow know, as soon as they talked with me, that I was a decent, caring human being who meant their sons no harm.

When I finally telephoned them, each mother's reaction was different. The first seemed distracted by a loud conversation taking place in her home, but when I told her who I was and why I wanted to interview her son, she agreed without question. This reaction reinforced one of my stereotypes: The boys' parents did not really care about them. After this successful phone call, I immediately called another boy's mother. This event marked my initiation into community-based research. After I had informed her of my reason for calling, the woman began asking questions. "Is this a minority study? What will the information be used for?" Although I tried to reassure her this was not a minority study and that the information would be used for nothing other than practice in interviewing and writing about a community, she was apprehensive and asked that I not use her son in my project. When I hung up, I felt strangely uncomfortable and ill at ease; no one had ever doubted my motives where children were concerned. I reminded myself the professor had warned the class that such things might occur: He had said that not everyone would be eager to help us with school research, but I had not seriously entertained the notion that it would happen to me. Maybe someone more abrasive might be refused, but not me.

I talked to a third mother in person. After picking up the first boy (James) for an interview, I asked him if he knew where the third boy (Lawrence) lived. When he said yes, I asked whether he thought Lawrence's mother would mind our stopping by to take him with us. He said he did not think she would care. After we got there, James and Lawrence walked into the apartment ahead of me to talk to Lawrence's mother.

I hesitated outside because I was not sure of my reception. Lawrence seemed happy to see us, but I was apprehensive about his mother. After being rejected by one mother, however politely, my confidence was definitely shaken. Lawrence lived in government apartments, most of which were rather run-down. I appeared to be the only White person there, and I was not comfortable standing beside my car. Two little boys were staring at me from their bikes on the sidewalk. Finally, I knocked on Lawrence's apartment door and went in. His mother was friendly and was eager for Lawrence to participate when I told her about my project. After agreeing to let Lawrence come with James and me, she asked casually if this was a study on criminals. I assured her that it was not and we left. I was stunned: Lawrence's mother's willingness to believe I was using her son as an example of a precriminal fueled the fire that kept my stereotypes alive.

The interview with James and Lawrence went well. After 2 hours of interviewing, playing video games, and washing my car, I took them home. I was relieved and happy to finally have begun my project. During the next week I planned to talk to the last two mothers and to interview their sons the following weekend.

The fourth boy's (Thomas) mother worked in the public library. As she did not have a home phone, I decided to go to the library to visit her. I was sure my presence would persuade her to allow Thomas to participate in my study. She did not seem to fully understand my request, however, so I repeated my initial explanation. After a few moments' silence, I thought that she did not want to give me an answer on the spot. I suggested she go home and talk it over with Thomas and then call me at home that night. I did not hear from her that night. When I saw Thomas at the district-wide, fifth-grade track meet the next day, he said his mother did not want him to be in the study. He would not look at me while we talked; he hung on the fence and looked down at the track.

I was not greatly surprised by the negative response, but it still hurt a little. Thomas stayed away from me the whole day although I did not note this fact until the entire project had collapsed. When I later reflected on events, I realized that Thomas had not spoken to me at the track meet except to say he could not be interviewed. His behavior was difficult for me accept because he had been friendly when I did volunteer work in his class, had included me in whatever he was doing, and had been the first student to ask me for help with an assignment. Now it appeared that he had been told to stay away from me, and even after the project had finished, he kept his distance.

I called the last parent the night after the track meet and asked whether her son (Martin) had told her I would be calling. None of the boys had told their parents I would be calling although I had asked them to do so, and Martin was no exception. I launched into my rehearsed speech about myself, however, and explained the nature of the project to her. Finally, on this last try, I felt I had delivered the speech perfectly, but I soon discovered I had made no impression on this woman. She began asking questions. "Why are you doing this?" "What is it for?" "What kind of questions will you be asking?" I told her that I was doing this project for my community-based ethnography course at the university and that the paper would be used for nothing except practice in using information-gathering techniques. I explained I would be asking questions about school, friends, home, but she cut me off and said she did not want me to interview her son for a project or to speak to him at all. Then I heard a click as she hung up on me.

This event had a devastating impact. I sat listening to the dial tone and slowly began to realize what had just happened. First I felt insulted at being cut off in the middle of a conversation; then the full weight of the situation hit me. My emotions became a jumble of fury, frustration, and pain. I was confused because the woman had judged me negatively without ever meeting me and furious because she had destroyed my project without knowing about it. There was a burning frustration at having lost control of the project when speaking to someone I did not know. I deeply resented the audacity of this woman who had questioned me and then not given me a chance to defend myself. My chest felt tight from trying to control my tears and anger.

In this state of mind, I made a few quick decisions. I vowed I would never again talk to anyone except White people and decided to move to the suburbs. I told myself I did not have to put up with such treatment, that I had other options, and that I would teach in private schools where parents appreciated me. I was certain I had spent more time on these boys and their mothers than they deserved. I felt completely unappreciated and thought it best to remove myself from the situation. I called their teacher and told her I would cease doing volunteer work in her room.

I was angry because I had not been given the benefit of the doubt and had been judged harshly by people who did not know me. I was irritated with African Americans for having "a chip on their shoulder." I was also angry because I was unable to make these women trust me and was incensed that they appeared to hold me responsible for social ills for which I was not responsible.

Because I was unable to study the community I had planned to, I had no project as the end of the semester neared. The most painful frustration came when I realized that because these mothers had rejected me, their sons' perceptions of me were tainted.

Had I been able to put my feelings aside for a moment, I might have appreciated the protective instincts of the three mothers who had not let their sons participate. These women were responsible, concerned parents who were guarding their children from a stranger. They were protecting the boys from a situation in which information they provided could have been used to present a detrimental picture of themselves and their community. I was condemning them for reacting as most parents would have done in a similar situation. The women had shattered the stereotypes I had set up for them in my mind, and I did not like it.

Aftermath

As I limped disspiritedly into my professor's office a few days after the resounding no from the fifth boy's mother, I was "projectless." By interviewing only two of the five boys I had not fulfilled the requirements of my project. I had not recovered emotionally or psychologically from what I felt was a personal attack; in fact, as time went on, I felt worse. When Martin's mother had abruptly ended our conversation, I had experienced only boiling anger, but after the initial surge of emotion had passed, I was left with a bruised inside, simmering anger, and a strong tendency to say, "I don't care."

I told my professor about the demise of my intended community and of the trauma I had suffered as a consequence. He talked with me for some time and described the history of relations between White researchers and the African American community. Over the years, he informed me, there had been an excess of studies of and investigations and reports about African American people. White researchers had entered communities, formed superficial bonds with community members to get the information they needed, then disappeared back to their research institutes and universities never to be seen or heard from again. The only outcomes of many of these studies were reports in academic journals in which communities had been often portrayed incorrectly, negatively, or both.

My professor also reminded me that the history of relationships between Blacks and Whites in the United States had often been unsettled. At the time I wanted to scream, "But that is not my fault! Why should I be blamed for things I have never done?" In retrospect, however, I realize that the mothers were protecting themselves, their families, and their community. The information could have been used in ways, common in such research, that ultimately associates these people with crime, poverty, unemployment, welfare, gangs, poor education, and homelessness. I can now understand why they did not give me the benefit of the doubt.

I also spoke, on my professor's instigation, with two African American professors from the university. They pointed out several facts about

Black–White relationships that had not occurred to me. The most unpleasant fact was a reminder that in the past, Black men in any way involved with White women were hanged. My reaction was, "These things happened hundreds of years ago!" The truth, however, is that in some states, even though it is illegal, African American men are still punished for socializing with White women. When I consider this act, how can I fail to understand why parents would be wary of allowing their young men to ride off with me for the afternoon?

The professors also reinforced my professor's comments about the re-searcher–subject relationship. They noted that the African American community in this town felt alienated from the university because students and professors, after performing many studies of their community, had eventually retreated to the ivory towers of campus and had left them psychologically stranded and wondering what had happened with the information they had shared.

I felt scared, apprehensive, and defensive as I talked to these African American professors. Although I tried to keep my face expressionless and my responses to their questions guarded, they pointed out that I was personalizing the episode and ignoring the larger issues. At first I felt even more defensive, but I was able to understand that the events did not represent a personal attack on me by the three mothers.

When I thought about their comments later, I realized that past and present events had influenced the project's outcome. The three women's negative responses probably related to events that had occurred long before my project. Their responses were part of their history, which included slavery and recent civil unrest in Los Angeles and Harlem.

Although still hurting, I was reassured that the problems I had encountered had not been in vain and that much could be gained. All three professors informed me that few people had faced such an experience and I had to decide how to handle what I had learned. I had to decide, in other words, whether to run away (to the suburbs), or to use this occasion to enhance my future teaching; whether to take the rejection personally or to realize how these experiences fit into a large picture.

As time went by, I was able to come to terms with the situation in a positive way. After a 2-week cooling-off period, I summoned the courage to call the teacher and returned to volunteer work in the same classroom. I was glad to see the students and thought they were glad to see me. Thomas would sometimes forget that he had been told to stay away from me and would show me something he was working on when I stood beside his desk. Yet although we would talk for a moment, it was never the same as before. The seed of suspicion planted in his mind seemed to have taken root. Martin and Charles acted as if nothing had ever happened and treated me as they always had, but I was apprehensive about talking to Martin because of his mother's anger. James, Lawrence, and I still get together, however, and they love to go to the university park to look for frogs, turtles, snakes, duck eggs, and mussels.

I now see that although James and Lawrence live at a low socioeconomic level, they are far from pitiful. I have since visited their homes and neighborhoods and found that their sense of family and neighborhood is much stronger than I could have imagined, far stronger than for youngsters from many middle-class neighborhoods. The boys have good manners, considerably better than most kids from "good" families. Most important, they are not uncaring, unfeeling, tough guys. They are fifth graders with the same worries, desires, likes, and dislikes as other kids their age. The family involvement in their homes, although sometimes different from White mother–father relationships is strong.

As I have become better acquainted with James and Lawrence, I have developed a sense of hope for their future. Had I not continued to meet with these boys, I would have believed there was little or no chance of their escaping a downward spiral toward self-destruction, crime, and apathy which society associates with young people in minority cultures. As I learned the hard way, change in attitudes and perceptions must stem not from pity, but from friendship and relating to people in their own realities. This sense of friendship and acceptance seems to be missing in many highly acclaimed middle-class communities.

When I first read Denzin's (1989b) definition and description of epiphanies, I associated them with psychotic behavior or life-threatening diseases. My interpretation was too narrow. As Denzin wrote, epiphanies are turning-point experiences, interactional moments that mark people's lives and can be transformational. My own experience demonstrates, however, that epiphanies can stem from the unlikeliest of sources—a book, a conversation, or the click of a telephone.

CONTEXTUALIZING EXPERIENCE

As I reflected on these events, emergent themes helped me understand the nature of my experience, organize my thoughts, and think constructively about a situation that had once seemed hopeless. Seeing the contradictions, assumptions, stereotypes, expectations, ignorance, and indifference inherent in my responses to the situation, I can understand these events differently.

As I attempted to formulate explanations for the problematic events I had experienced, I also discovered that many of my responses derived from childhood experiences, family relationships, and upbringing. That the influence of my family should surface so readily in my reflections was something of a surprise to me, but according to Denzin (1989a), "It is as if every author of autobiography or biography must start with family, finding there the zero point of origin for the life in question" (p. 18).

Contradictions: Expectations and Experience

Because I am not what Bruner referred to as a "letter-perfect copy" of my culture "with no discrepancy between outer behavior and inner state" (Bruner, cited in Denzin, 1989a, p. 30), I have grown accustomed to the contradictions with which my life is riddled. My background played a significant role in coloring the perceptions and expectations associated with my project. I grew up in a White, middle-class context and learned that I should be content with the world as it was given to me. I am accustomed to feeling or believing one thing, but acting and living another.

Biographical Note

My family's culture is based on the pioneer ethic that anything is possible when people work hard enough. The world is to be conquered and made to fit personal desires. To a certain extent, I agree, but certain aspects of this view make me uncomfortable, especially the discord between personal beliefs and public actions.

I believe some people need more economic, academic, and social assistance than do others, that some lack confidence in their ability to function in and to manipulate the U. S. system. Rather than thinking that such people are lazy or stupid, I have believed (from the beginning, I think) that with acceptance, guidance, and patience they can lead a comfortable existence. I have become increasingly uncomfortable with the ambition and competition I grew up with, traits expected in "successful" people. That everyone should be driven by financial success makes me uneasy. People should offer support to those who cannot or do not know how to help themselves. My lived experiences, however, have been based on the "pull yourself up by your bootstraps" mentality.

My life might have been emotionally safer had I accepted this way of thinking. Outwardly I have appeared to agree with all aspects of my culture, but internally I know that there is another, more compassionate way to function. This situation has led to self-questioning about my beliefs and my approach to other cultures.

The discrepancy between beliefs and actions which is part of my own experience contrasts to the mothers I came in contact with. They seemed uninterested in hiding their displeasure at my intrusion, and their outward behavior probably reflected their real feelings. They did not like my project and let me know it in no uncertain terms. Nothing in my background prepared me for this reaction; I was accustomed to humoring people and being humored in return.

Other key events showed that my expectations about this project and the participants' reactions were poorly related to the actual events. My expectations were based on the boys' classroom behavior and on the fact that they were African Americans attending a "bad" school. I categorized them as poor, needy children whose social, academic, and psychological development was severely retarded. My expectations, however, were not matched by the events that occurred in the time I spent with two of the boys.

A week before the mothers rejected my program, I had a revelatory experience during the first afternoon I spent with James and Lawrence. In class they were sullen and disrespectful, argued frequently with the teacher, and often referred to her as prejudiced. They created many problems for her by flicking staples off the end of their pencils at other students, throwing paper, talking at inappropriate times, and so on. I expected such behavior during the time we spent together in interviews, but James and Lawrence were so sweet and charming that I told their teacher they were not the people they appeared to be at school.

My first interview with them took place at a Dairy Queen and lasted about 30 minutes. Before we started I asked them whether they would like to order something—a banana split, milkshake, hot fudge sundae? They ordered only a small cup of plain vanilla ice cream, not what I anticipated from my "poor street kids." I had expected to tell them to order a medium, not a large size, because I thought that they would be greedy; I was surprised when they ordered small cups. When I had finished asking questions after half an hour and suggested going to the video arcade, Lawrence was immediately concerned that I had sufficient information for my project. He asked whether I was finished and had done everything I needed to do.

> *Expectation*: James and Lawrence would jump at the chance to spend my money on ice cream and video games.

> *Experience*: They were concerned about my work and needs and about helping me.

There were many more surprises that afternoon and others that followed. When I asked them how I could repay them for helping me with my project, I was again amazed at their responses. I expected them to ask me to buy them something—video games or university sweatshirts. Instead they suggested a tour of campus, a bike ride, a cookout, a movie, or a swim, and I felt ashamed for thinking they would take advantage of the situation. My expectations were once more proven wrong when I gave each boy two quarters to play video games, for once they had used their money, neither asked for more.

I was to have another learning experience as I drove them around in my car. Each made sure the other was wearing a seat belt, and they took turns riding in the front seat. Each wanted the other to be taken home first, but they did not argue when I made the final decision. In my care they were definitely not the rude, aloof 12-year-olds I had seen in the classroom.

I expected these boys to be so different from others I knew because of what I perceived as their pitiful circumstances—living in low-income households in poor neighborhoods and attending a school without many minority students. Although their environments might not have been the most advantageous in which to grow up, James and Lawrence showed enthusiasm and delight in all our adventures. When they walked through the mall parking lot from the video arcade, they competed to see who could locate the car first and then raced to it. At the mall an aquarium contest captured their attention. Each had his own ideas about which aquarium was the best decorated and why. They insisted on washing my car and, naturally, squirted water at each other. I had expected them to be indifferent toward most things we did and saw and to ridicule things, like aquarium contests that were not "cool."

Through these events and activities, I became aware of the discrepancy between the expectations with which I entered their social world and the reality of the events that occurred. Not only had most mothers failed to live up to my expectations, but their sons also surprised me.

Assumptions and Stereotypes

My stereotypes and assumptions in this project went hand in hand. I assigned stereotypes to everyone involved with my project, assumed they were accurate, and waited for them to be fulfilled. When the mothers did not live up to the stereotypes I assigned to them, I projected yet more stereotypes and assumptions. After I had been rejected by three of the women, I replaced my "uncaring, ignorant Black mother" stereotype with the "White-hating, Black women with a chip on their shoulders" label. I assumed these women were ganging up on me because I was White. I was using skin color difference as a basis for my stereotypes. In *Between Race and Ethnicity*, Marilyn Halter (1993) suggested "One of the first things we notice about people when we meet them ... is their race. We utilize race to provide clues about *who* a person is" (p. 13).

The assumptions I brought to the project were a product of my background. Because I had always heard stereotypes assigned to minorities, I interpreted people's behaviors according to these stereotypes. Instead of realizing that people in similar situations would usually react in similar ways, I accepted the stereotype that certain minorities behaved in predestined, predictable, and less-than-desirable ways. I was mistaken, therefore, when I assumed the away-from-school behavior of the boys I wanted to interview would reflect their in-school behavior. I was continually surprised, therefore, at their delightful behavior when we met outside school; they failed to live up to my assumptions or to manifest the behavior my stereotypes predicted. Assumptions and stereotypes, therefore, were an integral part of the story of my project.

Ignorance and Indifference

When I first identified the key elements in my writing, I commented, "Ignorance, although a small portion of the problem, was a factor in the disintegration of my project." As it turned out, ignorance was the key element in the project. I suspect I unconsciously chose to be ignorant about obvious danger zones. I chose to ignore problematic racial issues because I thought they were silly, including the problem of the relationship between the researcher and subject. I chose to ignore the fact that a White researcher interviewing members of a Black community might not be met with popular approval although I had been warned of such reactions. I ignored the warnings because I did not think race should be an issue. In general, I chose to completely ignore the fact that racial tension usually exists between Blacks and Whites. My unconsciously purposeful ignorance showed my indifference.

Biographical Note

"Unconsciously, purposeful ignorance" refers to my choosing to push sensitive aspects of White–Black relationships into my unconscious and behaving as though there were no unresolved racial issues. I was attempting to use one of the behavior modifications I had learned in classroom management seminars while a first-year teacher. The thinking behind this concept was that ignoring an undesirable behavior makes it go away. This concept did not work when I was not dealing with one unruly child's behavior. When I encountered an issue hundreds of years old, one entailing powerful emotions, ignoring it just made me appear foolish and naive.

I applied my unconscious indifference to a culture that does not view the world as I do and to people who have not experienced life the way I have. This arrogance may stem from my past experience; White adults in my hometown rarely, if ever, publicly acknowledged racial problems in the community. They privately lamented the racial and cultural differences, but never discussed them or tried to alleviate the problems. People seemed to assume that if the problem was never spoken about openly and was disregarded then perhaps it would not become larger. People appeared to act on the premise that if everyone continued to behave as though nothing were wrong, then the situation would go away or at least not escalate. In large and small ways, this thinking still prevails in my hometown. As I worked on my project, I thought that my acknowledging potential problems would make them go away and that my accepting the situation would make the mothers act similarly.

SURVIVING QUALITATIVE RESEARCH

Reflecting on events, I suspect that many of my problems were linked to my belief that I knew enough about ethnographic study, and people in general, to throw together a quick, easy project. I did not take my assignment seriously enough, although I had professed the desire to do something meaningful.

"A little learning is a dangerous thing" typifies my situation. Spradley (1979) stated, "Ethnography starts with a conscious attitude of almost complete ignorance" (p. 4). I did not accept the approach of complete ignorance or treat seriously the suggestion that "the researcher must become a student" (p. 4). I believed I should be in charge from start to finish and that I had information to give.

Naive Realism

I am now aware of my "naive realism," leading me to assume that although cultures speak different languages, each has basically similar meanings for similar concepts. "This almost universal belief holds that all people define the real world of objects, events and living creatures in pretty much the same way" (Spradley, 1979, p. 4). I thought I was being straightforward in my speech with each woman, but what I said was probably heard and understood in several different ways, reflected in the different responses I received. I was speaking in a language probably foreign to them. I was speaking the language of a university student with a vocabulary full of ethnographic terms still new to me and almost certainly unfamiliar to the women with whom I spoke.

As a researcher, therefore, I was unable to view the project outside my cultural lens. One particular statement sums up the overriding flaw of my project: "Whenever people learn a culture, they are to some extent imprisoned without knowing it. Anthropologists speak of this as being 'culture-bound,' living inside a particular reality that is taken for granted as 'the reality' " (Spradley, 1979, p. 10). I viewed the project in terms of my own cultural reality and tried to make sense of the confusion and frustration I experienced through my own cultural lenses. What I learned from the experience was all the more painful because I had difficulty in letting go the idea that my culture was common to all involved parties.

Working under the assumption of common cultures, I failed to alter my behavior when I entered a different cultural scene. Spradley commented, "As people move from one cultural scene to another in complex societies, they employ different cultural rules" (1979, p. 12). I did not employ different cultural rules because I did not realize I was walking into an African American culture whose perspectives were unrelated to university courses, university students, and university research projects.

I also neglected to consider that the mothers knew a great deal about themselves and their own situation. As Spradley (1979) wrote, "Any explanation of behavior which excludes what the actors themselves know, how they define their actions, remains a partial explanation that distorts the human situation" (p. 13). I reacted to the rejection I encountered in my project according to my assumptions about these women and their circumstances; with little or no real knowledge about the people, I explained their behavior on the basis of stereotypes and surface knowledge. I knew little about the other people who might be influenced by the outcome of my project and tried to deal only with the boys who could give me the information I wanted. I was attempting an ethnographic study with a partial and incomplete understanding of the actors in my selected community.

Support for Survival

I was fortunate to have nonjudgmental people with whom I could discuss my negative experiences. I was able to vent my feelings of anger, frustration, and apathy to those who would listen and respond appropriately. I continued to work through these experiences and to explore my responses so that the events became a learning experience. Eventually I learned not to be defensive about what I had done or about the consequences. I hope to be able to use the experience as a constructive reference when similar situations arise. I also feel more objective about myself and am less angry when I confront such situations in everyday life.

In the article "Research Alert! Qualitative Research May Be Hazardous to Your Health!" Linda Dunn (1991) recommended that people engage in an activity such as exercise at least three times a week to help reduce the stress of qualitative research. At the time of my project, I had many personal commitments to family, study, work, and community. I was tired most of the time, and although I tried to exercise daily, I was emotionally drained. I felt guilty about complaining or taking time off and now think that my stress was intensified by working as a volunteer with these fifth graders. I interpreted their behavior as a need for attention and expression and assumed they had few people and places for receiving or displaying either. I felt their desire to be special and grieved for them when all they could convey was crudeness and roughness. I felt I had no right to complain about my tiredness or unhappiness.

When the project collapsed, therefore, so did I. I was apathetic, no longer felt compassion for the children, and did not care whether I failed my course because I had no project. My circuits were overloaded and shut down. Talking became the only way for me to piece together the events and make sense of them. Had I taken heed of my professor's previous warnings about qualitative research or remembered Dunn's warning about researchers' emotional and physical health, I might not have slipped so deeply into apathy. In retrospect, this experience was epiphanic, but I might have weathered it better had I prepared myself.

I regret not keeping a daily journal; I can remember the overall experience and my emotions, but details of many important moments now escape me. Had I kept a daily log, I might have avoided some pitfalls by reflecting on my actions during the project and by altering them.

My professor was supportive and endured my defensiveness until he could see that the healing process had begun. He not only listened to me, but encouraged me to speak about the situation with other professors and with students. This support system has been the most important part of the qualitative research experience for me. Had I been forced to carry the burden of my emotions alone, I doubt that I would have experienced a positive change in my attitudes, and I would have learned considerably less.

Dunn (1991) suggested that qualitative researchers share their experience with others, and I am in the process of doing so now through this writing. As

I write, I am teaching third grade in a public school and, at times, can actually see how my "bad" experience has enhanced my awareness of my students' perceptions, actions, and reactions to me and has changed my actions and reactions to them. Sharing the experience has been very difficult because I had to dredge up my pain, but each time it stung a little less. I hope the hurt never goes away completely so that I forget what I learned and return to base zero.

WHAT CAN BE LEARNED FROM MY EXPERIENCE

"Persons ... often mistake their own experiences for the experiences of others. These interpretations are then formulated into social programs intended to alter and shape the lives of troubled people ... But often the understandings these programs are based upon bear little relationship to the meanings, interpretations and experience of the persons they are intended to serve" (Denzin, 1989b, p. 11).

An important distinction to be made about qualitative research is that such accounts describe and analyze ungeneralizable personal experience. A social program based on my initial superficial responses to the disintegration of my project would have been a program based on stereotypes about African American women. By continuing to reflect on the events I have recounted, however, I have come to a much better understanding of these five women, their relationships with their sons, and their responses to White university researchers. I also understand myself in a different way and, I hope, have altered my relationship to and perceptions of African Americans of all economic backgrounds.

The experience has altered my perspectives about policies related to racial issues. I now believe it far more productive to work at the level of individuals and schools than to introduce policies that attempt to force people to "be understanding." My past experience suggests that policies "telling" people how to behave tend to build resentment, and blanket "shoulds" or "should nots" about working with minorities are unhelpful. I now think it preferable to train faculty and staff to learn through personal experience, to train them in ethnographic process, and to give them opportunities to interpret their day-to-day interactions with students. People like principals, teachers, and counselors should keep logs of their daily experiences and then interpret and analyze their written reactions to become aware of the thinking underlying their practices. Increased understanding might result from situations that enabled educators to explore personal experiences and to derive their own ways of working with people. My experience suggests that not only would understanding and cooperation increase, but also that the quality of personal philosophy would improve. Denzin stated "Programs don't work because they are based on a failure to take the perspective and attitude of the person served"

(1989b, p. 11). In my opinion, programs also fail because they do not consider the perspectives and attitude of those required to implement them.

My belief about what is needed to improve understanding between people of different cultures and races has gone through many transformations, as I moved from being overly gracious to being aggressively friendly. In the end, I realize that developing a genuine connection with someone of another culture or race requires an approach that acknowledges the person as authentic rather than as someone with quaint customs or unexplainable beliefs or desires. In *The Clash Of Colour*, Basil Mathews stated, "Something very real is needed—not a vague atmosphere of kindliness but a brotherhood won through blood and courage and sacrifice" (1925, p. 165). Like anything else worth having, this brotherhood requires work.

REFERENCES

Berreman, G. D. (1968). Is anthropology alive? Social responsibility in social anthropology. *Current Anthropology, 9*, 391–396.

Denzin, N. K. (1989a). *Interpretive biography*. Newbury Park, CA: Sage.

Denzin, N. K. (1989b). *Interpretive interactionism*. Newbury Park, CA: Sage.

Dunn, L. (1991). Research alert! Qualitative research may be hazardous to your health! *Qualitative Health Research, 1*, 388–392.

Halter, M. (1993). *Between race and ethnicity*. Urbana: University of Illinois Press.

Mathews, B. (1925). *The clash of colour*. Port Washington, NY: Kennikat Press.

Spradley, J. P. (1979). *The ethnographic interview*. Fort Worth, TX: Harcourt Brace Jovanovich College.

6

The Impact of Group Interactions on Meaning-Making: Learning Qualitative Research Methodology

Patricia Gathman Nason

When educators hear the term *qualitative research*, many are challenged by an unfamiliar paradigm. When doing qualitative research, researchers not only attempt to take on the perspective and attitude of those being studied, but interpret interactions in the context being studied to reveal participant meanings and perceptions. This approach to research presents many problems for those who are familiar only with quantitative research methods because it seems to contradict many principles traditionally associated with rigorous inquiry.

These same problems emerge for graduate students who wish to do qualitative research because the new paradigm challenges traditional ways of thinking about research and requires researchers to become familiar with a set of skills and understandings that enable them to ignore their own ways of interpreting phenomena and to report events through the eyes of the research participants.

This study examines a collaborative approach to learning ethnographic research that significantly changed the epistemological assumptions of participants. It focuses on a graduate ethnographic research methods class that became a unique community of learners engaged in a unique educational experience. As they built the course agenda *together*, they determined its direction based on their own learning needs; they participated in collaborative working groups that allowed them to construct an increasingly sophisticated understanding of qualitative research. Course participants learned what knowledge is and how it is acquired and practiced; they shared and discussed qualitative research methodology so it became an authentic experience. The processes of interpretation central to their work enabled them to understand the reality of community-based research in ways that made a significant difference in their professional and personal lives.

INTERPRETATION OF SHARED EXPERIENCES

The participants in the class were mainly graduate students from a college of education in a large university and had varying degrees of experience with ethnographic research education. The verbal and written expressions of their meaning-making activities were manifested in interviews, class notes, group and individual ethnographies and journal writings; the data for this chapter have been drawn from these sources. The experiences of four middle-aged females who wove their lives together in the process of doing ethnographic research is the basis for this story.

The experience of this class is reflected in the methodology of this chapter—in other words, what we did in class *was* the methodology. This account of the shared experience of the writer's community of learners is made sense of through my interpretation of events. The chapter is written as a story of four individuals passing through, confronting, and making meaning of ethnographic research in theory and in practice. As we confronted events together, old ways of knowing and understanding came to the surface, and new ways of knowing were created for each group member. These experiences were not only intellectual but also emotional and social.

This chapter thus reflects the history of our lives as ethnographers during a 5-week period in the summer of 1993. My intention is to present a polyphonic account of the learning adventure that the group encountered. I accept the notion of subjectivity that is apparent when, as the teller of the tale, I give meaning to experiences shared by and with others.

I struggled to compile data for this chapter to reflect the experiences of our group, as I knew that sharing the experience gave the methodology meaning. *All* participants in our community–group knew themselves and each other better through our shared, personal experiences. Each of us, however, constructed our own meaning of naturalistic inquiry in our professional lives as educators and researchers.

Through the application of bracketing procedures suggested by Denzin (1989), three categories emerged as salient to the experience of group members: personal relationships, a group project as a learning context, and the collaborative construction of meaning-making. These categories gave insight into the significant features of the group's experience and portrayed the effects of group collaboration on developing of ethnographic epistemology for participants in this community of learners.

Continual member checks enabled me to ask other participants to clarify verbally their feelings and constructions and helped me to represent the *others'* biographical story. I recognize that this account is autoethnographic in the sense that it is my interpretation of our shared experiences. It is an epistemological view point that illuminates the meaning of the life experience that we shared.

THE CONTEXT: QUALITATIVE RESEARCH
FOR EDUCATORS

It was 8 AM in the 1993 summer semester at Texas A&M University. Fourteen graduate students converged on a classroom that looked more like an industrial setting designed to disrupt all contact with the outside world, except for thoughts that might be barely stirring in students' imaginations at this early hour. The class, Qualitative Research for Educators, was offered by Dr. Ernie Stringer and attracted students with a variety of work and personal experiences from all areas of the College of Education—Educational Administration, Curriculum and Development, Multicultural Education, Adult Education, and English as a Second Language.

Along with the concrete walls and no natural light, the room contained work tables and chairs, which could be easily reconfigured to accommodate the changing activities of the class. A sink and counter served as a coffee area, and a work table held breakfast, supplied on a loose rotation by members of the class. The breakfast, according to Dr. Stringer, "serves a symbolic purpose, connecting the learning experience to real life, infusing the learning experience with enjoyment and pleasure." It also helped everyone awaken; appetites were small, but the caffeine intake was noticeably large.

On the first day of class, Dr. Stringer described himself as the project consultant. He established his role as a facilitator and learner and, in the process, introduced a learning climate that allowed intellectual freedom and inquiry to flourish. Class members soon began to share their feelings of frustration, including those about the short time frame of the class—3 hours a day, 4 days a week for 5 weeks.

Participants were particularly concerned that their different experiences with qualitative research meant that each had different learning needs. After a lengthy discussion, students compiled a list of "What we want to know or be able to do before we leave this class." The class goals that emerged from the resulting list of needs were twofold: to "acquire and extend knowledge of the nature, purposes, characteristics and processes of qualitative research" and to "develop skills to plan, implement and evaluate qualitative research" and "apply [them] to the solution of educational problems" (class notes). These goals became part of a shared experience that characterized the life of the class.

BECOMING A COMMUNITY THROUGH
PERSONAL RELATIONSHIPS

There were pockets of chatter and excitement in the room as groups listened intensely to each person being interviewed about his or her life. My group, made up of Beverley, Vicky, Mary Frances, and myself was characterized in another group's ethnographic paper, "Food for Thought" (Avila, Gaston, & Henry):

> Beverley is short. She has blond hair in a cute bob. She has a son who is almost fourteen. She teaches in Somerville. Mary Fran seems to be always meditating. She has black hair and wears wire framed glasses; she is thin. She has a little girl and shares time with her [because] her husband is in Houston. She often wears slacks. She said this was her fourth summer of summer school. Patti is elegant. She is friendly and intuitive. She has lots of experience in computers; she brings a computer to class to type in her notes. She has long, blond hair. Vicky has a soft voice. She is not a morning person. She is thin and friendly. She is from North Carolina. She is an English instructor at TAMU (Texas A&M University) and usually has four classes at the same time. She was in Ernie's class last semester. Sometimes she speaks Spanish with Carol and Enrique.

One day we could be seen chatting over food at a table in the middle of the room and eating apple halves as we discussed our project. We had been asked by Ernie to "redefine your relationships and develop working relationships [within the group]; interview and observe [each other]. Get to know who [your group members] are, why they are here and why they are taking this course." We had previously interviewed each other using Spradley's (1989) grand tour questions that enable an informant to give a verbal description of significant features in her or his life. This assignment enabled us to find out about each other as we practiced interview processes, to learn how each person constructed his or her experience, and to develop a rapport.

Interviews quickly created a sense of community. During class time as well as at potlucks and other class events, group members seemed to naturally come together. They huddled around a table or computer, in classroom or patio, to engage in intense discussion, with body language and facial expressions showing interest and participation.

The first question we asked was, "Tell me about yourself," which led to "Tell me about a typical day in your life." Beverley revealed: "I feel like a Dr. Jekyll and Mr Hyde. I have this innate ability to communicate with children. My success is driven by intuitive ability rather than a direct act of instruction.

I [get] bored so I change teaching areas—eight changes in eight years. I've taught from kindergarten to P.E. (physical education)."

Mary Frances disclosed that she experienced two kinds of days: "the school day and the mom day. When I do the school day, I sleep at Mom's house. I start at about 8:00 or 9:00 and end around 11:00 or 11:30 when I stop reading … My mom days: I get up with my daughter when she gets up and start doing what's required—diaper, dress, breakfast, reading period—child oriented activities."

After outlining her daily activities, Vicky revealed that she had "no real personal time in the day for me. That bothers me a lot." She further explained her interest in breaking down patriarchal structures: "I think that I've been examining power structures and reading feminist theory—less in private life than in my professional life. In this department, especially in the university, it [the patriarchy] is in place. My interest in patriarchal structures comes from my whole life experiences—from intellectual and practical issues in marriage."

Thus, as a group, we developed relationships by attempting to describe in our own voices the ways that we perceived ourselves. Over the 5-week period, we became Mary Frances's psychologists as we listened to her describe her crumbling marriage. She said that just doing ethnography "helped me become a better listener," and explained: "I used to be able to listen superficially, but now I can sort of get into someone else's life and I value what might seem to be trivial stories but that people see as important."

As part of community building the interviews also created the conditions that enabled group members to act as a mutual support system. The details of Mary Frances's personal life were not easy for her to share, but she found sympathetic ears in listeners who became more than classmates and fellow graduate students. Distraught and somewhat hesitant, Mary Frances told us the details of a marital relationship that had deteriorated to the point of disintegration. "This class hasn't made life more stressful, but it's made me think about things. I share this kind of stuff in this kind of class. I wonder, 'should I tell?' But I need a counselor."

Vicky wrote of this in her journal: "Sharing anxieties and the work load is a tremendous help. Mary Frances really feels the group has been like an ongoing therapy session for her. It is true that we all are listening and that we care about the stress that she has. Her marriage is really dissolving before her eyes. Life is strange."

The sense of community that evolved through the developing personal relationships and emotional bonds in our community of learners produced many characteristics important in community-based ethnography. As active participants in what was effectively a research process in our groups, we became aware of the significance of the emerging topics. This awareness contributed an emotional quality that enabled individual needs to be met while furnishing a natural setting for our qualitative research processes.

A GROUP PROJECT AS A LEARNING CONTEXT

About a week into the class, Ernie asked us to develop a group project using ethnographic research that focused on the context of the class. Vicky was distraught at first as her previous group project experience had been difficult. "We are going to be doing ... a group class ethnography," she wrote in her journal. "When Ernie first announced it, I wasn't pleased, [but] having met with my group, I feel like I won't be able to keep up [with the work that is required]. It will be a good experience." Later she wrote, "The project is finished (first phase). Needs more work—more development. More editing. It is truly an ongoing process. Working with Mary Frances, Patti and Beverley has restored my faith in the group project. It has been really positive for me."

Having shared our seemingly exclusive predicaments, we determined that our group project would focus on the issues that plagued our personal and professional lives. Vicky wrote about our topic in this way:

> We decided on the focus for the paper. It really has emerged from the interview process. What we all seem to be talking about is the stress we feel from the graduate school experience. It is hard to separate [our] student and private life; in fact, I think what we are getting from the interviews is that the demands of graduate school are really bleeding into all our private lives and putting stress on relationships as well as evoking guilt about family/personal responsibilities for everyone.

As we performed our assigned tasks, we began sorting through and giving meaning to our encounters with each another. Vicky wrote, "Verbalizing thoughts and problems ... We had high aspirations for what we wanted to get done but also realized that we were limited by time and circumstances. The days were filled up with writing, research and interviews."

We interviewed several members of the class to determine whether they were encountering the same ordeals. The lens that gave meaning to these experiences, however, came from our own community of four researchers. Although many other class members seemed to be having similar experiences, our discussions cemented the sense of community and the personal aspects of shared events. I wrote in my journal, "How can we interpret what [the other members of the class] are thinking and saying when they aren't sharing from the depths of their souls as we have been? We don't really KNOW them like [sic] we know each other."

Another issue we found ourselves exploring was whether our circumstances were specifically female experiences. Our interviews with Enrique and Ernie provided insight that negated this "theory." Enrique told us:

> [My personal life] is one of my concerns ... [My children] begged me to take them to the mall Saturday. But I can't afford to spend two hours with them ... they have to be very quiet because I need a very quiet room to work ... I can't find time for them. I feel very family-oriented but I didn't even have time to

take them to the mall. It has been a hard time for me. I don't feel I'm fulfilling my role as a parent.

As we worked on the group task, our daily encounters with one another helped us learn how to get to the heart of an issue and to give meaning to the lives of the people involved. In capturing the data used in our research paper, we learned how to see through the lenses of the other members of our distinctive community. The ongoing interaction enabled us to verify that we were accurately representing the other's voice and, in turn, facilitated the development of a deeper understanding of each other and of ourselves. Vicky wrote:

> From a theoretical sense of my understanding, if you do ethnography, you study groups of people and we became the group we are studying. ... We "found" ourselves; we enabled each other to be free to be ourselves, in essence. We became either part of the group we were studying or we began to understand our relationship to a group and how that relationship was power, gender and race related. The relationship we have to [people in] that group—either alike or different—[enabled us to] see ourselves [through] a constant give and take of information and [comparison].

The group project, therefore, was a significant feature of the class. Not only did it enable people to practice the processes of formulating an ethnography, but it provided a context in which they were able to explore the lived reality of their own experience. As they explored their own experience and attempted to formulate a text that portrayed the experience, they became more aware of the processes involved in providing accounts of people's lives. They were sensitized to the deeply personal aspects of ethnographic work.

THE COLLABORATIVE CONSTRUCTION
OF MEANING

The processes of working in a group assisted us to learn from one another and to develop feelings of responsibility for individual and group scholarship. A system of checks and balances enabled group members to discover each other's viewpoint and to draw on each other's expertise and experience. Members supported each other as they engaged in skill-building exercises, including the design and conduct of interviews, the analysis of data, and the formulation of an ethnographic account. Beverley described her experience in this way:

> First, modelling and listening to other people do [ethnography] gave me the confidence to say I could do it, but [also] the emotional support (cheerleader idea) saying "You can do this." There was a support group there. My first interview with Vicky was disastrous but you two [Patricia and Mary Frances]

held me up. Not only did it feel good, it created a successful process; it wasn't a complete disaster.

Also, something else added [to the process]—when we were working [in the computer lab] like wild women, I sat there [thinking that] this product done collaboratively was infinitely better than anything that any one of us could have done alone. I don't write so badly that it would be an embarrassment but [the collaboration] made it rich with polyphonic voices that was [sic] not only beautiful but a higher quality. It was aesthetic, to me. I learned an enormous amount by hearing Patti's writing and Mary Frances' writing and Vicki's writing. Going through the process of editing enhanced my ability to understand.

We found relying on each other's strengths refreshing and exciting. Mary Frances wrote in her journal during the course:

I said I'd do the methodology because I'd done it before and that allowed the others to do what they said they were best ... there was a sense of self-monitoring ... filtering. We had to have some degree of self knowledge because we knew our [own] strengths. [We used] good common sense, classroom experiences, the ability to relate to people; [we] could jump in and help [when someone was having a problem].

But the most important impact that learning from and with each other had on our lives was that we began to change: We began to understand ourselves as well as one another in differently. Vicky described our personal interactions as "energy consuming." Beverley wrote, "We relied on each other's strengths. We were able to take people where they were and let them learn. We accepted [people] where they were by sharing knowledge, [formulating next] steps and providing feedback."

Our circumstances may have been unique because of the particular mix of group members, but the interaction among us was real and life changing for each of us. The dynamics of the group allowed us to share our thoughts, feelings, and ideas and to learn through the experiences we were living through together. Beverley explained: "If the composition of the group had been different, it wouldn't have been the same from my perspective. It couldn't have been equal or better. It is positive because of the people with whom I worked. I'm capable of doing it and it makes me feel I'm being empathetic. The collection of these four [people] with all of our individual strengths—and, Lord, we're different."

Constructivist approaches to teaching emphasize the meaning-making involved in any educational situation. Although traditional approaches to teaching and learning are often based on the assumption that individuals need merely acquire a predetermined body of knowledge, the reality is much more complex. People learn, according to a constructivist perspective, only when they can accommodate new information or knowledge within their existing frameworks of knowledge and understanding.

As we worked together we began to understand that a constructivist process works at several levels. People must not only negotiate the different systems of meaning that they bring to the learning process, but they must do so with different degrees of personal and emotional involvement. As we discovered in our group, the potential for extending a learning process through authentic interaction is enormous. Meaning-making does not become just a process of acquiring understanding at an intellectual level, but of engaging the full social and emotional possibilities of a learning context.

LOOKING BACK ON OUR LIVED EXPERIENCE

People often view education in technical terms, and the literature tends to emphasize techniques of teaching and learning that focus on individual learners in a relatively competitive learning environment. The social processes we, the community-based ethnography class, shared were in marked contrast to this educational perspective. These processes caused our lives to intersect in ways that encouraged the formation of a community of students, each with a unique interpretation of the experience he or she shared. The processes in which we engaged were part of the institutional structure of graduate school and although many people experienced epiphanies that were cumulative and re-experienced, the full meaning of these events emerged only as they began to interact and exchange thoughts and ideas. Graduate school came to include a progression of unique experiences that enabled us to share our "private troubles" in the public context of our classes.

Our group project, though personal in perspective, provided us with a communal task of fostering collaboration, which, in turn changed the way we perceived ourselves and each other as graduate students. To some extent our work was different from other groups: We chose to work in depth, in a way that required personal involvement in the learning processes.

Although these real-life experiences seem to be unique to the people and place, I would like to believe it possible to establish a productive, life-changing similar sense of community among my own students. Guba and Lincoln (1989) suggested that the successful hermeneutic process includes interaction, sharing of power, a willingness to evaluate oneself and emerge a different person, a commitment to integrity, and a commitment of time and energy. All these qualities were present in our community of learners and can be replicated in any educational context when the conditions and processes allow them to emerge.

The power of these constructivist processes is determined, however, by the extent to which people are able to invest themselves in the process. The willingness to face and share personal matters—to be vulnerable to others within a community—is an underlying contributing factor that gives meaning to the adventure of learning. My experience in this group suggests that the strength of our experience was enhanced because we were willing to disclose problems that confronted us in our shared situation, to treat each other as unique individuals, and to trust each other. By collaborating with each other we learned to look beyond our immediate experiences in ways that helped us understand the professional and private aspects of our lives. We capitalized on each other's strengths and empathized with each other's weaknesses through a perspective that said, "We are in this together."

In a later interview, Beverley summed up the communal experience:

A family feeling resulted from having to do a big task [together]. I see three people and I want to hug you. There were different dynamics [in this group] than [sic] anything I've ever experienced. I never felt incapable or alienated from you more experienced graduate students. My opinion, comments were not ignored. The fact that I could make a contribution made it a very important experience. It's not something that [I] could get from a book, but it was something that came from working with women, Ernie and the other class members in a collaborative setting ... People came out on the other side changed because of the experience Ernie constructed and the sense of emotional power that the class had.

Universities and schools in general sometimes teach learners that collaboration is cheating, unprofitable, unfair, and unproductive. Doing things together, however, is natural for human beings. The activities in which our class engaged gave the participants opportunities to learn from each other and to build positive relationships as they did so. It also gave us an apprenticeship in a model of teaching that we can replicate in our own classrooms. By *doing* ethnography together, we evolved into a community of learners who changed the way we thought about learning, teaching, and research. Such is the educational power of group interaction that enables people to make meaning together as they interact in a constructivist learning environment.

REFERENCES

Denzin, N. (1989). *Interpretive interactionism.* Newbury Park, CA: Sage.
Guba, E., & Lincoln, Y. (1989). *Fourth generation evaluation.* Newbury Park, CA: Sage.
Spradley, J. P. (1979). *The ethnographic interview.* New York: Holt, Rinehart & Winston.

7

An Illuminative Account of Personal–Professional Conflict: Loss, Redefinition, and Re-emergence of Self in the Process of Ethnographic Research

Mary Frances Agnello

This chapter focuses on the journey on which a group of graduate students embarked when they enrolled in a community ethnography class that was part of the research core classes of their program. Most students knew that this class would enable them to focus on learning an alternative to quantitative research. What they had not expected was to experience the personal involvement and self-revealing process that emerged as they pursued a class project. The following is a construction that reveals how four women researchers lose their self-identities, redefine them according to the demands of their rigorous programs, and re-emerge as different people, experiencing the etic and emic aspects of their research work and lives as interwoven and inseparable.

COMMUNITY-BASED ETHNOGRAPHY

The group research processes encountered in a graduate qualitative research methods class proved to be different from the sterile, text-bound, and solitary experiences graduate students often encounter in their educational careers. This narrative provides an account of the success experienced by individuals in a research class that featured community-based approaches to ethnography.

The four-member group ethnography project described herein ultimately became a means to an end as it exposed and re-exposed the professional and personal conflicts in graduate students' lives. To write about the epiphanies that we verbalized and contextualized, we relied on written and oral data drawn from the class context, the setting, a small-group project, and interviews. These provide the basis for a story which is both the product and an interpretation of our personal experiences.

Early in the course, the professor set the tone of the class as he presented his vision of the class. "Wisdom derives from being able to share ideas rather than [just] hear them, and working in groups achieves this." A community orientation framed our research, but the data derived from practice interviews in the group set the parameters and focused the group's project agenda. In a sense, the project created group dynamics that should be an integral part of ethnographic research (Lincoln & Guba, 1985) but often are not because of the solitary nature of much academic work. The pursuit of a community-based ethnography in this class sought to achieve consensus building through a process of triangulation that took account of all perspectives within the group. Ultimately, participants perceived themselves as in a state of transition while they explored who they were and what they became during the project.

What surfaced as the most salient issue was that the more we looked at the class' experiences, the more we understood ourselves. The work we completed became secondary to our understandings of ourselves as graduate students. By reading and rereading the data, we saw reflections of ourselves in transition. We were becoming people other than we knew ourselves to be; these changing definitions of ourselves afforded us a better understanding of where we were, where we were going, and the dangers we needed to avoid as we journeyed. We discovered, for instance, that other priorities in our lives needed nourishment, even though our graduate careers did not seem to permit us this luxury. The pedagogical processes that facilitated these glimpses into self-knowledge set the stage for the drama *we* lived in our setting.

PRACTICING ETHNOGRAPHY

We learned to do ethnography by practicing it. Interviews became the vehicle for group members to practice descriptive questioning techniques outlined by Spradley (1979), and served to build interpersonal relationships in both group and class. Interview sessions also enabled members to decide on a focus that would later merit the special attention of the group.

The phenomenon of personal–professional conflict was captured through a process recommended by Denzin (1989). Each group member recorded, typed, and shared detailed notes from in-group interviews. Interview notes were then reviewed, broken into units of meaning, and used as the basis for item analysis. Using Denzin's bracketing procedures we identified four common elements that illuminated the personal–professional conflict we experienced: setting and atmosphere of the class; schedule–time constraints; personal relationships; and relevance of the ethnography class to personal or professional lives or to both.

After three group meetings, we divided the work so that each would investigate one of these four elements. A meeting in the computer lab enabled us to synthesize these elements to construct the report. A final group meeting yielded a proposal for analyzing the way group processes had functioned.

Using interviews, journals, and the retrospective commentaries, verifications, and explanations that emerged from class discussions, I constructed my own interpretation of these events (Denzin, 1989). Direct and indirect quotes illuminate this account, which includes three distinct discussions: loss of self, redefinition of self, and re-emergence of self. Finally, I present the implications of this study and suggest the need for a more humanistic approach in amorphously inhuman institutions that usually deny us the opportunity to consider the subjectivity we inevitably bring to our investigations.

FINDING OUR PLACE: DIMENSIONS OF THE
GRADUATE STUDENT EXPERIENCE

Class Setting and Atmosphere

Despite the fact that the class was held in a barren setting, the professor and students attempted to counter the sterility in many ways and to create a community of learning by sharing ideas and food and by engaging in collaborative projects. The joint building of an agenda gave all participants a stake in the class, and group projects were instrumental in assisting students to accomplish their educational goals.

Physical location of students in the classroom was also a key source of success. Dr. Stringer experimented with chair arrangements to facilitate communication between participants, but also respected students' wishes by allowing them to stay connected with a table surface, a factor that seemed important to them.

The "breaking of bread"—we took turns bringing breakfast—and the relaxed atmosphere contributed to our general well-being. This sentiment was expressed by most participants. Patti commented that the class functioned as a low-stress environment in contrast to the high-stress feeling that graduate students usually experience. She emphasized, "This class is helping me a lot to discover individual human beings [and it] has humanized learning [in] the graduate experience."

Pedagogical and Learning Processes:
Stress, Struggle, and Solidarity

The environment created with the professor's guidance provided the possibility of relaxed learning processes, even though students expected a stressful class. Despite the professor's attempts to create a relaxed learning environment, however, Beverley, the most inexperienced researcher and a newcomer to the graduate program, was having a difficult time comprehending what was expected of students, a concern complicated by a lack of time. In one interview she commented on personal, private goals for the classroom and some personal, private conflicts she was having as she tried to juggle marriage, parenthood, full-time teaching, and being a part-time doctoral student. She said: "[This class] is coming at a difficult time for me personally, in addition to the normal summer school schedule. Too much is coming; the class is new to me. I am experiencing frustration taking the class. What does it mean? ... The small stuff seems big to me ... As a result of this class, I'm personally having lots of stress. I have stress and the class is adding to it. I either eat or sleep in reaction to it."

The group in which Beverley worked was composed of herself, Vicky, Mary Frances, and Patti, each distinguished by varied professional experiences and different levels of mastery of qualitative research which lent interest and strength to the group. As the neophyte researcher in the group, Beverley managed to scaffold on the three other members' knowledge and contributed to the quartet from a perspective untainted by past research experience. Nonetheless, even the more experienced members of the group felt insecurities as they struggled with the work that was expected of them and—perhaps even more stressful—the work they expected of themselves.

Vicky said, "This class is harder for me than the philosophy class; the ethnography class is the one breaking my back ... I would like some relief time from research courses." For Patti, the big picture was giving her stress. The stress of taking this class in conjunction with another one bothered her considerably. Mary Frances commented, "[The class] didn't make my life more stressful, but it's made me think about things ... It made me realize the choices one makes and how in reaching for the intangible one will give up a lot."

Similarities in the group, however, contributed to feelings of solidarity. Several members shared similar professional teaching backgrounds, an interest in furthering their credentials, and, ultimately, the desire to teach at the university level. The path to future career possibilities was the point at which their lives became intertwined.

Awareness of Personal–Professional Conflict

In my own interview script, I described a compartmentalization of my life into "mom" and "student" days. The permeation of graduate student life into every waking moment of my "mom" days indicated the degree to which personal–professional conflict was a continuing part of my life. Beverley's comment shows how guilt results when family obligations are not met because of the pressures of student life:

> I was at the computer yesterday afternoon [experiencing] a high fatigue level. My son came into the L-shaped surface area where we work and said, "There is no more relationship"—that he and Sandra had broken up. I said, "And what happened?" He said, "Too much of an age difference." I realized now that I had not talked to him during this crisis time of his life. He feels like [sic] I don't think that he's important. I confessed during spring that I was being self-centered … (I have) 50% conflict about whether I can do this and 50% wanting to get the degree.

Analysis of interview data reveals that the personal–professional conflict that emerged was relevant not only to this class but to graduate student experiences in general. Subsequent interviews conducted at potluck dinners in student homes confirmed the emotional conflicts that graduate students felt as a result of their study programs.

JOURNEY OF RESEARCHERS IN TRANSITION

Loss of Self

When we began a PhD program many of us knew hardships would present themselves in the form of financial difficulties, stress, time conflicts, and a dehumanizing bureaucratic system. What we did not know was the extent to which all of these dynamics would tug at our lives and pull us away from what we thought to be dear. Patti's emotional expression captured the loss of time for self. She said, "My nephew says I'm his favorite aunt because I'm still a kid at heart. This part of me is missing now and that's sad … As far as this class, I'm starting to think about whether or not I'll ever have time to do things for me." Vicky shared this sentiment: "There is pretty much no real personal time in the day for ME and that bothers me."

Ironically, a quest for self-development had inspired our research endeavors and had helped, perhaps inadvertently, determine that we would leave parts of our life behind in the furtherance of our quest for the life of the mind. The summer schedule precluded time for many family activities, exercise, down time, think time to satisfy the rigorous demands of an eat–sleep–study routine. All of us rose at 6 AM, worked all day, returned home for dinner, then resumed work until 11 PM or midnight. The weekends usually brought no respite because they often provided the stretches of uninterrupted time that enabled us to make steady progress in our writing or reading.

Redefinition of Self

In this context we immersed ourselves in the rigor of Dr. Stringer's qualitative research class. For us the class became "the thing." We put aside our private selves and developed our qualitative research skills as we executed a project from beginning to end. As we accomplished each stage, we became sounding boards for each other; we processed data, wrote, typed, shared, and edited. Debriefing sessions provided opportunities for introspection and discussion which helped us develop a consensual picture to capture, we thought, the essence of what we were doing. We were redefining our research paradigms and the intellectual perspectives through which we interpreted the world around us.

Cognitive processes guided us to the knowledge that we could complete this project, but our affective sides knew there were emotional issues confronting us constantly. The net effect on Patti was to make her question whether she would "ever have time for her." She "wondered if this phenomenon is a result of not teaching public school anymore." Her husband's insight into her rigorous lifestyle was "If it weren't graduate school it would be something else." She acknowledges a small effort to nourish her own needs: "I go to Jane Long [School] and check out children's novels—this keeps me up. But I always feel that I should do things that have a dual purpose." She had difficulty in separating her personal and professional lives as a graduate student.

Vicky also had difficulty pulling away from the demands of graduate school. The pressures it puts on a marriage were evident in her comments: "I don't have time to have a relationship with Robert and that's problematic. He wants me to do things with him and talk to him. The pattern is that days, days, and days go by and I don't interact with him, and he demands interaction and I get negative because he's demanding."

She explained the way she dealt with this dilemma: "One thing I did was go away with him. This past weekend I dropped classes on Friday and Saturday and came back Sunday. It was really hard letting go, but at some point, I let it go and this is where I am for a few days. Even though work was piled up when I got home, it was good. It was time to give myself permission to take time off. It's just extremely hard to do in summer school."

I too attended Dr. Stringer's class at a time of great stress as I found that an imminent divorce represented a crucial fork in my life. I thought:

> Perhaps in my zeal for the Ph.D., I had not realized that the "we" for whom we were doing this is no longer a "we." I feel great release in a way. It makes life easier. I will not have to compromise what "we" have to do but can do what "I" want to do ... The advice I would give anyone entering the [doctoral] program: you have to have a strong relationship in order to endure the process this experience will put on it. You become very preoccupied.

The net result of the reflective processes inherent in this class was the realization that we were redefining ourselves, our marriages, our families, and our academic lives.

Re-emergence of Self

Sometimes long-term goals seem far away as graduate students feel robotically propelled through arduous work weeks that never end; after projects and papers are completed, they are immediately replaced by others. Some would argue that we love this stressful life with its pressures and challenges or we would not do this work. Others comment that the grueling reality of a graduate student's life is dehumanizing in spite of our goal to study the art and science of education. Pedagogical processes, however, can be more or less humanizing, as the experiences of people in Dr. Stringer's qualitative research class suggest.

Patti

Patti said that as a result of taking the ethnography class she was "taking more time for people." She elaborated: "I realize[d] that everything that I was doing was for me and the degree, [so] I really started re-examining my purpose for being at Texas A&M." She has made more effort to communicate with her husband, who shouldered more household responsibilities since she went to graduate school.

In the process of becoming a more self-reliant woman, Patti saw her relationship with her husband change and her spiritual life develop. The doctoral studies made her so busy getting the degree that she was not thinking about the things that were really important. Taking this class and working on a small group project "made me re-examine where I was, where I was going and why." In the group context, "We talked about things that we don't normally share. We all had personal things that bothered us. By being a support system, we examined ourselves. Developing a relationship with other people is something we do not have time for as graduate students and the class gave us that opportunity." She spoke about what others have referred to in educational research as the "ethic of caring" (Denzin, 1994, p. 510).

Patti now thinks of her teaching in terms of her experience of the qualitative research class. She would like to be able to do for her students "what we were able to do for each other. We provided an environment for each other that enabled us to be ourselves. I want my students to feel free to be themselves." Ultimately she feels that "by modeling, we can be caring and allow our students to do so later in turn in their [own] classrooms."

Beverley

Beverley said, "A family feeling resulted from having had to do a big task [together]. I see three people and I want to hug you. There were different dynamics than [sic] anything I've ever experienced." The first thing that came to her mind about the ethnography class was the "institutionalized room" where we studied Denzin's ideas. The alien setting, however, was not reflected in her experience of the people. She never felt incapable or alienated from the graduate students who were more experienced than she was. She emphasized that "[she] had an opinion, a comment and was not ignorant." She also described her insecurity during the whole experience, but the fact that she "could make a contribution" made it a very important experience. She surmised that "it was not something that she could get from a book, but rather it was something that came from working with women, Ernie and the other class members in a collaborative setting." Her statement is a reaffirmation of the "ethic of caring" calling for "personal expressiveness, emotions, [and] empathy [which are] central to the knowledge/validation process" (Denzin, 1994, p. 510).

Perhaps the biggest impact for Beverley was made on her sense of spirituality. She was proud to have heard the professor comment in the presence of the other class members that "she made a contribution to the class." She described the "fullness of spiritual aspects that she experienced as she was learning qualitative research." She explained that "people came out on the other side changed because of the experience Ernie constructed" and noticed "the sense of emotional power that the class had."

Vicky

Vicky was able to describe professional and personal epiphanies she had experienced in the ethnography class. Because her first community ethnography the previous semester was problematic, she had very negative feelings about group work. She regained confidence in the group work concept because working together this summer in our group made her realize the possibilities of group efforts. The second epiphany was a re-enforcement of her commitment to her personal life. She felt the need to manage her time in a manner that provides more time for personal activities.

Mary Frances

I came out of this ethnography class with the knowledge I had been pushing very hard for 2 years and, as a result, had finished my course work but had not had time for other aspects of my life. I knew that if I pushed hard for another year without a husband's help and support, I probably could write my dissertation but at too great a price? I knew that as a single parent I would need much more energy. At that stage my daughter became my main priority. I found a good babysitter, because I knew I would need even more help than I had. I realized that it would be difficult to endure divorce proceedings and motherhood *and* to write a dissertation. I also decided that my heart and soul were bound up in language arts and internationalism and that I needed to do some international research on educational issues. I felt determined to "follow my bliss."

The people around me, particularly my research group, were supportive and concerned with my newfound circumstances. I found that, with their support, I could carry on my academic work and study. I never regretted that I had entered academic life, even though I have become more cognizant of its pitfalls. I have taken time to consider what it might be like to spend the rest of life as a single parent. I have received solace from two female deans in our college who assure me that they were once in my position. I was reinvigorated by my assurance that I would survive and finish my degree, but that it might take me longer than I initially hoped. I became happy with the process of becoming a doctor of philosophy rather than focusing so much on the final goal. I re-emerged from this class with friends, a support group, and self-knowledge.

OTHER INSIGHTS: FROM THE PRIVATE
TO THE PUBLIC

Elliot Eisner, an artist, educational theorist, and philosopher, described a personal odyssey in a recent discussion of his journey to "understand the development of mind and forms through which its contents are made public" (1993, p. 5). By becoming a teacher of art, he felt that his efforts would be of greater value than if he confined himself to art itself. In similar vein, we four graduate students and others like us in this class felt compelled to study for advanced degrees in our fields. I suspect that all of us, having gone through the educational mill as students and teachers at schools and at universities, would agree that one of the most important goals of the educational process is to help people develop their abilities to the utmost. Part of the process involved spending time finding ourselves, time for personal discovery. Ironically, we found ourselves driven to the pinnacle of achievement in our field, only to discover that we had been forced to give up a large part of what we considered to be important to us as educated and fully developed people—leisure time, time with family, and time for activities that contribute to physical and mental well-being.

"Outsiders in the Sacred Grove"

Recent feminist research supported much of our new understanding about this process of metamorphosis. In *Women of Academe: Outsiders in the Sacred Grove*, Aisenberg and Harrington (1988) illustrated how women who deviate from the "marriage plot"—that is, adherence to the traditional female role of wife and mother—undergo profound transformations to begin at the same place as male academic professional. Our four group members found it necessary to abandon parts of themselves that were defined by marriage and motherhood to invest the time and effort required by academic study. This investment did not present an insurmountable agenda, but monopolized our time and energies and thereby took us away from other equally demanding roles.

This analysis speaks to the conflicts between personal and professional life that emerged as the focus of this study. Group activities encountered in a qualitative research methods class helped us come to a better understanding of the way we suffered loss of self in the process of bettering ourselves in the process of furthering our professional and educational lives. Dewey (1916) suggested that the most important reason to be educated was to be a better world citizen. The dichotomy between private life and school life was not one that he clearly reconciled, although he thought that education ultimately must relate to all aspects of life. As doctoral students in education, we knew from our classroom experiences that the more concrete and relevant learning is to students, the more they learn.

Some concrete features of our lives and our citizenship became relevant as our group reflected on the educational aspects of our interviews, debriefing sessions, and triangulation activities. We found our citizenship put into jeopardy as we struggled to survive the rigors of summer school. In the larger scheme of citizenship, we found ourselves struggling with love-ship, family-ship, and friend-ship. None of us had much time to gain insight into the broader community or, ultimately, the world to which Dewey alluded; yet, paradoxically, we were pursuing doctoral studies to better the world of education at a level higher than had previously been possible for us.

What surfaced from our analysis was complex, yet simply related to our educational experience that summer. My journal entry for June 3rd shed some light on this analysis. I wrote, "There were a couple of things that were interesting ... if I were doing a more in-depth look at Beverley's teaching philosophy that I would have extended on." In retrospect, the issue that Beverley was concerned with was her self-concept as a "Dr. Jekyll and Mr Hyde" personality. She felt that one personality revealed itself in the classroom, and her personal self was something else. Reconciling the two with the added variable of university life confounded her attempts to define her concept of self.

Developing this chapter and coming full circle to some understanding of the importance of the group processes in which we engaged, we see that the interview is the key that opened the doors of our personal lives. Because we were able to verbalize our problems, thoughts, and struggles, we could see the gaps in our lives created by the graduate school experience.

Equally relevant to this reading of our graduate school lives and particularly to the role of ethnographic researcher, we learned about "respecting the form of the telling [of the story] as being bonded to its meaning" (Grumet, 1991, p. 68). Although the interview process initially seemed straightforward, we learned that the art of a good interview allowed us to know ourselves in much more complex ways; as Sartre suggested in the *Transcendence of the Ego*

(1972), familiarity and knowledge are not synonymous. By sharing our personal perspectives with each other, we could better understand the process of metamorphosis in which we were engaged.

We began to understand the dynamics of finding ourselves "outsiders in the sacred grove," for as Eschbach (1993) indicated, "The entry into professional life [for women has] remained, despite the abundance of higher education, slow and difficult" (p. 185). We learned from our experience of group ethnographic research how much our personal experiences, attitudes, and philosophies affected the way we view the people we observe. We learned that if the etic or outsider view is one end of a spectrum and the emic or insider view is the other, both ends are tenuous and neither extreme is attainable.

As educational researchers we must understand that our position varies as each observation fits or diverges from our own life experiences and is colored by the concurrent forces in our lives. There are no static phenomena observable by uninvolved researchers—because we ascribe to the philosophy of the ongoing learning process that makes up our journey through both individual and collective life.

REFERENCES

Aisenberg, N., & Harrington, M. (1988). *Women of academe: Outsiders in the sacred grove.* Amherst: University of Massachusetts Press.
Denzin, N. K. (1989). *Interpretive intreractionism.* Newbury Park, CA: Sage.
Denzin, N. K. (1994). The art and politics of interpretation. In N. K. Denzin & Y. Lincoln (Eds.), *Handbook of qualitative research* (pp. 500–513). Newbury Park, CA: Sage.
Dewey, J. (1916). *Democracy and education.* New York: Free Press.
Eisner, E. W. (1993). Forms of understanding and the future of educational research. *Educational Researcher, 22,* 5–11.
Eschbach, E. S. (1993). *The higher education of women in England and America 1865–1920.* New York: Garland.
Grumet, M. (1991). The politics of personal knowledge. In C. Witherell, & N. Noddings (Eds.), *Stories lives tell: Narrative and dialogue in education* (pp. 67–77). New York: Teachers College Press.
Lincoln, Y., & Guba, E. (1985). *Naturalistic inquiry.* Newbury Park, CA: Sage.
Sartre, J. P. (1972). *The transcendence of the ego* (Williams & Kirkpatrick, Trans.). New York: Octagon Books.
Spradley, J. P. (1979). *Participant observation..* Fort Worth, TX: Holt, Rinehart & Winston.

8

Reaching Consensus and Writing Collaborative Accounts

Deana Lee Philbrook Henry

FOCUS

Many people who work in arenas where community development is important prefer consensus as the means for making decisions. Older, authoritarian styles of leadership are replaced by participatory, democratic processes that are manifested in concepts such as total quality management (TQM), flatter management hierarchies, shared authority, and partnerships in decision making. These concepts are now evident in many areas of public and professional life, from business management to school administration. In education there is a continuing debate about the efficacy or desirability of collaborative and constructivist approaches to research and learning implicit in these concepts.

A recent graduate course in community-based ethnography provided a group of graduate students with direct experience of collaborative work as they experimented with corporately written ethnographic texts. By the time they had completed this project, the group came to realize that the manner in which they had achieved consensus while composing a paper was relevant to research or report writing in communities, organizations, classes, and other group contexts that aspire to democratic modes of operation. This chapter offers an interpretive description of the group's experience of participatory process and shows how it is possible to develop accounts or reports that represent a shared vision.

Definitions

Webster's Dictionary (1986) gives the following definitions for the major concepts in this chapter: *Collaborate*: to work jointly with others or together especially in an intellectual endeavor; *consensus*: group solidarity in sentiment and belief, a general agreement, unanimity, or the judgment arrived at by most of those concerned.

FORMULATING A NARRATIVE ACCOUNT

This account is based on the experience of 17 doctoral candidates and 1 master's candidate in a graduate course in community-based ethnography. As part of the course requirements, participants worked in groups of four or five to write ethnographic narratives of their class experiences. This chapter describes the experience of one team—Joseph, Lois, Shelia, and myself—that included people with different levels of expertise in ethnographic work and a rich and diverse range of professional and social experiences.

Data for the narrative were drawn from class ethnographies, interviews, field notes, and written evaluations. Field notes included records of classroom observations, class notes, notes from interviews with the professor and other class members, and individual reflections about the class. As each team prepared an ethnographic account of the course we exchanged material with each other to increase the body of information at our disposal. I taped and transcribed conversations between Lois, Joseph, and myself about 5 months after the course had ended, and Shelia mailed me her written reflections at that time. First names identify speakers or writers.

To analyze the data I reviewed all information at my disposal and made a preliminary list of elements or themes, then identified categories and subcategories within the data. The approach to analysis is based on procedures recommended by Denzin (1989): "In bracketing, the researcher holds up the phenomenon for serious inspection. It is taken out of the world where it occurs. It is taken apart and dissected. Its elements and essential structures are uncovered, defined, and analyzed. It is treated as a text or a document; that is, as an instance of the phenomenon being studied" (p. 55).

For Denzin there is an intensive struggle to interpret meanings in the data, and it is necessary to use the subject's interpretations as part of the process of becoming an "informed reader." Bracketing enables people to derive the "essential recurring features" of the phenomenon under study from in the experienced world of the subject.

Using these bracketed categories, I created an outline for a narrative. When questions about interpretation of data arose, I contacted one or more of the three other members of our group and/or reviewed the original documents to gain greater clarity, or both. This process took place in another course—Advanced Qualitative Methodology—in which participants reviewed ethnographic method, reflected on each other's writings, and shared efforts to gain understanding of other realities. Because Lois, Shelia, and some others had also been part of the community-based ethnography course, I was able to share my manuscript for verification and member checks (see Lincoln & Guba, 1985, pp. 236, 314–316, 373–378).

THE CONTEXT OF OUR GROUP NARRATIVE

Collaborative Classwork

Dr. Ernest T. Stringer (Ernie) came to us as a visiting professor from Australia. He is a unique teacher who demonstrated collaboration and consensual decision making in the process of leading our class. An almost tangible openness exuded from our instructor because of his informal manner. On the first evening of our course, he commenced class sitting in a chair rather than standing, a position we later learned, that he consciously took as a means of conveying a feeling of equality. This attitude contrasts to the dominating stance of most instructors who emphasize hierarchical professor–student relationships. Ernie set the scene for what was to prove a very different class experience for many participants: According to Shelia, Lois, Joseph, and Deana:

> There is an enthusiasm about him. The word had spread through the grapevine from those graduate students who had met Ernie that he was delightfully interesting. We intuitively knew this would be an excitingly different course than [sic] others we had taken at A&M ... We now realize we were undergoing a new paradigm in community-based research as Ernie guided us to greater autonomy and [a sense of community] among people who come from quite diverse backgrounds.

Lois wrote in her field notes:

> I like the freedom we have had in everything in this class. I liked this type of collaborative emphasis that was similar to my experience at another university I attended. This university is too traditional, structured. It is like stuffed shirt city. I took a midterm on a Scantron for a graduate class! It was really easy to grade but I was shocked. I like the research being collaborative with the community. In other courses the researcher's anonymity is stressed. I like helping people take action, empowerment, helping them help themselves.

Collaborative processes were a central feature of the course and were enacted in a variety of contexts as participants practiced consensual decision making, collective "remembrances," interviews, introductions, and, later, collaborative writing. According to Shelia, Lois, Joseph, and Deana:

> A collective remembrance, a term that sounds almost sacred, was one of the first strategies Ernie employed. In the second class meeting he had members recall the events of the previous week, so that bit by bit, piece by piece, we were able to put the pieces of the puzzle together and collectively recall the first class. Through a process of consensus our common story was built upon the multiple realities of the participants, so that, collaboratively, we were able to arrive at a comprehensive understanding of the events of the previous week.

We also engaged in collaborative activity in our work groups as we presented and discussed summaries of readings, memorized frameworks for interviewing and observing, and facilitated class meetings. Shelia described one of these experiences in the following way:

> When we moved into our work groups to discuss the readings, Deana started us off with a summary of Ernie's chapter from the book Theory and Concepts in Qualitative Research (Flinders & Mills, 1993) in which she stressed her appreciation of Ernie's clarity in writing an understandable description of postmodern research. For her second reading she provided a diagram that showed the steps and details presented in Chapter 3 of Denzin's book Interpretive Interactionism (1989). This was helpful and provided a clear reference tool for later use. I followed with a short description of the article "Is Anthropology Alive? Social Responsibility in Social Anthropology" by Berreman (1968). I summarized the article with quotes that explained its general thrust—that researchers should be responsible to individuals they studied and to related public issues. Next, I drew a web or map of descriptive observations from Spradley's (1979) book Participant Observation. Joseph completed our discussion with summaries of Doing Anthropology of America (Varenne, 1986) and Pearls, Pith and Provocation (Dunn, 1991). The former talked of the need for American anthropologists to study mainstream society instead of concentrating on the exotic, while the latter spoke of the dangers of deep personal involvement. Lois concluded with a summary of Chapter 1 from Denzin's (1989) Interpretive Interactionism in which she provided definitions of some of the terminology. We had a healthy, fruitful discussion in our group. I really like being able to share the readings this way.

The manner in which each group facilitated a class session was yet another instance of the collaborative approach to activity we experienced in this class. As Shelia, Lois, Joseph, and Deana wrote:

> As a group, we had the opportunity to organize and facilitate a class session ... We met for twenty minutes before class commenced ... to discuss our strategy ... Deana became our leader and we opened the class, much to amusement of our fellow class members by dancing and singing the song "Getting to Know You" as a ritual of celebration. Ernie had mentioned earlier that celebration was an important aspect of activities that helped us grow as a community.

In a variety of ways, therefore, collaborative activities formed the basis for much of our classwork. In small groups and as a class, we participated in events that enabled us to share the workload, to provide opportunities for discussing and testing ideas, and to practice and refine our ethnographic skills. In contrast to many traditional classes, which emphasize individual performance, we worked together and, in doing so, created an environment conducive to learning.

Group Members

Our group was made up of four PhD students between the ages of 41 and 49. Joseph, Lois, and Shelia studied curriculum and instruction; Deana's specialization was adult education. We all tended to be vocal in class and to smile rather than frown. In later conversations we agreed that the importance of the individuals making up our group could not be underrated. We felt that the particular makeup of the group enabled us to work productively together so that we were able to use consensual approaches to such difficult tasks as a collaborative ethnography.

Our backgrounds were widely divergent. Joseph was from Singapore and, as lifetime member of an order of Catholic lay brothers, had been a high-school music teacher and principal. He had two university degrees from the University of Tulsa and had also studied in India, Sri Lanka, and Hong Kong. He had extensive training in tai chi, kung fu and Eastern religions and had also studied massage and dream therapy futurism. Joseph was a yachtsman.[1]

Lois came from a close-knit Italian family in Tucson, Arizona. She had been a teacher of bilingual students in elementary and junior high schools, for a time on an Indian reservation in Arizona and later in Alabama. Lois had been the director of religious education for a Catholic school and for the past several years taught student teachers at two universities. She has two children and has been married for many years.

Shelia grew up in Chicago and worked there as a social worker. She later returned to school to get a teacher's certificate and taught English as a second language and reading courses at high school for 11 years. Shelia also leads summer writing institutes for teachers and has worked part time with student teachers for several years. Shelia has three children and has been married for many years.

I was raised as a "preacher's kid" in six U.S. states and have since lived in five other states, the Marshall Islands, and two provinces of Canada. My work in these contexts has included community development, adult education, and small business accounting. Since my childhood I have been active in social justice issues as a member of a Protestant ecumenical lay religious order. I have three sons and, like the other women in our group, have been married for many years.

Despite the diversity of our experiences, we felt that there was a quality about the group that enabled us to reach consensus relatively easily as we engaged in corporate writing. Our group was noncompetitive, friendly, self-selected, responsible, and harmonious. We had all been in extended partnerships with individuals or groups, in marriages or a religious order, and the four of us had worked together earlier. These factors contributed to our ability to work as a team, to engage in class activities, and to engage in collaborative projects. The particular makeup of the group, therefore, was an important ingredient that facilitated our ability to work productively.

---

[1]Since this was written Joseph has left the Christian Brothers order, married, and returned to Singapore.

THE PROCESS OF COLLABORATIVE WRITING

Writing a collaborative account of events is a complex activity. Not only are there different actors, activities, events, and contexts to describe, but the ways in which they can be depicted differ according to the experience of each of the people and their various perspectives. In this instance the writing of our account was greatly assisted by the way our facilitator and teacher organized class activities. Ernie allowed us to take class time to compile observational data, to conduct additional interviews, and to analyze data. He also allowed himself to be interviewed and assigned each class member the task of writing 20 pages of field notes, an activity that added greatly to the data available.

To provide a framework around which a narrative could be constructed, we first shared our reflections on the experience of the class and then pooled the information we had gathered. From this mass of data we listed 29 elements and placed symbols beside each to identify those that were similar:

o community	x Ernie (facilitator)
o interviewing each other	* readings
+ working groups	+ presentations
* + frameworks	* + processes
o food	o potluck
+ agenda (routines)	o collective remembrance
x diversity among students	@ classroom
o conversation	x personalities
x humor	+ stories (examples)
+ questions	+ role playing
+ fish bowl	v projects
v writing class story	x personal histories
+v journals	v portfolios
* textbooks	vo + summaries

Next we added elements that had not been included in the original list, including: @—Ernie's apartment; @—Lois' house; @—Another classroom; @—Ernie's office; @—Chicken Oil Company (restaurant).

The categories were then identified as x—actors; *—resources; +—methodology; v—tangible outcomes; o—community building and formation; @—settings.

Then we added the category "Goals," which we thought was woven throughout all other categories and finally decided that each of us should compile an account based on one of these categories. Joseph later recalled this brainstorming and writing process:

> First, we went through the steps to interpretation. We brainstormed when we first got together, did a content analysis of the various parts and then each of us wrote about one part. We wrote the various sections separately and then brought all four parts together and made a decision to do it together, since all of us were present. When that process started, the actual interaction that was taking place was ongoing, [and] it refined and deepened as the semester went on.

By analyzing the data together, therefore, we were able to clearly delineate those aspects of the setting that were critical to an understanding of the class. These factors provided a framework around which we were able to weave the fabric of our story and enabled us to divide some of the workload among us. This initial analysis was followed by an intense period of activity as we worked together to develop a collaborative account we all could "own."

HOW WE REACHED CONSENSUS

Seven elements helped us to understand how our group was able to achieve consensus about the meaning of our class experience: During the writing process we worked together; during the writing we were together for an extended time; we worked spontaneously; we used the computer together for writing and editing; when there was disagreement we stopped writing and negotiated meanings until we had an agreement; our group interpersonal interaction was very positive; and we all were committed and made personal sacrifices to complete our group ethnographic narrative.

Through these processes we were able to work through the large amount of data we had accumulated and to derive an account that, we felt, reflected our corporate experience.

Working Together

Although some other groups completed almost all their work separately, our group discovered that we were able to be more productive when we worked together. We met one Sunday at Lois's house, enjoyed a pizza lunch, and then commenced work in her home office. Shelia described the writing process: "From that point we worked in a collaborative manner, with each of us taking a key element to work up and insert into the group effort."

According to: "Each of us shared our 20 page report and got down to business. We managed to achieve a lot ...in a relatively short time" (Shelia, Lois, Joseph, and Deana).

Joseph wrote: "One of us would write into the computer and the rest would be editing, rephrasing or asking such questions as, 'How does that sound?' 'Is that okay?' or 'Does that speak for all of us?' It was an ongoing thing all the time and as we worked we typed directly into the computer. So by the time the whole project was finished it was a holistic product composed by all four of us."

Working for an Extended Time

Our group started at 12:30 PM and worked until we finished around 8:00 PM. We did not break for snacks; each of us left the room separately as the need for a drink or a visit to the bathroom arose. Shelia later said, "That uninterrupted, large chunk of time was critical. … It enabled us to complete our task at one sitting [and comply with] the class schedule. We all felt good about getting the content of our narrative together without getting caught up in heavy duty revision."

Spontaneity

Although our group had intended to leave the final compilation to Joseph, once we had started working at the computer, it seemed better to continue writing until we finished. In this and a range of other ways we continually changed plans in order to go with the flow of activity as it emerged. This spontaneity enabled us to be more productive by allowing us to organize our activity around the conditions that applied at the time, rather than according to a predetermined plan.

The Computer

All of our group members agreed that the use of a computer greatly assisted our collaborative writing processes. We had intended to take turns, but the program and hardware proved awkward to Deana and Shelia, who were used to other systems. After a short attempt, Deana left the actual input to Lois and Joseph. It was obvious, however, that the use of computer technology had greatly facilitated our ability to cooperate directly in writing the account. Some time after the course had finished, Shelia, Lois, and Deana reflected on the writing process and suggested that this collaborative approach to writing gave a deeper sense of sharing and a feeling of equal participation. Joseph wrote:

> [We heard] that other groups had problems when they split up and allowed each person to write a separate part of the text … I don't know what the outcome was, but I think that the people in our group wrote pretty naturally because we were together rather than compartmentalized when we wrote the various sections … [We were able] to edit or change paragraphs … It was a big tool and I think I would continue to use it in collaborative writing."

Negotiating Meaning

Although there was only one significant disagreement during our marathon writing collaboration, there was an ongoing need to define the way things had occurred. Joseph wrote: "I thought that there was a lot of give and take at the session we had at Lois's place. A lot of negotiation [was required to establish] consensus especially between you (Deana) and Lois in that episode. In the end you gave in to her; it was a compromise. Shelia and I also had a different perspective. I thought it was fascinating to see how we interacted."

Shelia's recollection differed slightly: "We had some disagreement during the writing that required us to talk [things] through, but very little. I would add here, that we were all confused about the sequence of events at one point; that none of us agreed. Did we ever resolve that?"

Lois did not think the disagreement was a key part of our writing experience, though she felt it was critical that we stopped writing until we worked out disagreements in perspective. Through all this, though, we continued to negotiate until we came up with a solution that people in the group could accept.

Positive Interpersonal Interaction

Our group dynamics were an important part of our collaboration. Joseph and Shelia both made several statements about the way we had worked together: "There were no raised voices. We were focused. We had equal roles. We had respect for each other. There was a lot of sensitivity to each other's needs."

Joseph recalled how each of us brought our own experiences to the writing process: "We appreciated each other's richness. When we brought [all of our experience] together it came out in our writing ... I think all of us contributed in various ways, like your (Deana) strong point with editing and Shelia being an English teacher and myself and Lois mainly doing the typing because we were familiar with the software. We enhanced each other's talents and giftedness in the project"

In some ways this writing process reflected our experience of the course. Our group ethnographic narrative related similar processes taking place in class:

> Ernie talked about the definition of culture as being the sum total of the group's experiences and knowledge; all that they learned consciously or unconsciously and that permeated everything they did. With this definition, we felt that our class was evolving a unique culture of its own. All of us were in some way simultaneously shaping each other and though the results were not yet apparent, things were beginning to gel.

The positive tone of interaction in our group, therefore, contributed significantly to our ability to work harmoniously and develop a group narrative.

Commitment and Sacrifice

Our commitments to the group's success were also important in the writing process. Joseph recalled that we had all promised to finish the writing that Sunday and Shelia related how each of us had completed "our part of the designated work so that we would not let the other group members down. We stayed on task and, as a result, completed our group narrative on time." Joseph used the word *sacrifice* to describe our willingness to collaborate, despite the difficulty of getting all people together at the same time. "There was a lot of give and take and sacrifices on all of our parts—the common time to meet, all the various people [that we needed to include]."

Achieving Consensus

These seven elements helped us to understand the way in which we were able to work together to write a collaborative ethnographic text. They also helped us to understand that we were not merely developing an account of our class experiences but were also re-creating the meaning of the course for each of us. We experienced this process as reaching consensus. Because we worked as a group for an extended period, it is difficult to separate the influence of our writing experience from other course experiences; this dissolving of borders made our narrative almost a group autobiography or ethnographic memoir (Tedlock, 1991). The experience is probably best summed up in the words of those who participated. Joseph commented thus: "I think the combined influence of our group, especially while writing our community ethnography, was very important. It influenced what I got out of the course and affirmed the title, community-based education,"

Lois reflected: "Other folks did have resistance within their groups. I felt very fortunate to be a part of this group."

Shelia summed up the experience this way: "We were good! It was a most enjoyable experience for me. We felt our experience of writing together was very positive."

The processes involved in achieving consensus were obviously instructive in a number of ways. Not only were participants able to gain experience in negotiating diverse perspectives, but they were able to do so in a context that enabled them to extend the breadth of their experience and contribute to the production of a text far richer than might otherwise have been accomplished through their separate endeavors.

CONTEXTUALIZING THE EXPERIENCE
CONSENSUS IN PARTICIPATORY RESEARCH

The struggle to achieve consensus as part of the processes of collaborative ethnographic inquiry and narrative composition has far-reaching implications for adult educators, community development workers, and others who engage in participatory research. Tandon (1988) described the need for direct involvement of stakeholders in research on adult education. He suggested that much current research is alien to adult learners who feel themselves to be unilaterally controlled by researchers and treated as objects to be manipulated in the research process. Tandon described participatory research as a system of knowledge production that has been unrecognized, neglected, and delegitimized by dominant systems of inquiry merely serving to perpetuate the status quo. He presented alternative systems of knowledge production that provide opportunities for ordinary people to control events in their daily lives. In contrast to traditional approaches to inquiry, he presented participatory research as a methodology that explodes the myth of neutrality and objectivity and emphasizes the principles of subjectivity, involvement, insertion, and consensual validation: "Participatory research attempts to present people as researchers themselves in pursuit of answers to the questions of their daily struggle and survival. It recognizes the need for an occasional special input of expertise and contribution of certain skills, but it rejects the myth of professionally trained experts as the only legitimate pursuers of knowledge" (Tandon, 1988).

Participatory research is a collective process of inquiry that is opposed to the individualistic nature of traditional research methodologies. As a collective process, therefore, it rejects the separation of roles of researcher and researched and denies the authority of an individual researcher to determine the purposes, processes, and products of investigation.

Participatory research also sets aside the question of objectivity or subjectivity in ethnographic inquiry as being irrelevant to the main thrust of the project. Tedlock (1991) suggested there is an incompatible difference between the "subject's way of knowing and the scientist's way of knowing." She reported that some field workers "reject the sharp analytical distinction between Self and Other" and employed the phenomenological term *human intersubjectivity* to describe communication between the researcher and researched. Tedlock believed that the willingness and ability to be intersubjective separate the human sciences from the natural sciences. Her voice is one of many who now question the assumptions of objectivity embedded in traditional approaches to research and suggest the need to develop new ways of evaluating the quality of research. In this chapter, the use of collaboration and consensus suggests possibilities for new levels of intersubjectivity that enrich and validate investigation.

The processes of obtaining consensus become central to the task of writing collaborative texts, narratives, accounts, or reports. They are ways of responding to the philosophical and political implications of recent critiques by ensuring that the voices of all participants are heard and equally valued. These consensual, collaborative processes are relevant to many creative projects now emerging in settings as diverse as educational institutions, employee job discussions, small group planning processes, and composition course and other classes.

In *Writing from the Margins: Power and Pedagogy for Teachers of Composition*, Hill (1990) discussed partnerships and collaborations among writing teachers in schools and colleges and in the Maryland Writing Project. She suggested that innovation will increase with the attempt to cross the borders between text and context, learner and what is learned. In business contexts, Roszak (1988) explored the application of participatory management processes that must work in an environment placing a high value on concerns such as productivity and foreshortened timelines. The formation of consensus was also important for Moore and Feldt (1993), who presented plans for facilitating planning and problem-solving consultations with small groups. Consensual decision making is part of a process of defining problems, inventing solutions, choosing options and working through issues of implementation. In similar vein, Angeletti (1993) reported on her use of collaborative writing with second graders. She presented a step-by-step approach in which students work in small groups to write short stories that will be published as a collection.

By focusing attention on contexts where collaboration, writing, and consensus are an integral part of the processes of inquiry and investigation, people may better understand the processes involved in research and writing. The sweeping trend toward such management techniques as TQM and shared decision making, approaches similar to those discussed here, may lead to the acceptance of democratic processes in which people are involved in making responsible corporate decisions that are meaningful to their lives.

REFERENCES

Angeletti, S. R. (1993). Group writing and publishing: Building community in a second-grade classroom. *Language Arts, 70*, 494–499.

Berreman, G. D. (1968). Is anthropology alive? Social responsibility in social anthropology. *Current Anthropology, 9*(5), 391–396.

Denzin, N. K. (1989). *Interpretive interactionism.* Newbury Park, CA: Sage.

Dunn, L. (1991). Pearls, pith and provocation: Research alert! Qualitative research may be hazardous to your health! *Qualitative Health Research 1*(3), 388–392.

Hill, C. E. (1990). *Writing from the margins: Power and pedagogy for teachers of composition.* New York: Oxford University Press.

Lincoln, Y. S., & Guba, E. G. (1985). *Naturalistic inquiry.* Beverly Hills, CA: Sage.

Moore, A. B., & Feldt, A. J. (1993). *Facilitating community and decision-making groups.* Malabar, FL: Krieger.

Roszak, J. (1988). Community development in the workplace: Bridging factions with the participatory process. *Journal of the Community Development Society, 19*(1), 121–133.

Stringer, E. T. (1993). Socially responsive education research: Linking theory and practice. In D. J. Flinders & J. E. Mills (Eds.), *Theory and concepts in qualitative research* (pp. 222–242). New York: Teachers College Press.

Tandon, R. (1988). Social transformation and participatory research. *Convergence, 21*(2/3) 5–15.

Tedlock, B. (1991). From participant observation to the observation of participation: The emergence of narrative ethnography. *Journal of Anthropological Research, 47*(1), 69–84.

Varenne, H. (1986). Doing anthropology of America. In H. Varenne (Ed.), *Telling America* (pp. 34–45). Lincoln: University of Nebraska Press.

Webster's Ninth New Collegiate Dictionary. (1986). Springfield, MA: Merriam-Webster.

9

Community Ethnography: Reproduction and Resistance in Writing the Collaborative Text

Vicky Newman

> [Foucault was] the first ... to teach us something absolutely fundamental; the indignity of speaking for others.
>
> —Gilles Deleuze

In his book *Time, Narrative, and History*, Carr pointed out that Hayden White (and earlier, Louis Mink) "raises the question of narrative's capacity to represent" (p. 10). The question explored how the "plot structures" of telling an event shape the events themselves and therefore how the event itself can be represented only by preordered imaginative cultural constructs.[1] In the context of collaborative writing, the issue of representation becomes even more complex—first by offering the possibility of multiple perspectives on the telling of events, but then by raising the issues of whether narrative can represent events and can allow multiple voices to construct these events.

This account of a group writing project, which took place in a graduate course in community ethnography, is designed to both construct and deconstruct the stories of our experiences of writing a collaborative text and, in doing so, to articulate the reproductions and resistances that took place in the group. In using the term *deconstruction*, I am referring to opening the possibilities of making meanings as well as to exposing how some meaning-making or interpretations can be marginalized by normally accepted ways of seeing. These

---

[1]Derrida and other poststructuralists continued the critique of representation by maintaining the impossibility of representation because language fucntions as supplements or fields of substitiutions that can only move around the thing trying to be named. In other words, language substitutes narrative authority for narrative authority. See J. Derrida (1976), *Of grammatology*, Baltimore: Johns Hopkins University Press.

processes operate to unconsciously order the dynamics of collaboration. Recognizing the fictions inherent in describing the production and organization of meaning (Clifford, 1988; Denzin, 1989), I have organized this chapter around presenting multiple stories or fictions to expose the complexities and multiplicities of perspectives in representation and to offer insights into possible implications of these perspectives, as well as of the form of the text. The voices of the group members who appear in this chapter, along with my voice, were unfortunately not heard until follow-up interviews were conducted well after the class had ended. Thus there is a compelling need to understand the institutional power structures and concepts that can silence people's voices. The philosophical and political conflicts among students or group members can lead to silencing and to critical resistances to representation.

I participated in the community ethnography class facilitated and taught by Dr. Stringer. He defined community ethnography as:

> A form of qualitative research which is both academically rigorous and socially responsive ... [It] is intrinsically participatory, so that the products of the research are not portrayals or reports written by an outsider, but collaborative accounts written from the emic perspective of the group. Such accounts, grounded in the hermeneutic processes of dialogue, negotiation and consensus, provide the basis of powerful group and community action. (1993)

After the class was divided into small groups, our first major assignment was to write a collaborative ethnography of our class based on the perspective of our particular group. The assignment required understanding, defined by Denzin (1989), as "the process of interpreting, knowing and comprehending the meaning that is felt, intended and expressed by another" (p. 120). Writing this assignment, however, exposed the difficulty of such knowing or comprehending; it required that we represent our personal experience and that of others through language and a single text. The assignment also exposed the irony of our narrow, traditional definition of the idea of the text: We all assumed that the text should have a traditional format that would include quotes about the experience from all the group members, but would nevertheless be subsumed under and interpreted in one voice.

Although many groups in the class though they had positive experiences and were successful in achieving understanding, in building consensus, and in articulating the perspectives of the members of their groups, our group did not have that positive experience. This chapter emerges from, and is directed to the implications of, these problematic dynamics.

One problem that emerged for our group was the paradox of the desire for and the resistance to authority or representation. This paradox manifested itself in a concern for what was perceived by some members as a power grab in the class and in the relief and subsequent capitulation by most members of the group to a monological narrative voice in the ethnography.

Because ethnography is enmeshed in writing, our discourse can be interpreted as "the meaning of our longing ... [and] how we speak and write tells more about our own inscribed selves than about the object of our gaze" (Lather, 1991, p. 119). Thus the issue of the "specific strategy of authority" (Clifford, 1988) seemed pivotal in revealing this paradox. More specifically, what most members of the group experienced or chose to experience was what I interpreted or labeled as a marginalization or silencing. I read this silencing as representing a larger and more complex context that was repeatedly articulated by the members of the group, particularly those who felt most marginalized. Rereading the process of writing the group ethnography through follow-up interviews and through articulation of the stories that emerged from these interviews reveals how embedded structures operated to reproduce or reinscribe themselves, even in the context of a liberatory pedagogical setting.[2] But what also emerged from these stories or tellings are resistances to both the authority of the narrative voice and to the feminist reading that theoretically supported the ethnography, in other words, resistances to theoretical representation. Because the feminist reading I was offering was so far removed from the inclusion, plurality, diversity, and community building (and even fragmentation) that much feminist theory and pedagogy have encouraged another irony is apparent.[3]

My agenda in this chapter then is threefold. One is to examine in the specific context of our classroom setting and group writing project how the demands of the academy reinscribe or reproduce themselves regardless of attempts at subversive techniques and principles in the classroom. Although the aim of the collaborative ethnography was to represent the polyphony of the experience, subsequent articulations by group members suggested that the pressure to finish the project, one of the "demands of contemporary academic careers" (Lather 1991, p. 84), and the embeddedness of the desire for authority to accomplish the task, converged to create a hierarchy in the group and subsequently within the text itself. This hierarchy not only frustrated the attempt at polyvocal or collaborative articulation but it also revealed the pervasiveness of our concepts of the text's possibilities.

I also read as part of the experience, however, resistance to the hierarchy as well as to the feminist politics that were at the core of what was finally submitted as the collaborative text. My imposition of feminist theory as a way

---

[2]The *liberatory classroom setting* refers to the way Stringer allowed students to help build the syllabus by contributing to the knowledge base and practices that we thought were important. Many members of the class, however, needed the reassurance and familiarity of a conventional arrangement; indeed one group wrote its ethnography around the anxiety and subsequent stress they it felt about what it perceived as the "unstructured" nature of the class.

[3]See, for example, F. Maher and M. K. Thompson Tetreault (Eds.;1994), *The feminist classroom*, New York: Basic Books; also J. Gore, *The struggle for pedagogies* (1993), New York: Routledge; J. Roland Martin (1985), Becoming educated: A journey of alienation or integration, *Journal of Education, 167*(3), 871–884; and J. Stacey (1988), Can there be a feminist ethnography? *Women's Studies International Forum, 11*(1), 21–27.

to recontextualize the experience silenced the very voices it should have enhanced. The importance in presenting this case lies in recognizing and articulating this power structure and our complicity in cultural production and reproduction. It is important to recognize and acknowledge the often conflictive nature of groups: Resistance to others' representations can result in silenced voices.

Finally, in this chapter, I argue that this example may suggest something important about the processes of collaboration and writing. Although reading and sharing the ideas we explore through writing is the way we build community, we also need to recognize that part of the process is or sometimes needs to be autonomous or singular. Flax (1990) suggested that oppositionally constructing connectedness and autonomy is fraudulent. Collaborative efforts must take into account how meanings shift and are negotiated and how this process involves moments of both autonomy and "being in relations" (p.181).[4]

THE POWER OF THE STORYTELLER

To present the different ways that group members experienced producing collaborative ethnography, I have attempted to reread the experience of the group writing project by conducting follow-up interviews with two members of our group and by re-examining my own analysis of the process of writing the ethnography, an analysis that was written as my final writing project at the end of the semester. I have presented "my story" and paralleled critical comments from my follow-up interviews as a way to deconstruct my own reading, to expose the problems inherent in our collaborative process, and to present alternative readings or stories about the experience. Because I was the main author of the ethnography, because I embodied the power of the storyteller to write my own desires into the text, and because I critically re-examined the process through a subsequent text in the course of the semester, I have presented much of the reflexive analysis or commentary I wrote about the experience of collaborative writing. In doing so, I am deliberately reinscribing the power relations and dynamics that took place in the group and exposing my own desires and will to power as they manifested themselves in capturing, bracketing, and contextualizing (Spradley, 1979). The comments from other group members, transcribed from the follow-up interviews, serve to disrupt the authority of my story and to present alternative readings and critical assessments of the experience of writing the collaborative ethnography. Finally, I have contextualized or read the experiences of our group back into a broader context of reproduction and resistance through examples of critical and feminist theories.

---

[4]Flax (1990) observed that, "for adults, forms of being in relation can be claustrophobic without autonomy, and autonomy without being in relations can easily degenerate into mastery" (p. 181).

REFLECTIONS ON WRITING
THE COLLABORATIVE ETHNOGRAPHIC TEXT

Following are three stories about the experience of writing the collaborative ethnography. The first telling, "'The Captain' Reflects," is mine; the subsequent tellings are those of two other members of the group.

Story One: "The Captain" Reflects

Capturing an account of the class by using materials from interviews had seemed relatively easy for us: We simply used the model of the interview with Dr. Stringer that had already been conducted by the class. First, the group interviewed one member and gained experience in recognizing and formulating the descriptive questions we needed to ask as well as the opportunity to correct and redirect questions couched in language that implied value judgments. Additional one-on-one interviews followed until every member of the group had been interviewed. Having captured what we thought was enough information through this process, we met several times and finally decided that each person needed to bracket the raw data. We each took the transcripts of the interviews and bracketed the domains that seemed to emerge.

But how was this information to be interpreted? Who would be responsible for textualizing the domains we had identified? More meetings—those were what we needed—more discussions. We were getting weary and running out of time. I suggested we needed to just start writing, but who would begin? All of us? Could we then merge the texts through an editing process? No, we would each make an outline of the domains, accompanying examples, and discussion we should include, meet with this information in hand, and then construct a master outline. From the master outline, we would all go to an office on the fifth floor of the building and together write the rough draft. I decided to begin writing the ethnography that evening after the meeting and I came to the next class with a partial draft in hand. I was hesitant of the issue of authority. After all, one of the domains we had bracketed was the grab for power in a class not modeled on the prevailing patriarchal pattern.

The group was relieved, however, that I had begun textualizing the information. In fact, they agreed I should continue. The partial draft seemed fine to them and one member even said she trusted whatever I decided to do because she was tired of, and lost in, the process.[5] Only one group member, Terresa, hesitated to hand over authority to me. We agreed that she and I would finish writing the text together.

As I wrote, I moved quickly over the thick description of the actual experience—the "you are there" of the text; the focus of the ethnography

---

[5]When Stringer read our journals at the end of the semester, he reminded me of how much power I had appropriated in presenting a "finished" product, of how different it is to construct or write than to edit.

became analytical and theoretical for me. In other words, locating the experiences in a historical and political context was the way my narrative authority operated in textualizing the experience. The issue of impositing authority emerged again. For example, as I read a comment about the "abrasiveness" of the women in the class from the interviews, journals, and conversations, I interpreted the comments as evidence of our engendered concepts of women. I imposed not only the authority of my own voice but another authority as well. From all the issues and domains that surfaced from the group, I chose to foreground the issues of women.

From the interviews and other conversational observations in our group and from the bracketing phase of the assignment, the "aggressiveness" of the women in the class emerged as a domain. From my perspective it was problematic. Negative comments were made about the "abrasive style" of some of the women; these comments suggested that the women lacked good listening skills, that they were unwilling or unable to compromise, that they handled a perceived power vacuum badly, and that they needed to learn to argue like men. For one member of the group, these women were offensive, had discomforting styles, and were unhelpful. Another member found the women's attitudes less troublesome, but the connotations of his comments were also negative. He attributed their behavior to aggressive personalities and to lack of experience in the field. I began to question where these negative associations with strong and forceful women came from. It seemed to me that historically they were located in the patriarchal power structure; that is, these reactions were based on engendered notions of women in our culture. Feminist theory, in my opinion, spoke to our associations and reactions to the behavior of some women in our class.

This theoretical framing, however, had begun for me in the very first interview. We had assembled as a group at one member's apartment. The interview was underway, and fairly soon the issue of the "abrasive women" surfaced. We asked questions. I was transcribing furiously while one member talked. But my thoughts were an example of the filters and lenses that were imposed from the onset of the interview. While the member was expressing distaste for the women and lauding the way men handle things by comparison, I was engaged in drawing a thousand conclusions and actually judging what she was saying. I was simultaneously transcribing, theorizing, and making value judgments about everything being said. "How can she not be aware of her sexism?" I thought. "Doesn't she see the connections between her comments and her own oppression? Doesn't she recognize her judgments and comments as sources of our oppression as women? When she praises the way the men in the class offer to 'see her through,' doesn't she realize how patronizing that kind of attitude is? Is she going to teach school? What will she teach the girls in class about empowerment?"

Later, I realized how quickly I had set the agenda. Other members' comments on the issue only reinforced what the interview had revealed to me.

Nevertheless, in contextualizing the experiences of the class to write the ethnography, I believed strongly that the issue of our sexism was central to our experiences in the class. I believed we were responding to an engendered system in our paradoxical frustrations at not having an "expert" authority figure who directed us very specifically and in the negative reactions to strong women in the class. I had been careful to ask for criticisms but when the members of the group next reviewed the draft, they had no critical comments. There were no negative reactions to my theoretical framing. My sense was that except for Terresa, the members of the group were willing to accept the text for whatever it might become.

Because I assumed the task of textualizing the information, I replaced the experiences into my life rather than into the lives of the members who had actually narrated their experiences. Part of the problem lay in the failure of the triangulation process. Denzin (1989) emphasized the importance of triangulation in presenting the subject's point of view. But because of the lack of group participation and the pressure of time, this step in the process was accomplished only superficially. How is this important to an ethnography about the experience of being in a graduate seminar? How has it illuminated issues and understandings about participating in this class or community? For graduate students, coming into a new class is always fraught with anxiety. Concerns about workloads and grades are overriding. The system is designed to impose maximum stress, but it is also structured to impose, validate, and reinforce a power structure that privileges an "expert" authority, a structure that perpetuates the patriarchy and the accompanying notions of power and control. In order to "do well" in the class, we students sought the best means to "produce the goods."

What became evident was the nature of the power structure itself. The domains emerging were about this issue. Examining the function of narrative authority in the text, especially the constructed text of the community, revealed the nature of power and control at a fundamental level; it revealed how deeply pervasive structures of domination and power are inscribed in the day-to-day processes of education.

Story Two: "A Crew Member" Speaks

I feel it is the nature of groups that one person becomes controlling or becomes the leader. Otherwise, there is no direction; nothing is accomplished, and there is frustration. I chose to sit back in the group. Because I was the only male in the group, I did not want to assert myself too much, but I also liked being an observer. The class for me was a good experience. I think the method of teaching or facilitating is good, but it is designed for an ideal world and we do not live in an ideal world. In the real world, the process of consensus is too time consuming. As much as we would like the world to be different, it is not so now. I did not assert myself about that paper, not because of aggression by anybody, but because I was stifled by the agenda. For me, and for others in the group, personal conflicts and demands from other classes and the paper's deadline all came together to make that draft a welcome sight. Without it, aimlessness and anxiety about getting it done after the due date would have continued. The content at that point was not so important.

Story Three: Another "Crew Member" Speaks

I remember getting together in the group and wondering what the hell you all were talking about. When we were doing the outline, I was clueless. When I read that paper, I was thinking that it was not what I wanted the paper to sound like; it sounded sterile, like something from a clinic. The whole dynamics of the group was predestined. I hung back from the forceful personalities and felt I could not really contribute anything.

To me, the paper should have been more personal. It seemed as though we had been aloof when we did it. But maybe the paper was like the dynamics of the group. Maybe it was my personal style—"meat and potatoes," lots of myself. I thought that the approach was wrong, but I never said anything. I would have to read, then talk about the outline to understand it, but I felt inferior. The way we would do things would be much more professorial.

After the class started, I was shocked because I was the only masters' student. I thought about withdrawing on the first night. As things went on, I heard what you all knew. I was stunned; you knew everything, and I was really intimidated. People had to comment on everything. There was a power struggle in the class from the beginning. Terresa made me withdraw. Then it got later, and later and I jumped on the bandwagon. I felt alienated from the beginning, not just by the group. There was probably nothing anyone could have done to make me feel part of that class.

Terresa made reference to marginalization, but just that "someone" was often left out. I never responded. Terresa's personality was not going to change because I felt left out. I felt steamrollered. Terresa has a steamroller personality. The paper seemed so impressive when I read it. What does this paper mean? It must be really good because I did not understand it. I felt like the dumb kid who sits beside the smart kid—Yes! I am going to get a good grade. The paper meant nothing to me. The process meant so much. I am going to use this paper as an example of what I do not want to sound like when I write. I listened to you all talk about the paper, but I was never part of that paper.

What was written was not my story. Sometimes the interpretation of me was wrong; it was not what I said—or meant anyway. I would not have overlaid outside quotes and philosophies. I would have told the story more straightforwardly. No lofty title—off-putting from the start. I liked the way the quotes were used, but each person should have interpreted his or her own quotes. As for the feminist interpretations, I do not like anything that has to do with feminism. The comment about the engendered sense of role models—I do not like pushy people; that is what the comment was all about, not so much male–female as a matter of etiquette. I had no ownership in that text. I felt nothing for it. Philosophically, I felt like the Rush Limbaugh of the class. As a real conservative Republican, I felt like Rush. But I did not speak up, and part of the reason was deadlines. I wanted to get this thing turned in on time for a grade. That was more important than to get to tell my story. If there is a leader, I follow. I was more than happy to jump on that bandwagon.

CONTEXTUALIZATION

The issues I have chosen to focus on are among many that emerged in the dynamics of our group. I have chosen these issues, however, because I believe they are significant to problems that students and nonstudents experience in collaborative settings. I recognize the importance of relocating the experiences of writing the ethnography into larger issues that have emerged from these tellings in a way that retains the basic integrity of the voices of the storytellers while avoiding an approach that reads these experiences or stories under a totalizing theory or allegory: a "story of stories" (Tyler, 1986). I also see the need to contextualize the issues that emerged as a way to look critically at the process, to expose the underlying structures perpetuating reinscription or reproduction, structures that marginalize some voices and stifle critical exploration of the implications of the structures themselves. The philosophical and political conflicts of groups and the resistances that emerge from these conflicts can also be read and addressed through the example of this collaborative experience.

REPRODUCTION AND RESISTANCE

Foucault (1977) examined the nature of power as it changes and operates in different historical periods and under differing specific circumstances. His analysis of power in the modern state has been cited frequently as a way to understand the power–knowledge relationship and its manifestations. According to Foucault, in the modern state there has been a shift from overt power to a more invisible or disciplinary power that is exercised through "normalizing technologies of the self":

> Traditionally, power was what was seen, what was shown and what was manifested. ... Disciplinary power, on the other hand, is exercised through its invisibility; at the same time, it imposes on those whom it subjects a principle of compulsory visibility. In discipline it is the subjects who have to be seen. Their visibility assures the hold of power that is exercised over them. It is the fact of being constantly seen, of being always able to be seen that maintains the disciplined individual in his subjection. (p. 187)

Disciplinary power becomes an internalized power: "He who is subjected to a field of visibility, and who knows it, assumes responsibility for the constraint of power; he makes them play spontaneously upon himself; he inscribes in himself the power relation in which he simultaneously plays both roles; he becomes the principle of his own subjection" (pp. 202–203).

Foucault's reading of the internalized power structures that become "technologies of the self" is one way for graduate students to read the part of the story of writing the collaborative ethnography that emphasizes the desire for and resistance to power. Gore (1993) understood Foucault's "regime of truth" as conveying "the connection between power and knowledge, which is produced by and produces, a specific art of government" (p. 55). Gore pointed out that these regimes of truth can be understood only when contextualized at the micro level and that according to Foucault, "it is in discourse that power and knowledge are joined together" (p. 56).

And as Foucault also noted: "Discourse is ambiguous ... a form of power that circulates in the social field and can attach to strategies of domination as well as to those of resistance ... Discourse can be both an instrument and an effect of power, but also a hindrance, a stumbling block, a point of resistance and a starting point for opposing strategy" (1977, pp. 56–57).

In this case, the discourse seemingly attached itself to strategies of domination, that is, the anxiety about time constraints and the pressure and demands from other courses caused the participants in our group to fall back on what is perceived as the most efficient way to accomplish writing a text: entrusting the task to a leader. In the process, the content or validity of the story was compromised to meet the goals of the class, which gives the 3 hours of credit necessary for the degree plan and which assigns the grade.

Disciplined by the educational system, we internalize the concept of success and the way success is often defined in the educational institution, as connected with negative concepts of power such as domination, control, and competition, and with the subsequent encoded desire to reproduce these models. Even in the context of a liberatory classroom setting, these desires still reproduce the same regimes of truth or dominant educational practices.

Scholars of feminist pedagogical theory have shared with Foucault and other critical theorists such as Giroux and McLaren a recognition of this paradox of reproduction and resistance and have examined how it operates in the classroom setting. Weiler (1991), in writing about the power issues of feminist pedagogy, commented on institutional reinscription and its implications for democracy and collectivism: "The issue of institutional authority raises the contradictions of trying to achieve a democratic and collective ideal in a hierarchical institution. ... This hierarchical structure is clearly in opposition to collective goals. ... Not only does the university structure impose this model of institutional authority but the students themselves expect it" (pp. 460–461).

Hayes (1989) examined the collaborative process in the context of feminist pedagogy. She pointed out that the "collaborative process is at the heart of feminist pedagogy" and that "individuals must share a group goal and efforts must be made to equalize the contribution each member can make toward the attainment of that goal" (pp. 59, 60). The pragmatics of our project, however, did not bring the group members together in pursuit of the intended goal of articulating their experiences. Rather, the pragmatic issue became producing the paper by a certain date, regardless of the story it told. Finishing the paper took priority over telling a polyvocal story of the experience of the collaborative task and did not resolve the issues of conflict and contradictory subjectivities in the group.

As Audre Lorde observes: "The conflicts among groups trying to work together … among teachers and students in classrooms, or among political groups working for change in very specific areas can lead to anger, frustration, and a retreat to safer, more traditional approaches" (cited in Weiler, 1991, p. 451).

The encoded desire for this retreat operates constantly in the classroom setting as it represents the way to get things done, the technique of the efficiency model, and does not entail the time or pain of reading the world when this reading involves contradictions, conflicts, and struggles (Weiler, 1991, p. 455). Yet the retreat signals our impoverished sense of possibility for the form of the text itself. What if each of us had written our impressions and experiences and shared them as a way to develop community, and, more important imagined how they might represent all our voices in an other format that would challenge the reproduction of the hierarchy of the very text itself?[6]

As already discussed however, discourse can also be "a hindrance, a stumbling block, a point of resistance and a starting point for an opposing strategy." The desire for authority was also accompanied by resistance. In the third story, the group member clearly articulated her complicity in surrendering her voice to the dominant narrative voice in the story, but ultimately she resisted the surrender and used the text itself as her "starting point for an opposing strategy": The ethnography was an example of how she never wanted to write. It was not about her, and it did not articulate the process in which she was involved.

Because reproduction and resistance operate in the classroom and specifically were operating in our collaborative writing group, how can the urge to reproduce a monological authority in the story of the group experience be avoided? Weiler (1991) pointed out that "in settings in which students come from differing positions of privilege or oppression, the sharing of experience

---

[6]Here a look at poststructuralists like Derrida would be helpful. To imagine and create alternative forms for the purpose of telling the story would perhaps challenge the historicist structuralism of Hayden White, as well as the theories of other structuralists, Barthes and Saussure, for example. This imagining would also echo feminists such as Irigaray, Dristeva, and Cixous. For helpful overviews on structuralism and poststructuralism, see T. Eagleton, *Literary theory: An introduction* (1993), Minneapolis: University of Minnesota Press. For overviews of feminist literary theory, see T. Moi, *Sexual textual politics* (1985), New York: Routledge.

raises conflicts rather than building solidarity" (p. 469). If as Weiler suggested, coalitions must be built by recognizing the complexities of people's different histories and the tensions of these differences, how can the marginalization of group members be remedied?

Bruffee (1993) reminded instructors that students do not come to class "as blank slates," that they appear "already deeply acculturated, already full-fledged, competent members of some community or other" (p. 17). What Bruffee saw as the pivotal issue in collaborative work was the process of reacculturation. According to Bruffee, to join a larger community of peers who come from different experiences and communities, group members must "overcome resistance to change that evidences itself as ambivalence about engaging in conversation at the boundaries of the knowledge communities that we already belong to" (pp. 23–24). In my reading of our group experience, one of the issues that emerged was the resistance to political and intellectual differences. This resistance manifested itself in a withdrawal from the process of even discussing the collaborative experience. Feminisms and feminist writings represented a boundary, a conflictive difference that needed to be explored from a historical and cultural perspective—and at a personal level—in the context of the experiences of others in the group. This particular scenario suggests to me the need to explore these differences as the basis of the collaborative experience. To critically examine the way I had imposed feminist theory on the account of our experience would have brought out the conflict inherent in its exclusionary language and application and would have exposed the paradox of its intended liberatory purpose.

Trimbur (1989) concurred with this viewpoint in his essay on consensus and difference. He acknowledged the difficulty and controversy that have surrounded the notion of consensus (enforced conformity or group think) and conceded that "consensus in some of its pedagogical uses may indeed be an accommodation to the workings of normal discourse and function thereby to promote conformity and improve the performance of the system" (p. 209). He then offers his notion of "dissensus" as an alternative to accommodation, wherein collaborative learning "becomes a process of identifying differences and locating these differences in relation to each other" (p. 215).

Writing about her experience of teaching Cuban revolutionary films to a predominantly White, middle-class group, Worth (1993) articulated the need to explore the historical construction of identity "as a vital part of the textual encounter" (p. 20) and as a way to avoid what she referred to as "textual anger." Realizing that her pedagogical technique encouraged students who were working together to ignore their differences and seeing the negative reactions and withdrawals from the projects that occurred, Worth shifted gears and implemented an exercise in which students began to examine and identify their culturally constructed conflicts. "We had to develop a double focus that took into account the construction of the subject as well as the construction of the object of critique" (p. 17).

A POLYVOCAL STORY

Clifford (1988) contended that "intrinsic to the breakup of monological authority [is] the multiplication of possible readings" (p. 52). In this case, the collaboration did not yield a polyvocal story. Instead, what would more likely have brought the voices of the marginalized members of the group into the story would have been an exploration of the constructedness of our differences, followed by separate accounts or stories of the experience. In one story, a member of the group pointed out that she liked the quotes, but thought that each person should have commented on or interpreted those quotes for her- or himself. But more important, she felt the story was not in any way about her. She resisted the way she had been represented in the text and the theoretical framing of her experience. How would her story have read? Must a collaborative text be a single story to give, as Clifford suggested, "a coherent presentation, presuppos[ing] a controlling mode of authority" (1988, p. 54)? If theory building, rather than theory imposition, must be a part of collaborative work, these multiple stories, wherein position and recognition of the regimes of truth operate to create positionality, must be articulated and acknowledged. In our group, had all the stories been told, the final ethnography could have been constructed as conversation or even argument; the theory building would have been inclusive, an example of the articulated aims of feminism and of feminist pedagogy. Maher (1987) observed that one aim of feminist pedagogy is "to help students and ourselves listen to and come to terms with our differences and the multiple capacities and social responsibilities within ourselves" (p. 192). In addition to the inclusion, we might have explored together the possibilities of the gaps and silences of the text and discussed and applied theories that could have led us all to a better understanding of the power of representation and the theoretical basis for the ways representation can be deconstructed to expose other possibilities. Grappling with our thoughts and struggling to write about them become modes of self-discovery; reading and discussing these accounts with others become ways to build community and make attempts at shared understandings. The pain of reading the world, as a part of praxis, might have avoided the reproduction of the hierarchical and negative power dynamics that occurred and, rather than a denial of difference for the sake of efficiency and expediency, our group could have struggled toward a more meaningful common goal.

REFERENCES

Bruffee, K. (1993). *Collaborative learning: Higher education, interdependence, and the authority of knowledge*. Baltimore: Johns Hopkins University Press.
Clifford, J. (1988). *The predicament of culture*. Cambridge, MA: Harvard University Press.
Denzin, N. (1989). *Interpretive interactionism*. Newbury Park, CA: Sage.
Flax, J. (1990). *Thinking fragments: Psychoanalysis, feminism and postmodernism in the contemporary west*. Berkeley: University of California Press.
Foucault, M. (1977). *Discipline and punish*. New York: Random House.

Gore, J. (1993). *The struggle for pedagogies.* New York: Routledge.

Hayes, E. (1989). Insights from women's experiences for teaching and learning. In E. Hayes (Ed.), *Effective teaching styles* (pp. 55–65). San Francisco: Jossey Bass.

Lather, P. (1991). *Getting smart.* New York: Routledge.

Maher, F. (1987). Inquiry, teaching, and feminist pedagogy. *Social Education, 51*(3), 186–192.

Owens, C. (1992). *Beyond recognition: Representation, power, and culture.* Berkeley: University of California Press.

Spradley, J. (1979). *The ethnographic interview.* New York: Holt, Rinehart & Winston.

Stringer, E. (1993). *Teaching community-based ethnography.* Unpublished paper, College Station, Texas A&M University.

Trimbur, J. (1989). Consensus and difference in collaborative learning. In P. Shannon (Ed.), *Becoming political: Readings and writings in the politics of literacy education* (pp. 208–222). Portsmouth, NH: Heinemann.

Tyler, S. (1986). Post-modern ethnography: From document of the occult to occult document. In J. Clifford and G. E. Marcus (Eds.), *Writing culture: The poetics and politics of ethnography* (pp. 122–140). Berkeley: University of California Press.

Weiler, K. (1991). Freire and a feminist pedagogy of difference. *Harvard Educational Review, 61*(4), 449–474.

Worth, F. (1993). Postmodern pedagogy in the multicultural classroom: For inappropriate teachers and imperfect spectators. *Cultural Critique, 25,* 5–32.

10

High-School Students' Participation in Action Research: An Ongoing Learning Process

Shelia Conant Baldwin

When Dr. Stringer first talked to us about doing a community-based research project for a graduate course in community-based ethnography, I thought of involving students from the access committee at the high school where I teach. Our high school fit the description of a community—a group who identified itself as "we"—and the access committee was formed 3 years ago as a result of racial problems that erupted after cheerleading elections. Because no African American student had been elected cheerleader, the African American football players boycotted spring training.

The principal, after discussing the situation with the superintendent, formed the access committee by selecting students and faculty who represented most of the different cultural groups in the school: African American, Hispanic, Asian, Native American and White. The committee's purpose was to hear any grievances about racial and ethnic issues and to promote cultural awareness among the student body and staff. As I have an intense interest in this area, I thought that a study of the different cultural groups in our school would be of service to the students, the school community, and the district. Students acting as ethnographers to study the culture of their school and community were significant because they would be working in the communities to which they belonged. Our school's population of 2,771, in Grades 9 through 12, reflected the diversity of the community; the students had White, African American, Hispanic, Asian, and Native American heritages and various socioeconomic and academic backgrounds.

The focus of this community-based research project was to engage a group of high-school students in roles as ethnographers to study their own cultures and the cultural groups of the school. Six seniors, two juniors, and one sophomore, representing White, African American, and Hispanic cultures, committed themselves to this project. This chapter presents an interpretive account of how these students used ethnographic research methods to explore cultural diversity in their school and community. It portrays the process of the study from my perspective as the teacher, acting as facilitator and active participant in the project. Thus, the chapter is both ethnographic and autoethnographic. I include my voice as well as the student participants' voices as an integral part of the account of the project (Denzin, 1989).

ETHNOGRAPHIC METHODS

This descriptive account is based on data collected through various ethnographic methods. The student ethnographers had multiple opportunities to present accounts of their data gathering; we debriefed what we had learned, and I kept field notes during every meeting. Following the meetings, I recorded detailed accounts of the happenings and conversations and made reflective comments after each encounter with student participants. A 3-hour taped session was transcribed. Finally, data were analyzed from the final write-ups turned in by three participants.

EMERGENCE OF THEMES

The themes that emerged were all associated with *place* which had an impact on the way in which role relationships, community–school interrelationships, and temporal and school context affected the development of the project.

In terms of role relationships, a journey toward understanding new roles became a significant factor in the evolution of this study, with teacher becoming facilitator and students ethnographers. My teaching philosophy is changing: I no longer think of myself as teacher but rather as a guide to learning. I promote this role by offering my students the direction, tools, and environment to take responsibility and ownership for their own learning. My assumption of the role of facilitator was in keeping with my evolving teaching philosophy, but, it was difficult for the students to change their perceptions of their roles as students to their new roles as ethnographers engaged in research.

Another element that emerged was the interrelation of school and community. When I originally approached the students to invite them to participate in this project, I proposed a study of the cultural groups in the school community. Then, after talking to Ernie, who suggested we begin the study with the community, the focus became our identification of our own cultures through family and community. If time allowed, the study would continue with the school culture. Some student ethnographers resisted exploring their own identity and continued commenting on their observations of the school community. In the sharing sessions, however, the discussions revealed that school and community culture cannot be separated, that there is a merging of the two.

During one meeting, Clyde talked of his observation that "The Whites stay with Whites and the Blacks stay with Blacks."

Guy offered his interpretation: "Yea, that's how we live. Like where we stay. That starts way back … It's because of neighborhoods. Black people all live together so they hang together." Charles added: "I think it's the way we're raised as kids."

Temporal and school context played a major part in the outcome of this project. With the exception of two sessions held at my home, all other meetings were conducted in the morning before school started. The bell schedule governed our meetings and allowed only bits and pieces of time to come together for talking about findings and problems. Why was the group limited to before-school meetings? The students' schedules were full; they had extracurricular activities, part-time jobs, and academic demands that prevented after school and weekend get-togethers.

From another perspective, the time allowed for the project (3 months) placed constraints on the unfolding quality of ethnographic research. Time affected the way that I directed the project to ensure having some data to analyze.

Finally, the physical surroundings of the school hindered the students' adaptation to expanded roles as ethnographers. They had difficulty seeing teachers in different roles and found it hard to view the project as something other than a school assignment.

GETTING STARTED

Eight volunteers from the student access committee and one student recommended by his teacher, who had known of this project, made up the group of ethnographers. Twyla was of medium height; she took great care in her appearance, her dress, her varied styling of her thick, black hair, and her use of makeup to accent her café au lait skin. Her soft-spoken voice characterized the sensitive, reflective nature of her personality: "The involvement in the ethnography project helped me to realize the complex diversity in human relations, despite race." Twyla planned to work after her graduation in May and to attend college in January, 1994.

Charles, Twyla's boyfriend, volunteered through her to be part of the project. Although a member of the high school football team, Charles's first love was singing. He not only sang with the high school choir and his church choir, but was also founder of a male a cappella group. He entered the Navy after graduation. I found Charles' lack of positive academic experiences to be in direct conflict with his sincerity and insightful interest in this project: "I'm really interested in ethnic relations in school … I believe if we continue to make known of the many things that different cultures have in common we will get somewhere racially and culturally."

Maria, petite, with naturally curly bronze-colored hair and fine Latin features, had come to the United States from Honduras 8 years ago. She was bilingual in Spanish and English and, because of her French stepfather, has had a special interest in learning French. Although she planned to do something with her knowledge of languages in the business world, her immediate concern was to pass the state-mandated test in math to graduate. Her pleasure in being part of the ethnography group could be heard when she expressed in her husky voice: "This is fun. All of us together eating."

Another senior, Gary, is currently in the honors program at the University of Houston. His dreadlocks hairstyle, in direct contrast to Charles's shaved pate, seemed to represent his confidence in being different. Color was not a boundary: He was a member of a multiracial rap group, and he had an Asian girlfriend. Gary's desire to participate in the project was expressed when he told me: "I really am interested in learning more about the Black culture in Chaney."

Clyde, now attending the University of Texas at San Antonio on a tennis scholarship, was also a senior. His confident voice spoke of his interest in this project: "I would like to do something with ethnic relations in college." He believed a group like the access committee was going to be a part of every school and college in the future.

Jan, the last of the senior volunteers, maintained a fresh, youthful look with her straight hairstyle and no makeup. Although a talented dancer, she revealed her desire to study adolescent psychiatry during our discussion about the nature of our research. She commented: "Not statistics, numbers … I do not want to label people."

Linda and Flor were the two juniors in the group. Linda wanted to be a bilingual teacher. Although she was born in the United States, most of her family resides in Mexico: "And when I go over there, it's family. Here, it's just school"

Linda was fair, with dark-brown eyes and curly reddish-brown hair. She displayed leadership qualities and was at ease talking with the multilevel Hispanic culture in our school. Her enthusiasm could be heard when she said: "I think we need to know more about our school. I think it will be so interesting!"

Unlike Linda, Flor's family resided in Texas, and they visited each other often. Flor, a big girl with glasses and shoulder-length black hair, was a quiet force who seemed to get things done in an unobtrusive way.

The final member of the research team was a sophomore from Mexico. Federico's neatly styled black hair and starched and pressed shirts and pants went along with his impeccable manners. Federico was on the soccer team and was friends with many non-English-speaking people from Honduras and San Salvador. At the first meeting he attended, when I asked everyone whether they knew each other, Federico stood up, reached across the table to Gary, Clyde, and Charles and said while shaking their hands: "Hi! I'm Federico."

The majority of our meetings took place in the high school library. The building was approximately 30 years old; the decor was that of the 1960s, with bookshelves lining the walls and wooden tables and chairs spaced throughout two carpeted levels. Two of our meetings took place in the main cafeteria (a room almost the length of a football field). On two other occasions—school holidays—we met at my house and gathered around the table in the kitchen. The student ethnographers, learning about their home and school cultures, conducted interviews, made observations, and kept field notes. We had seven scheduled meetings during which we shared our data and multiple conversations in the halls.

RELATIONSHIPS

Teacher as Facilitator

In one sense, my role did become that of a facilitator. Throughout our time together, I likened our project to a journey we were taking together to discover our community and school culture. "Let's discover our own identity. Look at our own culture. And our neighborhood where we are growing up and living. The community in which we live. After we learn about ourselves, and our community, then we might better understand our school community. What we are going to do and how will be a group decision."

When Jan expressed her uncertainty about what she was to do, I told her. "Ours will be an act of discovery. We don't know what we are going to find out. We will discover it along the way."

After offering a simple definition of the term *ethnography* as the study of a culture, I provided a job description: "You will take notes of observations and interviews. From those notes, you will write up a description of your findings."

I acted as a guide to help the students develop the tools necessary for doing ethnographic work and provided multiple opportunities to share their data. Each ethnographer received a spiral notebook in which to record his or her notes, a handout with tips about how to interview someone (Spradley, 1979, p. 86), and what to look for when observing a situation (Stringer & Hall, 1982).

A student and I modeled a beginning of an interview demonstrating a way to word questions in interviews to elicit information from the interviewee and to avoid alienation: "Tell me what it's like being a teenager in Chaney."

I shared part of an interview I had conducted with my daughter. I told them I was practicing. I read part of it:

Researcher: Describe a typical work day.

Interviewee: I get to work between 7:30 AM and 8:00 AM. I do paper work and make phone calls all morning. Meetings on some days. Then I go out in the field in the afternoon.

Researcher: Could you explain "Go out in the field?"

Interviewee: Make home visits.

Researcher: Do you make appointments?

Interviewee: Not usually.

Researcher: When does your day end?

Interviewee: Between 3:00 PM and 5:00 PM. That's usually the routine unless I have something scheduled.

Researcher: Describe your office. [*Interviewee described the physical structure of her office.*]

Researcher: What is your job as case manager? [*Interviewee offered a lengthy explanation of her job responsibilities.*]

Clyde had completed an interview with his mother and he volunteered: "It went really well. I started out with some general questions and then narrowed down to more specifics."

I asked whether he would give some examples of his questions: "What are some of the memories of your childhood? What was it like being a teenager? What was the feeling about different ethnic groups?"

While I read part of the interview with my daughter to the ethnographers, I discussed with them some tips on note taking, on how I had tried to capture the essence of what she was saying by writing only the key words. I explained to them the importance of writing up the interview immediately afterwards to fill in the gaps and reconstruct what was said as best as can be remembered.

Another ethnographic method they were to use was observation. I gave them some specific examples: "While sitting in the cafeteria at lunch time, watch kids and then write down your observations. Or, as you walk down the hall, observe what's going on and then write a detailed account. Watch kids interacting in classes and record those observations and conversations."

Students as Ethnographers

Charles approached me in the hall after receiving a reminder of the first meeting of ethnographers: "I really like that word 'ethnographer.' It makes me feel special. I didn't know that's what I am."

They used some ethnographic methodology such as making observations, doing unstructured interviews, taking and field notes. Some students were already unknowingly engaged in ethnography before becoming part of the project. For example, Charles had observed the seating arrangement in the cafeteria: "There is a pattern there of how kids sit. Black kids sit together, then Hispanic, then more Blacks. Some kids like to mix so they'll sit at a table with Whites, Browns and Blacks. Others like to be isolated."

He shared another incident:

> There's a girl in our class who has something wrong. Her head always tilts to one side and she walks with a limp. Well, we had to get into groups. All the Blacks sat together, all the Hispanics. All the Whites. And this girl was left sitting in the middle by herself surrounded by the groups. Wow! Right here in my class it was happening. Not only do we separate by race, culture, but within by individual differences.

Another example of assuming the ethnographic role was a comment Clyde made during our first meeting: "When we had the racial problems last month, I wrote pages and pages of notes."

Similar observations involving two African American teachers, made by Federico and Clyde, demonstrated their ethnographic understanding. Federico shared his observations in an English class. Because this teacher was African American, Federico observed that students anticipated being treated differently: "At the beginning of the year, kids acted different, like they didn't know how she was going to treat them. She didn't treat any of us any different—Black, White, or Hispanic."

Clyde related the same anticipation of students with another teacher: "But that didn't happen. No, she's real cool. When we were having all the problems a few months back, they would talk to her about it and what she thought. She would just listen to them, not making any judgments."

Flor shared her observations when she attended the county fair. "A lot of White people, kickers. Some Hispanics. Not that many."

Clyde mentioned that he missed a good opportunity to observe people during his brief stay at the fair. When asked what he saw he answered: "A lot of brisket. We went to the cookoff and I saw a lot of brisket. How do you classify that?"

Charles used unstructured interviewing; at one of our meetings, he related his conversation with a Hispanic girl in one of his classes. She gave him some interesting information about the Hispanic culture in the school: "Like the Tex-Mex. She said something like the Hondurans don't like to be called

Mexicans ... Then she told me about how you have the kind of poor, the really poor and you see they wear really extravagant clothes to school, like really flashy dresses."

SCHOOL–COMMUNITY INTERRELATIONS

One theme that surfaced from the analysis of the narrative was that of the relation between school and community. It became apparent early in the project that school and community could not be separated. When I explained to the students the change of starting place for their data gathering, I said: "It is necessary for us to become familiar with and try to understand our own culture—our families, our community first. After all, this community feeds into this school. After we learn about ourselves and our community, then we might better understand our school community."

During our third meeting, a discussion about how people make groups ensued. Gary surmised: "Yea, that's how we live. Like where we stay. That starts way back. Like Dugan (an African American neighborhood), they all stay together. Then River Plantation, those kids all hang together. Then you got Robinwood, and where we live, it's a mix. It's because of neighborhoods. Black people all live together so they hang around together."

Charles had mentioned the value in interviewing children to find out about what they were learning at home and how it affected them in school. Gary later related other observations about the Black community and the factor of location:

> What I see is like where we live. Like if you live in Mellow Quarters, they go to Brookshire Brothers over there like to grocery shop and stuff 'cuz it's close. Like where I live, my mom shops at Albertson's cuz like it's closer. If she really wants somethin' rare, sometimes she'll go to Randall's or Kroger's, she'll travel, you know. But the people like go to rundown lookin' stores, you know, those kind a people don't travel, get a ride, walk, like the store you shop at depends what kind a neighborhood, what kind of social class you're in."

Another conversation involved a discussion about Hispanic gangs in the high school and the relation between the gangs and the size of the Hispanic community, as though one was contingent on the other. Charles related a conversation he had with a Hispanic girl about two Hispanic school gangs that disliked each other. Gary said he had heard about them and then shared his reaction: "Chaney isn't big enough ... You'd think any kind of gang activity would be racial."

Charles continued: "But this is between two of the same culture ... and they discriminated against girls who just sit by guys who are with the other gang."

Gary commented:

Yeah, I really don't understand that. There aren't a lot of people in Chaney and then they're goin' to be divided up by race and then inside, you know. I remember when the Black people tried to have gangs. It was the MQ Posse from Mellow Quarters and the Dugan Bad Boys. All the people that was in those two gangs lived in each neighborhood ... And then they died out. They went on about nothin'. Now we just like normal people just have disagreements but just not really a group thing. I was really shocked ... I used to say, "We don't have gangs." And then I look around the neighborhood and the school and Latin Kings ... There not a lot of y'all here. [Laughter] ... It's not like south central LA where there's a whole bunch of Latin people and whole bunch of Mexican people and then I can understand when there are a whole bunch of them.

From an interview with her stepmother, Linda shared: "My mom talked about the Latin culture in Chaney not being united. But it's hard to unite because people are from different places like Honduras and Mexico. They have different religions and customs. She also wished there would be more support for the children from the parents so they could progress more."

Maria mentioned that she had attended an Allianza meeting, a community organization that had been started 3 years ago by members of the Hispanic community. She said that few came to the meeting. In support of Linda's mother's remarks, Allianza was having trouble reaching all the different Spanish-speaking cultures in the Hispanic community.

Twyla cited religious differences between White and African American Baptists. She had a conversation with a White girl who said she was not going to the prom because her religion, Baptist, did not allow her to dance. Twyla related that she, too, was Baptist: "But we don't have any rule like that."

Charles had made some remarks about his church choir. Gary added: "That's a lot to write down just about the choir. Very strong choir ... Black culture and singing."

Charles concluded: "I think it's from the fact that we weren't able to assemble as much as we are now and we usually sang a song and that's why a lot of my people give their life to Christ. The White Baptists do a lot of singing but they concentrate on what the preacher is saying."

Another time the discussion turned to their experiences when talking to older people. Twyla shared this metaphor: "They're like old trees. If trees could talk, they could tell a lot about things. My grandmother? She can tell long stories."

She told a story her grandmother had told about an older blind man her family helped care for when the grandmother was about Twyla's age. On the completion of her story, Gary told a story that his grandparents had told.

Some talked about other ethnic groups that they had observed in Chaney. They saw the Asian community as close, driven, and committed. Clyde gave an example of a tennis player on the high-school team who was not necessarily a strong student but practiced 6 to 8 hours on the tennis court in the summer.

Charles commented that he had noticed that Middle Easterners had bought up several little convenience stores in Chaney.

It is apparent from their observations that the ethnographers knew a lot about their families and communities and relations with the school. Throughout the time we spent together, they made various references intertwining the two. The school was a microcosm of the larger community.

PLACE: THE TEMPORAL
AND PHYSICAL CONTEXT

In relation to place, the element of space in the context of time and place is another consideration to examine. Time played a major role in this project. All but two of our meetings were held in the morning before school started. Although the meetings usually were scheduled for 7 AM, they did not get started much before 7:20, after everyone arrived. With the bell ringing at 7:55 to end the homeroom advisory period, our meetings lasted about 35 minutes. I noticed that the students needed about 30 minutes to loosen up and to begin talking. No sooner would we get started when it was time to go to first period. At a luncheon meeting at my house, we assembled at about 12 noon. We talked before we ate; we talked while we ate; we talked after we ate until about 30 PM. The group talked openly about myriad things. We needed more get-togethers like this one to be able to reflect on the conversations we had to analyze our data together. I never got a chance to share what I was hearing from them.

What may have prevented us from meeting at a time other than before school was the busy schedules of all those involved in the project. When I asked for volunteers, Linda's question was, "How much time would this take?"

Linda and several others had part-time jobs that prevented them from staying after school. All were involved in other school activities that competed for their time. They would divide the 30-minute advisory period into two 15-minute segments so that they could attend both our meeting and another activity meeting that conflicted. I had hoped that we could agree on a set time to meet each week, but their overloaded schedules made this hope an impossibility.

Time is an important factor in ethnographic research. It takes time to build community and trust. By the end of the first month, a sense of community was developing as all agreed with Gary's suggestion, "Let's go for pizza!"

This project began the first week of March and was supposed to be reported on by the first of May, but I extended it until the end of May, the end of the school year. At the end of 2 months, the student ethnographers were beginning to take ownership when Twyla suggested, "Why don't we interview each other?" Unfortunately, with senior week arriving soon after this suggestion, the interviews never got finished; six of the nine were seniors. Other evidence of ownership was evident in the words of Gary when he mentioned his idea, "We should invite juniors to our next meeting so they'll know what to do next year."

It takes time for a group to realize ownership. The physical context of the school may have interfered with the student ethnographers' seeing the teacher–facilitator as anything but a teacher and the project as anything more than an assignment. Gary expressed this difficulty: "That's how I do 'cuz I think I'm in school and that's how we make do."

We held most of our meetings in the school library, already described as being an early 1960s idea of comfort, with wooden chairs and tables as the only means for gathering together to discuss. Usually when we started our meetings, the library was almost vacant. But soon after the homeroom bell, other student groups would descend and we would have to interrupt our thoughts to relocate to another part of the library and then try to recapture our thoughts. We met in the cafeteria twice because the library was too crowded. A comfortable place to meet did not exist in the school.

Despite all the drawbacks we experienced—lack of time, hostile space arrangements, and the like—the enthusiasm and interest of student ethnographers outweighed these material factors, and we were able to accomplish a great deal. Place affects activities but cannot prevent them from occurring when the spirit is willing.

THE TEACHER'S REFLECTIONS

Although I intended this project to be student directed, I realized from my analysis that I had maintained a degree of control and had not fully trusted the students to commit to the project. I did not know how much structure to provide. Instead of bringing my agenda for the project to them, I could have involved them in the decision making from the beginning. The team, as part of the community-building process, could have cooperatively determined the function of the group, and then each person could have assumed a responsibility such as scheduling, notifying, and conducting meetings. The students could have decided on the focus of their study. I invited the students originally to study the school culture, "We'll explore, describe the subcultures that exist within the school."

When asked by Gary, "How are we going to do this?" and Maria, "Are we going to talk to kids?" I replied: "That's what we need to decide. I am not going to dictate your moves. We would need to get together to find out what we are going to do and how."

Then the focus changed to a study of their own culture through family and community identity and then, if time allowed, a study of the school culture. I made this decision for them. Charles revealed to me about a month into the project, "I'm really interested in ethnic relations in school." I would like to have seen whether they would have arrived at the same conclusion as I did about the inter-relatedness of school and community.

In another instance Twyla asked about interviewing children: "I thought we could get a picture of how little kids see things in their community and in their school."

Charles added: "By talking to kids, we can find out about what they are learning at home. What they're being taught. How they think about things and how that affects them in school."

I could have done more to encourage them in this idea. I have learned that even though we were studying our own culture, we could do so from different perspectives. This suggestion was one way they wanted to approach their study.

The whole group could have determined how we would report our data instead of following my request for a final write-up of their findings. If I had relinquished my control, I may not have heard from the students: "What are you trying to find out?" "What do you expect to get out of this?" "I don't know exactly what you want."

My concern for their commitment was unfounded. These students showed their commitment in numerous ways and attended every meeting unless they had a conflict. The meetings held at 7 AM, were a true demonstration of commitment. They stayed with the project until the end. Their sincere interest was evident: Twyla suggested, "You should make this a course." Clyde affirmed, "This is a thing of the future." Charles pleaded, "Continue this next year or die!"

Some students also expressed their gratitude for my willingness to do this: "This is really good of you to do this." "Thank you for taking an interest."

Finally, Charles and Twyla met with me at Pizza Hut at the end of June to read my interpretation and to celebrate our accomplishment. Involvement in this project for the student ethnographers has made them more observant of what is going on around them. As Twyla wrote: "My involvement has helped me open my eyes and look through another person's pair of glasses."

They saw not only differences but commonalities among cultures. Charles believed, "Recognizing how we are alike will help us to get somewhere racially and culturally." Twyla finished her entry with: "Even though we may have different skin colors, different cultures, different religions, we're the same on the inside." Just helping students to be more observant may have made them more sensitive toward others.

Had I relinquished control by involving the student ethnographers in the decision making from the beginning, the direction of the project would have been their own. They demonstrated commitment. They volunteered to participate in the study of culture in their school and community because of their interest in something meaningful to them. They and I have learned from this experience. They have given me the confidence I needed to be a facilitator in community-based ethnography. Now I can allow the participants to take ownership.

AN ONGOING LEARNING PROCESS

Without a doubt, a project that engages participants to study the cultures in their community has great potential for building caring and understanding in a culturally diverse population. I consider that we, the student ethnographers and I, accomplished much in a relatively short time. What could be accomplished in a year? During this fall semester, the student access committee held class meetings for 3 days, and the entire student body had a chance to discuss ways make our school better. Throughout the 3 days, I heard support for dialogue groups, students talking to students. If I were to do this again, I would offer the suggestion that the students consider inviting a faculty member or two as part of our school community. We need to get to know each other so as to better understand each other. Understanding leads to improved human relationships in a culturally diverse society, and that is what we want to promote.

One result of my involvement with the student ethnographers was the writing of a curriculum to teach cultural awareness through literature and inquiry. The student ethnographers encouraged me to carry on with what we had started, and through the course I call Cultural Awareness, I am. During the access class meetings, I heard students expressing an interest in such a course as this one.

Being part of the study with students acting as ethnographers has had a great impact on my teaching philosophy. Throughout my descriptive account, I reflected on the student enthnographer's high interest in and serious commitment to this project. At one point I said: "We don't give students enough credit. We, educators, need to ... let them talk, offer ideas for study."

The subject of the study—school and community culture—was interesting and relevant to them because it dealt with their real lives. They were learning about themselves through ethnographic inquiry. Because of its relevancy, these high-school students became involved and took ownership and thus, were empowered. Their desire for our project to be perpetuated through a course or a continued study emphasized the importance they placed on it.

Our system of schooling perpetuates a teacher as transmitter of knowledge to students whose perspectives are rarely considered. Students are not considered part of the reality, a fixed reality. What they were invited to do in this study was foreign to most of them. It was a struggle for them to assume a different role from that of student, receiver of information.

The implications of this study further support my changing philosophy toward the use of inquiry as a methodology for knowledge construction.

Democracy requires citizens who can think, challenge and exhibit long-term thought. This means public schools need to become places that provide the opportunity for literate occasions, that is opportunities for students to share their experiences, work in social relations that emphasize care and concern for others, and be introduced to forms of knowledge that provide them with the opportunity to take risks and fight for a quality of life in which all human beings benefit. (Shannon, 1992, p. 20)

The term *constructivism* in relation to teaching is a new term to me. I did not know that the metamorphosis I was experiencing had a name. In this new paradigm, teacher and students work together designing an integrative curriculum with a central theme related to real-life issues (Beane, 1992, p. 48). The teacher's role becomes that of facilitator, providing the framework for student inquiry (p. 50) and liaison, connecting the curriculum to the outside world (Cohen, 1993, p. 793). Students internalize and transform new information (Brooks & Brooks, 1993, p. 15). Assessment is holistic and performance based when students apply what they have learned to real-life situations (Cohen, 1993, p. 794; Glasser, 1992, p. 693). The emphasis on questions posed by the students gives them a purpose; they have a stake in it, and at the same time, they enhance their self-esteem and become democratically empowered (Beane, 1992, p. 50). Learners see themselves as involved in constructive action rather than as passive recipients of teacher-disseminated knowledge (Brooks & Brooks, 1993, p. 7).

I attribute my willingness to try another approach in my teaching to the cultural study with nine volunteers last spring. They showed me that, when invited and when the purpose is relevant to them, students become involved and take ownership. I am involved now in a constructivist curricular design with my English as a Second Language (ESL) class. I believe that by engaging students in inquiry into social issues that are important to them, I can help to enhance their second language development and their self-esteem. I am in compliance with Beane's suggestion (1992, p. 52) to try this project in a classroom rather than to offer this as an in-service workshop. To establish credibility, it is necessary to have concrete evidence that is acquired by doing, evidence that shows student involvement and success and that can be shared with skeptical colleagues.

Finally, acting as teacher–researcher has had a profound effect on me professionally. Every teacher we know who has done research is stronger than before—whether in knowledge, curiosity, ability, willingness to explore ideas, effectiveness in helping students learn, or in some combination of these (Patterson, Stansell, & Lee, 1990, p. 83).

The experience has given me confidence and has empowered me. Being involved in research with nine high-school students for 3 months has yielded pertinent, useful information about our school and community cultures from these students' perspectives.

"Reflection, inquiry and action are interrelated in teacher research because teachers act as thinkers, learners and practitioners." (Shannon, 1992, p. 10). I now look more critically at pedagogy and methodology, and I am more reflective. Through research, I have gained knowledge that has led to my changing instruction (Johnson, 1993, p. 68). I am not afraid to take risks because I know I will learn. The experience has affected my practice and my view on teacher effectiveness in helping students learn. I wrote a job proposal to become a reading specialist on my high-school campus so that I could work with content teachers to integrate comprehension strategies through direct instruction into their content. By putting theory into practice (Bennett, 1993, p. 69), and by working together with teachers who have content expertise and adding my knowledge of strategic learning, we can have a greater impact on all students. My position was approved, and I have a volunteer pilot group of 10 committed teachers from various disciplines who are willing to explore new ideas, to experiment, and to reflect. These teachers will serve as change agents as they share their discoveries with their colleagues and, at the same time, build teacher networks (p. 70), which can lead to staff development based on teachers' classroom experiences (Johnson, 1993, p. 68). Ultimately, because of topic relevancy, staff development will become a more meaningful investment of time than it now is.

Just as research has changed my life as a professional, action research can revitalize the entire learning community and can aid teachers in changing or reflecting on their classroom practices. It can support initiatives by individual teachers, schools, and schools working with communities and districts (Calhoun, 1993, p. 62).

REFERENCES

Beane, J. A. (1992). Creating an integrative curriculum: Making the connections. *NASSP Bulletin*, 76(547), 46–53.

Bennett, C. K. (1993). Teacher-researchers: All dressed up and no place to go. *Educational Leadership*, 51(2), 69–70.

Brooks, J. G, & Brooks, M. G. (1993). *The case for constructivist classrooms*. VA: ASCD.

Calhoun, E. F. (1993). Action research: Three approaches. *Educational Leadership*, 51(2), 62–65.

Cohen, A. (1993). A new educational paradigm. *Phi Delta Kappan*, 74(10), 791–795.

Denzin, N. K. (1989). *Interpretive interactionism*. Newbury Park, CA: Sage.

Glasser, W. (1992). The quality school curriculum. *Phi Delta Kappan*, 73(9), 690–694.

Johnson, R. W. (1993). Where can teacher research lead? One teacher's daydream. *Educational Leadership*, 51(2), 66–68.

Patterson, L. A., Stansell, J. C., & Lee, S. C. (1990). *Teacher research: From promise to power*. Katonah, NY: Richard C. Owen.

Shannon, P. (Ed.) (1992). *Becoming political: Readings and writings in the politics of literacy education*. Portsmouth, NH: Heinemann.

Spradley, J. P. (1979). *The ethnographic interview*. Orlando, FL: Harcourt Brace Jovanovich.

Stringer, E., & Hall, J. (1988). *Getting to know you: Fieldwork studies in multicultural Australia: Book 1. Discovering cultural diversity; Book 2. Observing the cultural building blocks; Book 3. Observing cultural events*. Unpublished manuscripts, Perth, Western Australia, Curtin University of Technology.

11

Digital Distance Education: Qualitative Research in a Corporate Context

Patsy S. Tinsley-Batson

As a practitioner in distance education for more than 20 years, the focus of my professional career has been on developing and operating interactive-in-structional distance-learning networks (both microwave and satellite) to meet the educational needs of learners of all ages. After founding and managing the first satellite-based distance-learning network in the nation to serve public schools in the mid-1980s, I realized my interests were shifting from the challenge of designing and operating networks to the challenge of not only improving the quality of distance-learning programming but also of encouraging innovation in the distance-learning industry.

I was fortunate to register for Dr. Stringer's community-based ethnography class at Texas A&M University early in my doctoral study. Under Dr. Stringer's leadership, I not only studied but also experienced what was, for me, new, tradition-breaking processes and frameworks for teaching and conducting research. I found it very easy to transfer this new knowledge to my distance-learning consulting projects.

The first consulting project to which I applied this new qualitative approach to research was conducted for a national nonprofit organization charged with funding and oversight of a system of educational broadcast networks across the country. The following account is derived from the extended, final report of this research project. Although the organization and services described in the following text are somewhat similar to those studied for the client, the name of the organization and the services described are purely hypothetical.

DISTANCE EDUCATION AT A CROSSROAD

Distance education is considered a growth industry in our nation's system of educating lifelong learners. It increases access to needed educational resources in the home, as well as in schools, the workplace, and other settings. It is also a field of study in many of our nation's leading universities. Digital education as a new paradigm of distance education has emerged from the convergence of traditional distance education (live and interactive complete course instruction delivered via technology), and traditional instructional television (passive videotaped instruction used by a classroom teacher to supplement in-classroom instruction), in the context of emerging digital technology.

Digital technology enables distance-learning networks to integrate a variety of technologies to establish new and better ways to teach and learn at a distance. Interactive data, voice, video, and multimedia services for schools are possible through the integration of such technologies as satellite, computer, telephone, and broadcast video. The success of digital education depends on its adoption and successful implementation by existing and emerging distance-learning networks and on their willingness and ability to help schools access and use the new digital services.

The emergence of digital technology presents the distance-learning industry an opportunity to offer new programs and services to public schools. Over the past several years, many existing distance-learning networks have been laying the groundwork (both technical and programmatic), for establishing multichannel digital education services via satellite. As a result, change is now imminent for all distance-learning networks if they are to stay competitive. Networks can no longer simply explore ways to maximize services to their subscribing schools via single channel broadcast systems offering programs on a fixed schedule. They must also now consider how to plan for multichannel services offering programs on an on-demand schedule. For distance-learning networks to take advantage of the potential offered by digital technologies to meet the needs of the public school market, however, both the technical infrastructure needed for multiple channel programming and interactivity gateways and the organizational infrastructure needed to implement and support new programs and services must be put in place. As a result, local, state, and national distance-learning networks now find themselves at a crossroad of technical and programming changes. On the technical side, individual networks are beginning to deploy the state-of-the-art digital technology that will provide the needed distribution and interactive infrastructure. On the programming side, distance-learning networks are not only beginning to define and develop innovative programs and services to deploy via the new digital technology highway, but are also beginning to explore the changing staff roles required to implement and support the new programs and services.

In this emerging environment of multichannel digital education services, distance-learning networks can play a critical role in bringing the full benefits of educational excellence via distance-learning to U.S. schools. To fulfill this role, however, a framework must be defined in which networks can provide both the human and the technical infrastructure needed to implement and support multichannel digital education programs and services. The challenge is to match what is *needed* or *required* to implement and support the emerging technologies, programs, and services with what is *possible* and *attainable* by each local, state, and national network. To assist in this process, a national nonprofit organization, The Digital Learning Alliance (DL Alliance), was formed in the 1990s to advance innovation in the use of digital technology in distance education to meet the needs of lifelong learners.

The barriers to successful implementation of any new distance-learning technology or service are significant. Existing distance-learning networks across the country, however, make up a potential infrastructure of technical and human resources required to initiate and support digital education in U.S. schools, an infrastructure unparalleled by any other educational technology or service provider. This research project was undertaken for the DL Alliance to define ways of organizing the steps to be taken by existing and emerging distance-learning networks in the transition to the new way of doing business in a world of digital technology.

Research Process

This research project was designed to define a process to be used by distance-learning networks in implementing emerging digital educational services and in providing the infrastructure needed to support the process of change. The methodology employed to guide this research was a multi-tiered approach to data gathering. The process specifically included the following data-gathering activities:

Participation in a DL Alliance meeting of the Digital Education Advisory Committee.
Participation in a DL Alliance audioconference meeting of the Digital Education Advisory Committee.
Viewing of a DL Alliance national videoconference on digitaleducation.
Participation in conference sessions at national distance-learning conferences.
Personal and telephone interviews with network managers and staff.
Site visits and personal interviews at distance-learning network offices.
Review of selected readings in digital technology innovation.

When possible, the data-gathering process included observations and interviews conducted at places where distance-learning network executives naturally interact in business. It also included observations of discussions of groups of network managers and staff relating specifically to emerging digital technology and education services and, more generally, to the opportunities and changes facing distance-learning networks. Follow-up telephone interviews were conducted to clarify information and to gain new perspectives. Recording activities primarily included field notes, audio recordings, and video recordings.

The majority of distance-learning network personnel selected to be interviewed were members of the Digital Education Advisory Committee. Others were participants in national conference sessions on emerging digital programs and technologies. Still others were subjects of previous case studies conducted by the researcher. Together, the personnel interviewed represented varying governance structures; varying resource levels (financial, technical, and staff); varying levels of current educational services; and varying market sizes, interests, and needs.

The findings of the study were considerably broader than those reported here and, as would be expected, have implications for all organizations (local, state, regional, and national) that make up the distance-learning industry. Action taken on the recommendations made here will impact all organizations whose operations will be involved in moving distance education into the new environment of multichannel digital technologies and services.

ISSUES AND NEEDS FACING
DISTANCE-LEARNING NETWORKS

The process undertaken to define the framework required to give distance-learning networks the support to offer digital education services began with bracketing the data collected in the study into the issues raised and the needs identified by network personnel. The issues and needs identified related specifically to the conversion to digital technology and the offering of on-demand educational resources provided by the DL Alliance. The most basic category of issues raised by network personnel concerned product definition and the associated business arrangements, both financial and marketing, to be made between individual networks and the DL Alliance before the new digital services could be introduced to the market. The second category of issues raised concerned the conditions, both at networks and in the school markets they served, that were causing considerable concern among network personnel as they examined their ability to implement any new digital education services. The needs identified by network personnel included staff and training necessary to implement the new digital education services, information and support from the DL Alliance and from other organizations in the distance-learning industry, and models and tools to help the networks develop and execute successful strategic planning for conversion to digital technology and services.

Issues Raised

As might be expected, those networks already in the process of converting to digital technology and actively preparing to launch digital education programming expressed the clearest understanding of the promise of converting to digital technology and deploying digital education programs and services. A high level of uncertainty was found among network managers and staff interviewed who were less familiar with digital technology and digital education programming. The basic issues raised by the more cautious network personnel did, however, parallel those raised by those with a better understanding of the changes required in both the technology and the programming.

To begin to understand the confusion that networks were experiencing about what the new DL Alliance services were, it is helpful to place the experiences of the network managers in the environmental context of offering multiple new digital education services concurrent with executing dramatic technological changes. In this broad context, the level of confusion expressed by network personnel of all levels of knowledge and experience is easy to appreciate. This lack of understanding about the basic services was expressed in several ways by network managers and staff in words reflecting both the confusion they were experiencing about multiple new services being introduced simultaneously by the DL Alliance and their lack of understanding about the technical capabilities required to implement the new digital education services. The following statements reflect some of this confusion: "What, specifically, do these services provide my network?" "How much broadcast time will be needed for the services?" "We don't have the technical capacity to offer new services to schools."

There was also considerable confusion expressed about how the broadcast services would relate to online services being introduced by the DL Alliance, as evidenced by the question: "How does the pricing and business of the broadcast service relate to that of the online service?"

Confusion was also expressed regarding the technology to be used to provide the new services: "The technical aspects, overall, are unclear … logistics of how the pieces fit together are unclear."

Another manager recommended that the DL Alliance exercise caution in implementing the new services: "If networks are frustrated early on, it will be hard to get them back. So [the Alliance needs to] focus attention on the user friendliness of the service and the technology."

From the transcript of the earliest meeting of the Digital Education Advisory Committee hosted by the DL Alliance to the latest interviews conducted over the course of this study, network managers continued to speak out with questions about the overall picture of the new world of multichannel digital education services:

A single service alone is too small. We need to bundle all of the new services together with other incentives.

Are all of the new digital services being developed at the same time?

The issue is whether the first service is part of a bigger picture, and if it is really the first of many services to be offered.

Specific product definition questions raised by network personnel reflected their own concerns about bridging their existing traditional distance education program offerings with the new digital education programs and services, understanding the financial structure of the services, and implementing the marketing program required to support the new digital education services. Bridging issues raised by network personnel included more than simply what the product components might be. The issue of providing a bridge between current offerings of networks and the new digital services focused primarily on integrating existing video product into the new digital offerings and, more specifically, why it is "important to integrate the existing programs into this for schools and students to show we are serious and capable, and why we should be doing this." One manager stated that it was "easier to transition to stuff you know, like offering interactive broadcast courses in a digital format will do, because we can support it simply by making minor schedule changes." The implication was that most of the new digital education programs and services being developed by the DL Alliance were made of stuff they do not know, and the transition would be difficult and would require bridging to resolve uncertainties.

Business-related issues focused primarily on two areas: the financial structure and the marketing structure of the service. The range of financial issues raised was very comprehensive and covered issues from the price to be charged schools to participate in the service and how the price should be structured to the revenue split between the DL Alliance and each participating distance-learning network.

As might be expected, the cost of capital equipment and ongoing services that schools would bear to participate in the new digital education services concerned network managers, particularly in light of the financial situation schools across the nation were facing. When the DL Alliance established a price for the first digital service, one manager combined the product definition issue with the cost issue by asking: "The fee to be paid by schools buys what?" The issue of analyzing the pricing structure was then addressed as various managers asked questions and made statements intended to reveal each of the costs a school would have to pay to participate in the service:

What other costs will be incurred by schools? Equipment, phone lines, modems?

What is required beyond [the] basic fee?

It is best fee based, but, technology in schools is a problem!

The plan must address not just the fee for the first digital service, but when more money for other services will be needed.

The central issue of the financial arrangement to be established between the DL Alliance and participating distance-learning networks for implementation of the new digital education services was expressed very clearly by an interested, but concerned, network manager: "How do we generate revenue out of this new service?" In fact, several managers asked the same question in only slightly different terms, an indication of how important early resolution of this concern was to securing network participation in the services.

The remaining business issues raised by the distance-learning network executives concerned how the digital education services would be marketed to schools. More specifically, network personnel expressed concern over the role each network would play in marketing the services and in providing support to schools using the services. The fear that a specific distance-learning network might be viewed by schools as an unnecessary element in the marketing effort was raised by networks of all profiles because of the national program-scope of the DL Alliance. Just as prevalent, however, were those networks that insisted their involvement in providing the service would be essential to the success of the effort—even to the extent that all materials should flow through the network to the schools rather than from the DL Alliance to schools. A common thread of discussion also involved the development of a nationwide marketing initiative—how it might be set up, how it might be implemented, and how the fees might be split. One manager defined the biggest problem not as "the product, but marketing. ... We need national, regional, and local marketing plans."

Managers from several networks also emphasized the necessity of involving state, county, and district-level personnel in the marketing effort and of having them "buy into" use of the service. One manager put the focus of the marketing issue specifically on the control of financial resources in districts: "Even though teachers say they want the services, they don't control the money." The necessity of helping principals and school board members understand the new services as policy makers and financial decision makers was addressed by another concerned network manager: "Dollars are short, and how to bring [school] boards and administrators on board and into focus is a marketing question."

As executives of distance-learning networks talked about their potential involvement in the new multichannel digital education services, there was a direct relationship between the levels of concern and uncertainty they expressed and the general strengths (and availability) of resources to support anything new at their networks. A dominant and recurring concern network managers spoke about was staff availability:

Staff at my network is already overwhelmed!

How will we do it all?

Our engineers are overwhelmed! They must push buttons and fix things, as well as plan and think and learn.

Many networks don't have the staff to take advantage of opportunities already provided.

What will we have to give up to do this?

A statement made by one network manager summarized what many other managers and staff members expressed: "How will we keep up with it all with the limited dollars we have?" Facing declining revenues, another manager spoke with obvious anxiety and uncertainty about an even deeper level of concern by questioning whether the network "can hold on at all, much less get into something new."

Significant concerns about selling the new digital education services to schools were expressed equally by personnel representing distance-learning networks providing a range of educational program offerings, from only a few hours per month to thousands of hours per year. Most of the concerns related to the lack of schools financial resources to purchase the new digital education services:

A "thanks but no thanks" attitude will be encountered due to lack of funds in schools, and the cost of the program.

Schools have no money to even reallocate to this program—they have reallocated everything already.

Schools have already postponed scheduled textbook purchases to redirect funds to provide essential services.

The perceived inability of schools to participate in the service was related not only to the lack of financial resources schools had to pay for the service, but also to the lack of access to the equipment and technology required to interconnect with the new digital services. Concerns expressed by network personnel about technology related primarily to the fact that schools did not have the required technology in place to access the services—including computers, satellite receive antennas, digital receivers, telephone lines in classrooms, and other associated technical components—that might be needed. One manager spoke of how basic the problem was: "There exists a lack of basic technology in schools that are just now getting funds for a single computer to go in the administrative office."

Even though it was acknowledged by some managers that the schools and states they served were prioritizing technology in schools, they expressed concern over the challenge that making the digital education services accessible in these schools had to be considered at the level of the end-user teacher. One manager spoke realistically of the challenge of getting teachers to use the new services: "We cannot assume teachers have the technology available to them." This concern related not only to schools having digital satellite equipment, but also to teachers having convenient access to a computer and to most schools having telephone lines only in administrators' offices. These concerns reflect in a very small way the level of consideration network managers were giving to making the new digital education services available to end-user teachers among their subscribing schools.

Needs Identified

Distance-learning network managers across the country talked at length about the issues and concerns they faced as they explored the possibility of providing the new digital education services as resources to the schools they served. They also identified their many specific needs that they believed only the DL Alliance could and must meet in order for the new digital education services to be successful. The needs identified included staff and training, information and support, marketing tools, and models of service implementation. It is important to note that these needs were stated by representatives of large, nationwide distance-learning networks, as well as by representatives of small, regional networks serving primarily schools in a single state.

The issue of limited network resources that was previously addressed provides a framework for understanding the need expressed by many network managers for additional staff "to be added for advertising, promotion, in-school marketing, and programming." The solution recommended by one manager from a rather small network was for a "full-time educational outreach coordi-nator for all new digital education services combined" to be provided each network by the DL Alliance. This solution would also answer the request from another manager who stated: "We will have to have staff to provide end-user assistance to schools." The need for staff crossed all network organizational structures and market sizes.

Closely related to the requests for additional staff were the requests for training—both to make the new services a reality for the networks and then to implement and support the new digital education services in schools. Many requests for training related to the use of online services—an unknown technology and an unfamiliar experience for most networks. One manager specifically requested "technical, content, and support training for network personnel working with on-line systems and services." Another asked for a "step-by-step process [that] managers can follow to prepare for providing online services." Other requests for training in the technical area were broader and asked for training to convert analog engineers to digital and to support operating, troubleshooting, and maintaining the new digital equipment and systems being installed. One manager lucky enough to have an experienced digital engineer on staff stated, "Engineers even with experience with digital technology will need training—there's so much new they will have to learn!" Another manager, concerned about his engineer's ability to handle all the changes to be encountered, also asked, "In terms of retraining and staff development, what will engineers have to understand? Do they need to be programmers?"

In addition to training in technical areas, network managers requested training on how to raise funds to convert to digital technology, to launch the new services, and to support marketing and selling the service. One manager, humorously yet seriously, requested *last mile* marketing training. More specifically, help was requested by many managers to train "those who were going to be interfacing with the public, with educators and with users of the system." It was repeatedly pointed out that network staff needed to know how these new digital education resources were going to be used in schools to be able to train and support the end-user teachers.

The importance of the timely flow of information from the DL Alliance to each participating distance-learning network about the new digital education services was a critical need that, like training, was raised by managers of networks large and small. At the most basic level, the information requested by network personnel would provide the answers to many issues raised in this account and could greatly lessen the uncertainty network personnel felt about their future. Specific information needed included details of what was expected of each network; assumptions underlying anticipated costs and revenue splits; a complete rundown of equipment needed by schools to participate in the new digital education services; a detailed product definition; an understanding of network responsibilities for technical operations; a statement of benefits to networks that participated in offering the digital education services to schools; and a continuous update on next steps in the process of implementing new digital education services.

As a national membership-based organization, the DL Alliance is viewed by member distance-learning networks as the key to providing not only the information they need to understand new digital education services, but also the support they need to initiate and sustain the services over time. Repeatedly, managers expressed concern about the volume of information directed to them from the DL Alliance. Many network managers and staff expressed the need for "a better two-way system for information sharing with the DL Alliance." More specifically, one manager recommended "an online service or 800 number with a person to call that can provide our network the opportunity to discuss its specific situation ... here's what we're doing ... and work through our problems and questions." Associated with requests for online communication were requests for "database-accessible information with user-friendly access" and a "computer link to help marketing ... including marketing data and contacts in the market."

Closely related to and interwoven with the requests for training, information, and support were requests for specific marketing tools and for how-to models. Three primary tools were requested by networks to use in marketing the new digital education services: an exciting videotape about the new services to help the buyer understand the "sell," a videoconference series for school administrators and one for network personnel, and a tool kit to support marketing and selling the new services.

In addition to requests for marketing tools, specific requests were made for service initiation and implementation models that would enable networks to develop their own successful strategic marketing plans. Networks requested models of how they could provide digital educational services to bring about greater economies, staffing models based on possible new functions to be added, and training models for technical and marketing staff, among others. (Specific models needed and identified by network executives are presented in the following section of this account.)

It is important to keep in mind that this account reflects a point-in-time snapshot of issues raised and needs identified by distance-learning network executives shortly after the announcement of the availability of digital educa-tion services. Because the DL Alliance digital education services were intro-duced to networks only a short time before they were interviewed for this report, many issues raised during the interviews have subsequently been resolved for some networks. These issues have been included in this report primarily because of the relevance they might have to the introduction of future technology and program innovations and because not all networks adopt an innovation such as digital technology at the same rate. Because of the number of distance-learning networks and the differences among them, certain issues and needs are significant to different networks at different times over the introduction of any new technology, program, or service.

MODELS FOR IMPLEMENTING DIGITAL EDUCATION SERVICES

A common theme that emerged from the discussions with network managers and staff was an overwhelming sense of uncertainty caused by change coming at them from every direction. The changes facing the distance-learning indus-try touch every aspect of the way the local, state, and national networks do business—from the technology they use to deliver the product, to the products and services they deliver, to the structure of management best suited to provide the product and operate the technology.

The reality of limited resources facing most networks, combined with the potential to offer significant new digital education services, presents a chal-lenge to the entire distance-learning industry. One of the greatest challenges the DL Alliance faces in providing support to networks converting to digital technology and program formats is to do so in a framework that allows individual networks to not only make use of the digital education services offered by the Alliance, but also to build their own capacities to implement unique digital services in a competitive market environment. The long-term goal of the DL Alliance should be to provide models and tools that can empower networks to develop and offer the levels and formats of digital education programming they each choose for their individual users in the public school market.

A major recommendation of this report is that the DL Alliance use the experiences of the earliest market entry networks offering its digital education services to develop models and tools that respond to the issues raised and needs identified in this report. These models and tools would then be used in the development of strategic plans for the offering of digital education services by other networks in future years. The following models were specifically requested by network personnel over the course of this research and should be developed based on the experiences of the first participants in the new digital education services:

Marketing models to be used by networks in developing strategic marketing plans, and detailing the processes followed and qualifications of staff used in marketing the services.

Models of the training needed to support networks in initiating and supporting the new digital education offerings.

Financial models detailing network revenues from the services plus costs associated with initiating and supporting the service in schools.

Model success stories experienced over the first year of offering the digital education services.

Role and function staffing models, with associated time and cost factors.

Models of the training needed to support networks in converting to digital technology.

RECOMMENDATIONS FOR INFRASTURCTURE DEVELOPMENT

What is possible and attainable at each individual distance-learning network to support the transition to digital technology and the implementation of digital education programs and services is impacted by the varying levels of resources (human, financial, and technical) available, the varying levels of interest among networks in providing new digital education services, and the varying needs of the schools each network serves. In this context of differences, services and support must be provided to meet the needs of networks as they enter the future of multichannel digital services. Network executives need assistance to better understand the possibilities that the emerging digital technologies and digital education programs hold for them in their futures. They also need models to help them identify the steps they need to take and the resources they need to commit in order to maximize their participation in, and return from, this future.

To meet these needs, the following recommendations are set forth for the consideration of the DL Alliance as it plans how to establish the national infrastructure of support required for successful implementation of emerging digital technologies and education services:

Use the experience of the earliest networks converting to digital technology to develop models and tools for use by other networks in initiating and supporting the transition to digital technology and the development of digital education programs and services.

Prepare and distribute guidelines on the information that networks need to gather and the processes networks need to put in place to help them develop critical partnerships and to help them better understand the potential of digital education.

Explore the possibility of involving other national and regional organizations in the distance-learning industry to meet the training needs of networks implementing new digital education services using digital technologies.

Develop and implement a national online service for use by distance-learning network managers and staff, as well as other distance-learning practitioners and researchers, not only to support the process of implementing new digital education services and new digital technologies, but also to support network restructuring of management and operations in the increasingly complex digital technology and service environment of the future.

It is with a sense of great expectation and excitement that individual distance-learning networks and the distance-learning industry as a whole are approaching the future of multichannel digital education services. In this context of expectation and excitement, digital education technologies and services are being introduced to distance-learning networks and to the education market. As uncertainties associated with the newness of this innovative concept are resolved, the decisions made and the processes established to support the first model services developed and implemented will undoubtedly contribute to the success of future digital education programs and services.

12

A Learning Journey (In Progress): A Personal Biographical Ethnography

Terresa Payne Katt

I am an excited, challenged, frustrated, inspired, devoted, committed woman who has chosen the public education of young children as her vocation and full-time graduate studies as her current occupation. How I achieved my current mental and emotional state, how the interactions of my experiences, my beliefs, my contexts, and my learning have been interwoven to form these states of mind and heart, and how certain of my fellow human beings have grown to influence, compound, and confound these thoughts are the focus of this chapter. This chapter, therefore, is the vehicle by which I travel from the past forward in an effort to describe ethnographically the evolution of my thinking; and, lest the trip becomes too long and tedious, I identify only major landmarks and milestones in my journey. Finally, I candidly admit that I write less sure of answers than I have ever been, while simultaneously growing more confident about what constitutes the questions. The landmarks on this journey are: The Public School Classroom, A Curriculum Project, A University Classroom, My Daughter's Classroom, and Graduate School.

THE PUBLIC SCHOOL CLASSROOM

After graduation from college, I was hired to teach young children in River Tree, a large midurban public school district. Typical of most large districts, River Tree had a clearly defined curriculum including content and activities as well as a specific delineation by grade and level of what was to be taught. I was determined to be a "good" teacher and, to the best of my abilities, attempted to implement the prescription to the patients, whether they needed or wanted it. After a while, it became clear to me that simply implementing, delivering, transmitting instruction to children on an assembly line basis, with frequent standardized monitoring, was not promoting success for all the children in my classroom. Confronted by fellow educators with tenure, power, position, and experience, I was ill equipped to argue that the prescribed instruction was somehow inadequate and that these children who were unsuccessful in the prescription were not the source of the problem.

I began to ask questions and to carry out inquiries in my prekindergarten classroom, specifically to develop explanations of how students learn and how language works. Through my own research, I became aware of what was happening in my classroom and gained confidence in the children I taught and in my power to help facilitate their learning. In fact, my prekindergarten children were learning so successfully that a waiting list developed to get into my classroom; my peers who inherited my students in kindergarten began to express anger that my kids entered their classrooms already reading when they were not supposed to learn to read until first grade!

As a teacher who became a researcher, I was able to confirm or dispute what I began to read in research journals, put the research in perspective, understand it, and criticize the research and my own practice when necessary. Because I was doing research in my own classroom, each research decision was also, directly or indirectly, an instructional decision. Amid dealing with both theoretical and practical issues I was, in fact, learning how to be a better teacher. Ultimately, this inquiry process became as important to me as the content of the research itself. The process of inquiry, rather than answering all my questions, produced even more questions. I became increasingly curious about everything children do and continued to question, observe, and record information as I visited other classrooms around the district. This experience led to my interest in exploring how teachers teach as well as how learners learn; thus my struggle to understand this process called learning began.

Equally important, I became able to stand my ground when confronted by the bureaucrats who arrived at my classroom door with the truth carved in curriculum documents of stone. My professional life fluctuated between the incredible power and excitement in my classroom and elsewhere as I watched children learn in ways perceived to be blasphemous and the incredible frustration and mounting anger at my professional peers, who believed they had discovered the truth about ways to teach children and were ordering me to be faithful to the canon.

I went first to my principal and argued for a holistic, meaningful, flexible approach to teaching children, an approach that relied heavily on the students' ability to construct their own meaning. She did not know what to do with me. She appreciated my passion and conviction for children, but I questioned, made demands, challenged the current system, and made her feel uncomfortable. She sent me to visit others in the organizational hierarchy. To my surprise, they were not thrilled by my "discoveries." In fact, I was told that I might damage children by teaching too much. I tried curriculum coordinators, directors, executive directors, and associate superintendents. The party line was well rehearsed and the answers I received were, in short, "Follow the prescribed curriculum." I knew too much to do that and was ready to quit. I was stunned by their less-than-enthusiastic response. As a last effort, I went to see a central office administrator and told him about my classroom research, what I had learned, and how the organization was responding to my learning. This administrator, who became a valued colleague, heard me! The next thing I knew I was offering staff development courses to interested teachers, based on what I knew and the success I had. These courses soon became standing room only, as teachers, hungry for new and meaningful ways to help kids learn, became learners themselves.

Those in the organization who were threatened by an instructional process that was not codifiable or replicable continued to create obstacles. I became convinced that those who believed they knew the absolute truth were absolutely wrong, and I took every opportunity to tell them so. These opportunities increased with the next landmark in my journey.

A CURRICULUM PROJECT

By the summer of 1989, I had made quite a name for myself as a classroom teacher. I was not only doing staff development at every opportunity in my district; I was being called on to present and teach throughout the state. I had written a chapter in a book on the teacher as researcher. I was presenting at an International Reading Association conference. I networked with the gurus of the whole language movement. I was "in" and I knew it. My kids were dramatically successful when using the instructional process that I believed in, and I had the research and evidence to support the success. I found myself increasingly in conflict with what I now thought of as "old paradigm" educators. They were wrong because they believed they knew a universal truth. I was right because I believed truth, as learning, is individually constructed, not universally implemented.

I suddenly had the opportunity to apply for a curriculum coordinator position in my school district. What an opportunity! If I could land this job as an administrator, I would be in a position to implement my beliefs! Surprise, surprise, I got the job!

It fell to me to rewrite the elementary language arts curriculum. Based on my knowledge of language and literacy development and my belief that the profession needs the leadership of classroom teachers, I organized the task. In curricular projects of the past we had merely allowed input into a predetermined framework or curricular structure that does little to empower teachers or promote their expertise. This project, I decided, would be different. This curriculum document and process would be constructed by the practitioners who would implement it. I decided that the success of the project would depend on the ability of a critical group of teachers, administrators, and parents to collaborate and learn more about philosophical and theoretical assumptions, about the context of the project, and about various methodological alternatives to instruction in language arts. I believed that when these stakeholders came together to problem solve and research the alternatives to instruction in language arts that they too would see the light and design a holistic framework for language and literacy instruction.

In the beginning, my dedication to a participatory process led to the establishment of the Language Arts Advisory Council. I wanted to move beyond a committee and involve as many people in the project as were willing to participate. Although I had to limit the number of people involved in the project, I was allowed by the bureaucracy to establish this group of educators from across the district, including one teacher representative from every campus, campus-level administrators, school district administrative personnel, and, eventually, parents. Such a large group of potential decision makers brought criticism and warnings from my fellow curriculum coordinators. They assured me that adding parents to the actual process of designing the curriculum would be the death blow of the project. It proved, however, to be a landmark event in River Tree, one of the most significant decisions made early in the project.

The Language Arts Advisory Council began its quest for a curriculum framework that would best meet the needs of the students in the River Tree Independent School District. As a group, we engaged in an extensive review and inquiry into language and literacy developments. We examined the three models of reading (phonics, skills-based, and whole language), the conditions necessary for learning to take place, and the change process. In light of district efforts to increase campus-based decision making, we discovered that revision, adding more of the same, or even making significant improvements to the existing curriculum structure would not conform with maximizing language and literacy development for the children in our schools and would not take into account the professional performance of teachers.

A review of the research revealed that in the last 20 years, the view of how language and literacy development take place has dramatically changed. The research suggested that language learning is an integrated, developmental process that includes both integration of the language processes (listening, speaking, reading, and writing) and the content areas. In River Tree we had taught skills and phonics in isolation; we sequentially focused on separate cuing systems as necessary prerequisites before meaning from text could be gained. In effect, we often limited rather than extended student learning. Through a collaborative and dialogic process, the Language Arts Advisory Council decided that the new district literacy plan, while not abandoning skills or phonics, would create a new instructional framework to facilitate learning the skills and letters and sounds of language. Our plan would provide the functional context necessary for children to begin to make sense of the pieces of language they were learning, as well as how and when to use them. We believed that a holistic framework would allow children to use the supports of all three cuing systems simultaneously, as they do naturally when they learn to speak. We believed that increased numbers of children would be successful in their encounters with written language through this new framework.

Another critical aspect of our plan was to totally support interactive and responsive teaching focusing on the needs of learners. Through our study we had come to know that the "cookbook" or "recipe" approach of the past prevented the transactions between theory, teachers, and students needed for learning to be fully realized. Our plan, therefore, was not a lockstep model but was based on the belief that a teacher must take what she or he knows about language and literacy development, assess each student's strengths and needs in light of this development, and provide curricular support to build on these strengths and meet those needs. The role of teachers in our framework had to be dynamic and recursive if learning was going to be dynamic and recursive. Our goal was to go beyond merely teaching students to read; we wanted to create a context in which students would become "self-winding," lifelong readers and writers who learned to read and "read to learn."

This plan, or curriculum framework, was more a philosophical position than a traditional curriculum guide. As a philosophical position, it asserted that teachers make changes by beginning from where they are in their understanding of language learning and progressing to where they want to be—moving from the known in beliefs and instructional practices to the new. Recognizing that this process requires time for people to grow, learn, and explore professionally led us to a unique implementation framework.

In an attempt to provide support and guidance, the Language Arts Advisory Council designed an over 40-hour interactive training and overview of this theory and appropriate practice consistent with our research. This training was an effort to demonstrate that transitions toward holistic reading instruction involve gradual changes; opportunities were provided to allow each campus to choose a 1-year implementation focus along six interrelated dimensions. This was choice, right!?

At this point I began to realize that the truth as we had constructed it was evident only to those who had discovered it together. The process of reading and talking and rereading led this group of educators to new levels of understanding and to many questions. My motivation in this project was to create a process and a product that would, in effect, free teachers from the bureaucratic restraints binding them to a rigid instructional sequence and methodology. The problem, as I saw it, was that teachers have so many mandates that they become automata in the classroom. They have learned to do what they are told; they are punished for thinking and questioning the existing system. I was amazed to discover that some teachers did not want to be free at all and were as disappointed by our answers as they were with solutions of the past.

In my effort to free teachers from the bureaucratic controls of the class-room, I too imposed my agenda on them, and, by my imposing my agenda I was controlling them. I think I believed this was theoretically sound, and morally correct and would help them grow by controlling them more than they had ever been controlled. As I began to talk to the people who were not directly involved with the project, I began to doubt whether the product should be implemented at all and suggested the process we went through to arrive at our conclusions was where the real power was. When I suggested that the process of negotiation and collaboration built a community of empowered decision makers and seekers of learning, however, I thought I would be murdered. All this work to create "the document," and all I wanted to do was to use the process of how we had created it. I started losing credibility fast. Conflict, *real* conflict, began to occur.

Further, after the document was written, I found myself in a new role as curriculum coordinator. Entering the next school year, I was assigned to assist and monitor the "implementation" of the framework. Suddenly I was a bureaucrat enforcing a program that I was determined to develop to free teachers to free kids! I was not the leader of a collaborative team of empowered professionals together seeking new horizons to better enable students than had previous programs.

Doubts about what I had done grew. How could this, of all district efforts, be treated like any other program? How could I become the enforcer—one of those I so resented myself in my own practice? How could constructing meaning become an absolute implementation?

As I struggled with the dichotomy I was living, it took little to motivate me to decide to leave the district and pursue my doctorate full time at Texas A&M. I left with a mixed feeling of pride in our efforts and a growing sense of dissatisfaction with what appeared to be the inherent bureaucracy of schools. Arriving at the university, I found a host of new experiences awaiting me.

A UNIVERSITY CLASSROOM

As part of my assistantship, I was assigned to teach a required course in the teacher preparation program which dealt with current issues and perspectives in education. I team-taught this class with a colleague, and we attempted to facilitate the class from constructivist frameworks and to develop the content and process for instruction as we went along. One of our goals for the course was to show ways in which the debates about education are related to the concerns about social justice and equality. This idea served as a framework on which to build the constructive process. Therefore, our instruction centered on how fairness, social justice, and education are related and on how we must deal with the purposes of schooling and education, how people expect to be treated, and how they are actually treated in schools and in the society. As a result it became increasingly important to us, as we facilitated the learning of these 40 undergraduate education majors, that they be treated with respect and that their voices be heard.

The text we selected provided the structure for the transactive dialogic approach to our class. The students sat at tables and became a group of learners. Together the members at each table took time to discuss and share understandings of the assigned readings. Initially, as we attempted to engage these students in serious dialogue about the issues surrounding public schools, we got blank stares and no responses. In the beginning, they simply would not talk. Instead, they went about the business of writing down everything we said.

Frustrated by the unwillingness of these students to engage in discussion, we decided to role play and to demonstrate what we expected by dialogue and response. We talked about the difference between a transmission-based approach and a transactive-based approach to learning and began to establish a classroom climate to encourage various transactions. To understand what was happening, or rather not happening, in our classroom, we began to ask the students questions about their reluctance to participate. According to one student:

> You have to remember that none of our classes since elementary school have allowed group discussions. I guess probably eight out of ten on the average of my undergraduate classes not only do not allow group discussions, you just go in and look at the backs of people's heads. You don't get familiar with the faces. You only see the professor's face. The professors are typically male in the 43 to 52 year old age range. You may know what the class is about but you are never sure about the professor and his goals. You don't always know what he is trying to achieve. The class doesn't interact. You don't interact with the people around you unless it's to get the notes from the previous class. You don't interact with the professor, because most of the time you feel intimidated. They use physical barriers like a podium. That is a mental thing. All you see is a head above a podium and that is really impersonal. I feel feelings of resentment, although unfounded, towards them because it's hard to believe they care. Too many professors treat too many students like they are not real people. They lecture you. You don't really see them as real people either, or as seeing them as having separate lives. You are learning to write as fast as possible what the prof tells you. You don't process the information until three weeks later, until it's the test. Then you cram it all in and hope it's going to be on the test. These classes are transmission. You don't transact. You feel detached. You can't be an entity of the class. There are no ties. You don't owe that class anything but to take the notes and make the grade.

In reference to the professors in these classes, she continued:

> Their job is to lecture to students and get in the requirements of the curriculum that has been set before them. There is no requirement to get to know the student so you can get the information across in the best way possible. They believe the fewer interactions the less complicated it is. The students are

responsible for the learning and understanding, if there is understanding. For the most part the feelings the students have are negative. We dread going to class. It's a burden. There is no pleasure.

This revelation, this candor on the part of our students, reaffirmed everything I have grown to believe about instruction, from my classroom days in River Tree. Again students were the victims of a top-down, absolute, preordained, transmission instructional model. The ways our students described courses at Texas A&M were identical to that of the model of instruction in River Tree when I first started teaching prekindergarten. My fervor, my commitment to a transactive, constructive, meaningful approach to teaching was confirmed now for 4-year-olds to 21-year-olds. My colleague thought the same way, and we were determined to teach this course using the paradigm we both believed was most supportive of teaching and learning.

But it was not easy. Team-teaching this course was one of the most difficult things I have ever done. We lived through the initial "Oh my goshes" as we agonized over the process of deciding what we wanted to do and how best to involve the students in their own construction of learning. We were constantly asking ourselves questions, asking our students questions, and questioning each other. Did we talk too much today? Did we talk enough today? Are we too process oriented? Are we too content oriented? Are the students meeting our objectives? Are the students meeting their own objectives? It was scary, because we were asking questions. If we did not ensure the content, were the students going to get the information they needed to be successful in this class and in the future? We felt as if we were in a recursive learning process of taking three steps forward and two steps back. Experiencing the agony of the lack of instructional control was one of the most powerful experiences I have had to date. As the course came to a close, one student described the class in the following way:

> First, you have to dismiss any preconceived ideas about any typical class. You can't put this class in a category. You can't put it with any other class. You can't blow it off. You learn MORE in there. You see it as a growing experience and whatever grade you get, you get. You enter most classes and you have the feeling students may not know each other really, really well. In 302 there is a bond. A class-like bond. Profs support this. It's like, no matter what you say, people may not agree but you are never afraid to say anything. The atmosphere is kind of relaxing. It's kind of like a study break. It's laid back. People enjoy being there. The profs sit amongst the students and they claim to be learning along with the students. They gave no promises from the beginning that they have all the answers because they probably don't. Who does? The profs are personal. They interact on a one-to-one basis with the class. They always have something personal to say to each student and that makes the student feel important to know that they know them. The students are developing their own ideology of setting up classrooms during the whole semester. We form this on a basis of achieved consensus of the group—on the whole we are consistent. When you leave this classroom you accomplish something. You don't have to go brush up

on it. You leave learning. If you don't understand it, you ask more questions so
you can form your beliefs, so that you can defend them one day. Everyone sits
at tables. They are scooted away so you are facing the rest of the class. By mid
semester you could put names with faces and, at the very least, you know voices.
You are able to see the structure at the end of class. It comes together and the
goals are met. We interact about the chapter and, when we feel exhausted, we
move on. It is transactional—student to student and professors to students.

She went on to describe the benefits of the team-teaching experience:

You collaborate—that's obvious. We are able to see different views, because you
have different expertise in different areas. You ask a lot of "what ifs." When
there is one prof it tends to be one sided and you don't ever hear another side
and, you don't say anything against it. When there are two profs you see them
interact and you see them as individuals that see more to life than just sitting
and lecturing. In this class, you both seem to have a liberal philosophy. The way
you approach this class it makes you think. You are not necessarily right or wrong.
You don't view us as students. You view us as people. If students are people you
have as much to learn from them as they do from you. That's good, because
students feel comfortable in that environment and they can be completely open
without the fear of being put down.

She then described the process of examining the thinking that occurred:
"You don't feel nervous—it'll be challenged, what you think I mean, but not
negatively. If you can base what you say on some philosophy then that's fine.
The content gets learned."
She described the course's content:

I've learned what a paradigm is. I've come to realize the basis of the whole
educational system and why people change and why they don't and who the big
losers are when the paradigm shifts. I've learned it is okay to question because
that is the only way we learn and understand things. We have learned the basics
within a real, strong foundation of the conservative and liberal philosophies. I
understand more about the educational system. Like how school boards are run,
the logistics and, I've learned *how* people change and how they don't. I've learned
all the logistical stuff. I've learned that some authors, like Yerkes and Bobbit
(1992), made me mad. I'm just really trying to rationalize the issues out as a
result of their thinking, but I can't figure out how Yerkes could even rationalize
out what he was thinking. That seems absurd to me. I have a lot of respect for
Dewey. He exemplified the values of the classroom and his intent was that the
whole class would benefit. He promoted self responsibility and independence,
NOT oppression. The group work has taught me self-control. You don't always
say what you can, you listen too. You learn how to bring a whole lot of ideas into
a cohesive whole. You get a fresh perspective from other members of a group.
My experience has been that differences set people apart, in here, we have
learned to bring differences together to make something good. I've learned that
this educator is screaming to come out and this class has helped me to see my
belief system and how I can run my classroom. I can go on now. Now I know
that I'm going to be a good educator because I am a really reflective person and

I take a lot in. I don't just act, I sit and listen and see how others respond to those actions. I use what I have experienced to make a risk-free environment. I've learned that the educator must not be afraid or the students will feel oppressed. Students can question without feeling intimidated, no matter what. If the teacher believes in the students and expects them to achieve greatness and supports them in that process, they will.

Team-teaching was difficult and challenging. It was also one of the most rewarding struggles I have ever participated in. By the time the class was over, we knew, really knew, each student had more than mastered content; they had internalized the notions of the course. My belief in the transactive, constructive approach to teaching and learning was now more embedded, more reinforced than ever. Constructivist transactions were not simply better, they were absolutely right. I knew that so well, believed it so deeply, that wherever I encountered the other paradigm I was ready, willing, and able to wage the great war of conversion. I became like a missionary ready to both convert and save the educational world. I would have this opportunity closer to home than I ever imagined as my daughter entered kindergarten the same semester I team-taught the course.

MY DAUGHTER'S CLASSROOM

Leaving River Tree and moving to Campus Junction was a traumatic experience for me, and more so for my daughter, Lynn. At age 6 she was reading, as though because of my skills and beliefs, she had any other options. She was a highly verbal, highly active, very tactile child who loved learning. I enrolled her in the kindergarten of the public school in our new neighborhood.

Several weeks into the school year I had a shocking experience. At the teacher's invitation, I visited my daughter's classroom. The invitation note read: "Lynn will be 'kiddo of the week' next week. Please feel free to come visit our room during that week. Give me one day's notice of your visit and don't stay longer than 15 minutes. You can read a book to the class while you are there. Thank you, Mrs K." I responded to the invitation and chose a time that would quite naturally lead to the lunch period and asked to stay to have lunch with my daughter. The teacher hesitated, but allowed me to stay.

As I entered the classroom the children were seated in neat rows on the carpet, each one painstakingly separated from the other. The adult-size rocking chair was waiting for me, and, as I walked toward it, you could have heard a pin drop. I asked my daughter to join me in the rocker so we could together share the book, *Red, Green and Yellow*, by Robert Munsch, with her classmates. She looked to the teacher for approval and, when given an affirmative nod, she approached the rocking chair. All my kindergarten teacher behaviors came flooding back to me as I sat in that chair ready to read with a captive group of 5- and 6-year-olds eagerly waiting at my feet. I held up the book to show them the cover and asked, "Look at this cover; what do you think this book might be about?" Several children answered at once. The teacher said in a sweet voice, "Boys and girls, remember you must raise your hand if you wish to speak. Show Mrs. Katt how well you know what to do when we read stories." They nodded. Then, I continued to ask questions, the children continued to respond without raising their hands and the teacher continued to remind them of appropriate "book reading behavior." Her voice became less sweet as the story unfolded. The story was very funny, and the children laughed aloud. This, too, seemed to frustrate the teacher as her directions became crisper and more clear. The children applauded as Lynn read the last page of the book. The teacher was relieved and seemed to take great pleasure in resuming control of the classroom.

With the story now over, it was time for lunch. The teacher called children to line up for lunch in categories. First, the "free lunch" children, then the "buying lunch" children, then the "milk only" children and finally the "home lunch" children. Whew! Finally, they were all in line, and, after a review of the hall rules, we began our journey to the cafeteria. The teacher, walking backward, dictating "hall rules" as she walked, led us to the cafeteria. We passed other classroom lines of children also led by backward-walking teachers. I counted 17 Shsh's by adults in that 3-minute walk to the cafeteria. I saw lines of children facing forward with their hands behind their backs and following their adult leaders to the awaited social half hour called lunch.

Actually, I thought it would be a social half hour, but things have changed since I was in the classroom a short 4 years ago! The children who were making a purchase of one sort or another went straight to the appropriate line, while the children with home lunches went to the appropriate table. I was amazed at the organization and efficiency of these small children in this huge cafeteria. I noticed how amazingly quiet it was in a room so full of young children. I started to talk to my daughter and was promptly scolded by the teacher. She said, "Lynn, you better tell your mom about the lunchroom rules." "Oh boy, more rules," I thought! "We have to wait until everyone in the cafeteria is seated before we can begin to eat. We are on silence for the first 10 minutes so we can get calm. We can only throw our trash away if it's our turn." In only a few minutes I, not knowing the rules, had broken two: I had talked and had taken a bite of my sandwich. The teacher, mistaking the look on my face for remorse, said, "It's okay, Mrs. Katt, you didn't know." Then she went on to explain that the rules were necessary because, if the children talked and ate as they were seated, they would not finish at the same time, and then they would be "hard to handle." We sat for 10 minutes in silence and then spent the next 15 minutes quickly eating lunch so we could go to recess.

Recess was next. I knew I had stayed far longer than the allotted 15 minutes, but I decided to take my chances and asked to stay to play at recess. I wanted to have an opportunity to see these children have fun. The teacher said, "We have nap right after recess, so you will need to leave right after recess." I thanked her for allowing me to stay.

As we got to the playground, I watched as she lined up 7 of the 22 children to stand facing the wall, hands behind their backs, as a consequence of failing to follow one or more rules.

As I left the school, anxiety building, I decided to test my interpretation of this prisonlike classroom against my daughter's interpretation. My 6-year old daughter began her description of her kindergarten experience in the following way: "In the mornings we do the calendar. We listen to the announcements, actually, before the calendar. The announcements are when Mr O., our principal, talks to us from the speaker. He tells us what the lunch is and then we do the pledge with him." [*She then recites the pledge*]

When asked if she knew what the pledge meant, she responded, "No. It's just what we say every day." When encouraged to think about the meaning of the pledge she responded, "Hm ... It means that you care about someone I guess—is that true? That's it. I think it means that you care about someone."

As she continued her discussion of her morning in kindergarten, she focused on the events of the day as well as the structure necessary for the successful completion of these events. She stated:

> We sing songs like "Good Morning, Merry Sunshine." We sit on the carpet in lines. We've got to sit in our places where we always sit. She [*The teacher*] gives you a place, and when you are there for a while you remember where you sit, and it's not confusing anymore. It's harder for the new people. We have three new kids this week. We always get new kids. Their names are Janine, Anna, and Julia. Some kids just leave, and then we get new ones. There is only one way to talk—you have to raise your hand to talk—and you have to whisper. If you talk and you are not supposed to, you get a warning; then you have to change your color.

The "color chart" was the districtwide assertive discipline plan adopted as a means to "avoid behavior problems" in school classrooms. Lynn's pace increased, and her tone became more dramatic as she elaborated her description of the schoolwide discipline code. She said:

> See, we have this chart and first you start on green. That's the good color. Then yellow, and you miss 5 minutes of playtime. Then, when you change your color again, it's blue, and you have to go to the thinking chair. That's not a good place. You just have to sit there, face to the window, put your hands behind your back, and think about how you are going to act. It's hard to do when everybody is looking at you. I've only had to sit in that chair two times. Like the time I had a battery in my pocket, and I took it out and looked at it. Then, I forgot and did it again. Well, it fell out of my pocket, and I was just picking it up, but I had to sit there anyway. You miss 10 minutes of playtime if you get to blue. Then, it gets worse. If you have to change your color again—you get to red. Then you have to miss 15 minutes of playtime and the thinking chair, and you get a note home. I've never been to red. Then there is the worst, black! Black is the most

terrible of the whole colors. If you change your color again and get to black, you have to go to the principal's office. He has a paddle in there, and you might have to stay all day. You might even get kicked out of school. I've never been to black, and I never want to go to Mr. O.'s office."

As her story unfolded, she continued to focus on the importance of the school rules. She emphasized:

We have hall rules. No talking. Face the front. Hands behind your back. At recess, if you have to stand out part of the time or the whole time, you have to "stand on the wall." You just stand there with your hands behind your back. It's not very fun, and it's not very fair. People have to ignore you and can't even talk to you because you are in time out. Now we've even started that when you don't bring back your report card, you'll have 5 minutes on the wall. Nap. Nap is important, too. You have to lay [sic] on your tummy. You can't move around. That's why I don't like to wear my dresses with buttons because they hurt my tummy, but you always have to lay on your tummy, even it hurts.

Although many of her responses centered on the way the classroom was managed, she also addressed the issue of learning in her classroom and gave the following description:

We learn new things. We learn *north, south, east,* and *west* and the letters and stuff. We're through already with the letters, so now I don't know what we'll learn. [Long pause] She [the kindergarten teacher] doesn't know during the week if we're learning unless she can read our minds, but if she would come check on me and see what I'm learning at home she would see that I can read. I can read *Mortimer, I Can Read, The Principal's New Clothes,* well ... I can read a lot of books. ... At home I can read books; at school sometimes I get to read words—just words—real words—like *blizzard* and *Chili's* and *Bennigan's* ... You know, food words, that you see in the world. Words I have been reading for a long time.

She asked, "You want to know how I learned?" I said, "Yes." She explained, "I kept asking what it said, and someone would tell me and then I would look at it and remember what it meant." She went on to emphasize why she included these comments in the interview: "Reading is very important to me, you know, because when I grow up I can learn stuff grownups learn. They are always reading books. That's why it's so important to me, and I'm so glad I have so many books to read at home. I learn at school and at home, but it's more fun at home because we read more and I get to learn stuff that's not boring. I have lots of books at home, and there is no color chart."

When asked if she liked learning in school, she responded:

Yes, but sometimes I don't like it though because we just have to sit there and listen all the time. You can't even fix your sock if you need to. You'll have to change your color. The mornings are better. You don't even have to ask to get a tissue if your nose is running, and if you are really early, you can go to the bathroom if you need to. Oh, yeah, you can go to the bathroom after nap if you need to, but not during nap. Once I had an accident during nap because I didn't go when I was supposed to.

As she continued her story, she shared what she liked most about school, "I like crossing the monkey bars the best, and I love to go to art. I love Mrs. Machs [the art teacher] because she loves me. Art class is my favorite part of school. Mrs. Machs puts my art up and says I am good at art. I am, you know; my art teacher says so." Finally, when asked to share her thoughts about the most important thing about school, she responded, "The teacher and my principal make sure you follow all the rules so we can have a good school."

Even now as I sit here writing, remembering my response to the school, its rules, its instruction, the way kids are treated, my anger almost overwhelms me. How could it be that the very war I waged in River Tree goes unwaged in my daughter's school? How could it be that I know so much about teaching young children, and my daughter must suffer through an educational experience where control means more than learning? How could it be that while I am attempting to lead a transactive, constructive classroom at the university, my daughter is memorizing letter of the week and classroom rules?

The inequity, the unfairness, was just too much. I went to the teacher and offered to teach some model lessons. I went to the principal and offered to do free staff development. I wrote notes, I visited the classroom, and I comforted Lynn at home. This school and this teacher are wrong, and I know it! My duty was to change it, to convert the adults at the school to a better way of thinking. If I could not effect such a change as a teacher, as a coordinator, and now as a parent, there was no hope for public school.

As the fire burned in my belly, as I prepared to wage the righteous war, I continued to take courses at Texas A&M.

GRADUATE SCHOOL

In the fall semester of 1992, I took history of education with Paul Theobald. What a surprise! Dr. Theobald did not lecture; he expected the class to read the assignment (a half a book a week!) and be ready to discuss it each class meeting. I remember staring at those six fat books and wondering whether I wanted to put myself through it. With encouragement I decided to accept the challenge of working in an area where my background was very limited. I remember the first night when several of my classmates, who were later to become friends, so easily dialogued about the Jeffersonian and Progressive Eras. I remember thinking, "Jefferson, he was one of our presidents, wasn't he?"

Dr. Theobald did not seem to care that some students in the class had rich historical backgrounds and others had a limited background of "dead men and dates." As the course unfolded, I began to realize the importance of the content we were studying. I saw that U.S. education is connected to the beliefs, practices, and values inherent in the structures of social, cultural, political, and economic life. I learned that throughout educational history, changes in these life structures have shaped major debates over the process and purposes of schooling in the United States. The ultimate purpose of the class, as it emerged for me and as a result of the analysis of these historical changes in schools, was to begin to examine how belief systems (ideologies) deeply ingrained in our culture come to shape the way we see schooling and how these ideologies are translated into school policies. For the first time at an explicit level I began to see the interrelatedness between schooling and culture.

I learned that the democratic purpose of schools today echoes the voices of 100 years ago and offers a paradigm shift, rather than a new strategy to improve school efficiency. It became increasingly obvious to me that as we enter the final decade of this millennium, we must think about education in the context of society. We are faced with a range of critical issues and problems such as poverty, social injustice, racism, sexism, the depersonalization of social and political life, the moral and spiritual decay of the culture, and the ecological deterioration of the planet. Education must become an ethically responsible endeavor with a serious commitment to democratic values. Our children must grow up to be humane and caring people so that they may use their skills in the service of the social goals. The purpose of education, therefore, must be more than preparing children for economic success. It must be an empowering human process, which promotes individual dignity and the meaning of community in a democratic society. Unless children learn to honor human and cultural differences, the shared, interdependent quality of human existence cannot be fully realized.

I further learned that schools are the way they are because of decisions made by those in power. Educators and historians have described the profound changes in power relationships of schools and communities occurring in past years and the ways in which a small group of need providers—parents, ministers, employers, politicians, principals, and teachers—were once seen as authority figures and holders of the truth. These need providers, because of limited travel and communication outside their communities, often interacted with each other in one way or another so that communication and consensus building were ongoing processes among them. These tight-knit social networks built a sense of community and cohesiveness that gave the need providers power that has since been lost.

But schools are not now controlled by community-based need providers. Rather than a sense of community, people are now in daily contact with strangers. Policies, programs, and practices are dictated by federal and state governments that operate on the assumption they know best what schools should be doing. Local boards are no longer made up of leading community figures who seek to serve the public good, but by local politicians seeking forum or by disgruntled single-issue patrons. Despite these profound changes in power relationships, the structure and operation of schools have changed very little. I learned that, unless people examine the bases and use of power in our society, they cannot understand the problem schools face today, much less plan effective and appropriate innovations.

In the spring semester of 1993, I enrolled in a qualitative graduate research course with Dr. Ernie Stringer. According to Dr. Stringer, community-based ethnography, was designed "to model the community-based approach in the class so that the student will be able to see a process of working with a group of people, or in a setting, and telling a story or producing a narrative about those people in that setting." He stated: "Most ethnographic work is done by an outsider who comes to that setting, observes it, interacts with the people and goes away and writes the story. Community-based ethnography focuses the work of going into a setting and working with a group of people, to assist them to write stories which enable them in some way to accomplish purposes they have together."

This approach of learning through negotiation and collaboration is one that Dr. Stringer has been developing through his work with Aboriginal communities in Australia for the past 30 years.

The class project in which small groups of students constructed ethnographies to describe our class was a long, explorative process. Members of our class came together collectively to try to build a picture of our classroom community to understand what our community was about and how it worked. It seems to me that most students in this class had unquestionably accepted a set of beliefs about learning that had their origins in what Arthur Koestler called "the dark ages of psychology." As long as people continue to hold these beliefs, they continue to organize their learning behavior in ways that reflect them. True, in this class we began to experience a different process or theory for learning from the one most of us have experienced to date but, on reflection, our group still made a collaborative attempt using our pre-existing competitive frameworks. Although a step, it was just a step toward truly realizing the power of collective learning.

In my view, the class process revealed that students' stories were motivated by pre-existing frameworks made up of what each of us believes about the processes that underlie learning (of course, this is *my* organizing framework). These beliefs about learning, or personal learning theories, are carried around in our heads and help us to construct meaning for ourselves and others. The multiple realities, or individual frameworks, of the class members became most evident on the last night of class as each of us described the process of constructing meaning in this classroom context. For some, the learning process might be described as painful; for others, the process brought pleasure. Whatever the outcome, I finally realized that each of these internal frameworks was different for each of us.

Now I have more questions: Is everything we hear, see, experience merely an interpretation made through our frameworks? If so, does truth exist? Is there reality? Should we discount our interpretation or be acutely aware of the implications of our interpretations for ourselves and others? Can we truly understand another person's reality if we translate their reality through our framework? Can we resist imposing our agenda on others if we perceive our agenda to be the moral thing to do? What is the moral thing to do? What is right? Is there right? Oh, my aching head!

"CONCLUSION"

Even as I title this section, I wonder whether there is such a thing as a conclusion. Do we ever really conclude? Do we ever arrive at a destination, or is there merely the journey, *this* being but one stop along the road of learning?

So where am I? Traditionally most schools, in my view, both historically and in my own experience, have supported a hierarchical system that was built on deficits in transmission of knowledge and focused on the product. They taught skills and tasks in isolation, controlled the learning, and minimized social interaction and group learning. On the other hand, some schools have supported a system in which the community would act advisedly and concertedly toward a chosen cultural outcome. This view seemed to emphasize engagement, reflection, and shared responsibility and to maximize social interaction and questioning. I have come to believe that, unless people identify the needs of collective humanity, current economic values will continue to create an entire generation of mechanistic, nonthinking automata. I firmly believe in the communally constructed, transactive, holistic, meaningful interaction of teachers and students as a process to promote real learning. This belief is reaffirmed by every course I teach and every course I take. I believe it so completely that I have served as a missionary, determined to convert the unknowing savage to my belief system.

It is this missionary zeal that I now question. If truth is separately constructed, can I claim to possess truth for others? By what right do I impose my construction? Do I use the rationalist base of supporting data and research to substantiate my claim and, in so doing, undermine my philosophical base? Do I argue that this way is best, based on my values, beliefs, and experiences? Do I simply share my constructions with others and recognize their right to accept or reject these constructions for their own brand of truth? What is the prime directive? Is there one? Have I been as guilty of absolutism as the absolutists in my fervor for relativism? If so, what do I do now?

These are not merely moot, esoteric questions for me. The answers will shape the rest of my life, personally and professionally. I have learned that questions and our own answers truly constitute learning. It is the tension of not knowing, the passion of the search, the uncertainty inherent in the asking that constitute my own path on this journey. I hope I never absolutely know that I have arrived!

ACKNOWLEDGMENTS

As I have continued my journey to grow and learn to make a difference in children's lives and in this world, I have been fortunate to have many travel guides to help me along the path to each major destination. Of course, at each major destination I thought I had arrived at truth and was ready to end my journey so that I might spread this truth to others less enlightened. Luckily, these travel guides kept me moving down the path, helping me to face obstacles and to seek opportunities to continue to grow and learn. It was their encouragement and belief in a greater good that kept me traveling on that often rocky road. In truth, no one travels alone.

As I was ready to wage war on the public school, the organization that was trying to control my classroom practice and ultimately my students, it was John Stansell at Texas A&M who offered me greatest support. Martha Bair, a principal, was also my advocate as I worked toward an organizational structure that encouraged research, learning, and improvement. As I was faced with daily struggles, I found myself leading a major curriculum innovation; Judy Stevens helped me begin to see the discrepancies and inconsistencies in my own thinking. It was painful but I learned to control less and listen more. As I struggled with how to respond to Lynn's teacher, Paul Theobald helped me see the historical context of all our current dilemmas and added, through his own open, transactive, constructive teaching, a rich background for my struggles, a background that I was unaware even existed. Paul helped me to see that it was I who was in fact limiting my own thinking. As I currently seek to know the next steps in my path, my friend, mentor, and colleague, Ernie Stringer, by giving me the opportunity to write this ethnography, has opened the door to my next journey and has raised questions in my mind about moral imperatives, rightness, truth, and intervention.

I owe a special thanks to you all, and others not specifically mentioned, as I continue along this path. Thank you for being teachers, fellow travelers, and learners. It is my hope that I, too, will give of myself to the other travelers along the journey as each of you has so honestly given to me.

13

Teaching Reinterpreted

Ernie Stringer

CONTEXTUALIZING TEACHING

The perspectives on teaching presented in the previous chapters are extended and complex, and the various interpretations are difficult to "hold in the mind" from account to account. In this section, therefore, I try to capture the essential elements of our narratives and provide a framework of concepts and ideas to enable readers to readily grasp and recall what we have presented.

The authenticity and credibility of this representation of teaching do not derive from scientifically verifiable procedures, but from descriptions and interpretations that have their origin in multiple iterations of a process of reflection, dialogue, analysis, and "member checking." Thus we placed our ideas squarely in our everyday experiences of teaching and learning. We do not suggest that these ways of thinking about and enacting teaching are generalizable to all teachers in all places, but that they are relevant to people who recognize themselves and their situations in these accounts. Taking our own diverse experiences into account, however, we suspect that these interpretations are relevant to people in a broad range of educational and community contexts. Our hope, articulated clearly by Kenneth during one of our discussions, is that our emerging vision of teaching "can happen to any group of people. Any teacher or other person can get similar results by doing these things."

RE-THINKING TEACHING AND LEARNING

Our experiences of classes that enacted a community-based approach to learning led us to conclude that we might enrich our understanding of teaching, learning, and education by thinking about these processes in different ways. Although presented in terms of their location in formal institutional contexts such as schools, universities, and colleges, teaching and learning processes are relevant to varied activities in settings like community organizations, human service agencies, and businesses. As Kenneth and Deana have demonstrated, teaching-as-facilitating-learning is relevant to many aspect of adult education and community development work, and Patsy's narrative demonstrated that facilitating learning is an important part of organizational development.

Indeed, teaching encompasses facilitating learning through processes of inquiry, it can be defined in terms usually associated with research—the production of new knowledge. As this text explicates, when knowledge is seen in terms of meaning and the acquisition of knowledge in terms of the discovery of meaning, then the distinction between research and learning becomes arbitrary. Teaching-as-facilitating-learning involves creating a context in which people discover new meanings or ways of envisioning their worlds that make sense and provide the basis for productive action. This process of discovery may be termed either learning or research largely on the basis of context, and the term *teacher–researcher* takes on a whole new set of meanings.

If the purpose of education is learning, teachers teach to facilitate learning. Learning, minimally, is about acquiring new information and socially desirable skills. This, we suggest, is a necessary but not sufficient condition for good teaching and education. Learning, in the sense that we advocate, is an active, ongoing process of discovery that reveals new knowledge, meaning, or under-standing and enables learners to know themselves and their worlds in new ways. Enriched learning processes enable people to make sense of new information because they have assisted in its construction and can understand its relevance to their own history and experience of life. In its fullest form, learning empowers individuals to act in concert with others to identify and transform problematic features of their world.

We maintain that community building is an essential feature of good teaching practice and has the potential to powerfully enrich the educational experience. Good teaching, in other words, requires a community of learners. The approach that is advocated here, therefore, could be typified as a com-munity-based, reflective, constructivist model of teaching. By enacting this model, teachers would effectively disrupt their student-participants' generally accepted, taken-for-granted views, and would use learning activities and conditions that reveal their worlds in new, different, productive ways. The processes, conducted in a safe and collaborative atmosphere, would enable students to come face to face with many of their underlying assumptions about life and the world, assumptions that are an intrinsic part of their social and human experience.

In such a learning situation, students would not transform their worlds in every class session. Traditional modes of learning may still be adequate for many classroom goals, but over time students will engage new dimensions of experience that work directly to enrich their educational experience and their understanding of the social and cultural universe. Students will routinely engage in learning as a meaningful, enjoyable activity that is relevant to their everyday lives, and each activity will contribute in some small but significant way to their understanding of the world.

Nor does a community-based approach to instruction mean that excellence or grades are unimportant. On the contrary, we believe that high levels of student commitment, high standards of competence, and high levels of skill and understanding are accompanying conditions to these new visions of teaching. In the brave new world of accountability and minimum standards, we consider that our approach to teaching can accomplish legislative mandates and administrative ends far more productively and effectively than does adherence to chalk-and-talk, teach-to-the-test approaches to education, which are often boring, repetitive, and stress inducing.

The following framework describes teaching that complements technical considerations and produces rich, meaningful learning environments. Techniques and strategies of teaching and learning are enhanced, we suggest, when encompassed in a vision of teaching that emphasizes the significance of the facilitative, modeling and creative aspects of teaching.

THE ART OF TEACHING: FACILITATING, MODELING, AND CREATING

A key observation that emerged in the process of our investigation was that teaching was clearly more than a process of transmitting information or passing on knowledge. We discovered that teaching is a complex art that requires teachers to facilitate learning, to enact or model what is to be learned, and to create appropriate organizational and social conditions that enabled learning to occur. This fundamental shift in perspective implies that a teacher should: facilitate learning by engaging students in learning processes that not only enable them to acquire discrete pieces of information, but also to engage in active inquiry and discovery that lead them to see and understand their real-life experiences in new ways. This way of conceptualizing teaching requires learning approaches that are consciously reflective, assist learners to understand the ways they best acquire knowledge, and enable them to understand the relevance of knowledge to their everyday lives.

A teacher should model what is to be learned, rather than merely talk about it. Modeling works on at least two levels. Teachers must demonstrate facility with the skills or knowledge they wish students to acquire. They must also enact what is being taught. If they wish to teach about democracy, for example, then they must organize classroom life in ways that demonstrate democratic principles and behaviors. If they wish their students to care for each other, then they need to demonstrate caring behavior themselves.

A teacher should create conditions that maximize the learning potentials of the context. The conditions of learning articulated in the literature on teaching relate to the need for teachers to be well organized, to plan carefully the scope and sequence of learning, to control the flow of activity, and so on. All are useful characteristics of good teaching. Our experience suggests, however, that these essentially technical qualities need to be complemented by other characteristics. Teachers need also to build communities of learners; to ensure their physical and psychological well-being; to maximize opportunities for them to actively participate in planning and other forms of decision making; and to ensure that learners are consistently engaged in various learning activities directly relevant to their everyday lives.

CREATING CONDITIONS FOR LEARNING

Where learning is considered solely in terms of the acquisition of isolated pieces of information, then linear and mechanistic approaches to teaching tend to predominate. Our experience suggests the need for a holistic and integrated approach to designing learning processes to ensure that learners can engage the full educational and revelatory potential of their activities. The following conditions that emerged consistently from our explorations and analyses suggest practical ways of enhancing learning processes.

Community Building

Our experience suggested that individual learning is greatly enhanced when students work cooperatively and provide each other with feedback and support. One of the primary functions of teaching, therefore, is to build a community of learners. A sense of community does not occur naturally, but can be carefully and systematically constructed through organizing classrooms and planning learning processes. Activities must provide recurring opportunities for participants to engage in dialogue, to collaborate, to share ideas, to explore many viewpoints, and, in the process, to experience the multiple realities that are part of any human social encounter. These community-building activities not only provide contexts that enable participants to learn how to negotiate agreements, but also demonstrate the importance and productivity of positive interpersonal relationships.

The cross-pollination of ideas and experience that derive from community building gives people access to a rich repository of knowledge and demonstrates that shared learning activities can be enjoyable and enlivening. This collaborative, cooperative approach to teaching-learning is in marked contrast to the ethos of isolation and competitive singularity that pervade many classrooms. In its highest form, community building enables the development of intimate, supportive relationships that become powerful learning contexts in their own right. The power of collective learning becomes synergistic and opens the possibility to an array of enjoyable, exciting, powerful learning experiences. Community building, we reiterate, should be a central element in the professional repertoire of all teachers.

"We shared ourselves, that's what made it human" (Lois).

Comfort and Safety: Physical and Psychological Well-Being

Among the most significant features to emerge from our explorations was the need to provide safe comfortable physical conditions and to ensure the emotional safety of participants. Although this feature might be read in a minimalist sense, we suggest the need for teachers to work proactively and consciously to establish and maintain these attributes of a good learning environment:

Classrooms are often poorly designed, with uncomfortable furniture. The furniture is often so arranged that productive interaction between participants is problematic. We believe that good teaching requires efforts to maximize the comfort of learners, to make the environment as attractive as possible, and to arrange furniture to maximize the possibilities for learners to communicate and to engage in diverse learning activities. This notion may be anathema to teachers who constantly engage in actions to minimize communication between students. We believe, however, that spurious or distracting interactions between learners are minimized over time, as students take ownership and responsibility for their own learning and become productively engaged in class activities. Learning, we believe, occurs in relaxed and comfortable environments those that enable participants to feel at home. By making space in the classroom a collective environment, by giving learners a sense of place, people can create learning environments that enhance participant learning.

Physical environments that maximize learning have adequate furniture, arrangements that promote communication, attractive decorations, a sense of place ("This is my/our place"), and space for collective, cooperative, and individual activities.

As for emotional safety; asking a learner a question in a typical classroom, writers have suggested, is equivalent to the experience of a duck caught in a hunter's spotlight. The fear of criticism or failure that often accompanies a focus on individuals causes many learners to freeze in the hope that the spotlight will leave them and find another target. Typical ways of motivating learners, of engaging their attention, focus on grades that, although ostensibly designed to indicate quality or extent of learning, are used to induce feelings ranging from elation to disappointment in learners. As a tool for motivation, grades often have the reverse effect and, particularly for poorer students, generate a couldn't-care-less attitude that masks feelings of embarrassment and ineptitude. Learning activities that result in grades or public criticism can be embarrassing and can inhibit learning. Evaluation or critique of performance is a necessary part of learning, but should be directed at specific performances and followed closely by opportunities to repair errors or improve performance. Good teaching–learning environments should foster an ethos in which error or failure is framed positively, as a necessary part of learning.

Emotional security is derived from:

Supportive, open, trusting, caring relationships.
Clear guidelines for behavior and activity.
Clear, easily accessible frameworks of concepts and ideas.
Freedom to express thoughts, ideas, and emotions.
Freedom from judgmental criticism.
Opportunities to improve specific performances.
Teachers who learn with and from their students.

Safety does not mean lack of challenge. In the previous narratives a number of us expressed satisfaction at the demanding nature of the learning activities we had experienced, but pointed to the conditions that enabled us to engage these challenges without fear. The guidance and support provided by all participants permitted risk-taking activity that would rarely be contemplated in normal classrooms. Conditions in the class enabled us to "[Get] to know the people in class and [be] free to express emotion, even to the point of tears" (Rhonda).

Participation

People have often interpreted participation as the willingness of students to take part in classroom activities, an outcome perceived to be a function of individual qualities or motivation. Our narratives, however, refer to participation in a much broader sense, where participants are not only actively involved in activities but have power to make decisions related to these activities. Good teaching, we suggest, requires teachers to limit the extent to which they engage their authority and to allow students to share in planning and decision making in fundamental ways.

This observation suggests a role for the teacher different from the one generally accepted in today's educational systems. Rather than being responsible for all decisions related to the organization of the learning environment and the curriculum, including objectives, content, and learning strategies and activities, we suggest that students should become actively engaged in planning such matters as curriculum goals, content and learning strategies. Students do not necessarily understand all that is to be learned, and they cannot always make decisions about all facets of their education, but we are convinced of the efficacy of procedures that allow them to actively participate in decision-making processes and to take responsibility for their own learning.

Although the extent of decision making may be somewhat limited in very young learners, we suggest that, over time, people who engage in decision making develop detailed understandings of their own capacities and capabilities that tell them how they learn best.

Participation that enriches student learning shares decision-making power, enables all voices to be heard, and accepts students' thoughts and feelings. Such participation includes taking action on ideas, issues, and concerns expressed by students; not marginalizing any student or group; and enabling students to construct their own explanations of events and phenomena.

Participation, however, goes further than decision making. Traditional school activities that focus on teacher or individual presentations to whole-class audiences foster passivity. Students whose only function is to observe and listen soon "turn off." Our experience suggests that learning strategies maximizing opportunities for small-group activity also maximize the possibilities for active participation of all students in a class. Active participation, we discovered, greatly enhances student learning.

Active Learning

An assumption reinforced by constantly expanding curriculum content is that teacher's task is to formulate knowledge in packages that can be "learned" by the student and regurgitated in tests and exams. The quality of education is often judged by the extent to which students are successful in exams. Teaching and learning, therefore, tend to be limited to activities that enable teachers to present large quantities of easily tested material. The prevalence of chalk-and-talk and individual paper-and-pen activities probably result from these pressures.

Our experience suggests that good teaching need not restrict itself to overly prescribed learning processes, but may focus on strategies and techniques that allow multiple and complex outcomes to emerge from learning activities. Active learning processes enable learners to extend their understanding of the knowledge and skills to be learned and their relation to life experiences. Active learning, we suggest, is not just about learning prescribed, objective knowledge unrelated to real-life experience, but is also about meaning-making, reflexivity, and the accumulation of knowledge and experience. Active learning, we suggest, has no compartmentalized, natural end; it leads to open-ended insights that often produce more questions than answers. Learning, we suggest, is a hermeneutic process that should privilege meaning-making over memorization.

Active learning promotes activities that emphasize inquiry, reflection, review, and recursive thinking (thinking that turns back on itself). These activities include deconstruction, reconstruction, critical consciousness, and sharing, as well as dialogue, understanding, application, and learning by doing something, not just talking or writing about it.

Active learning may result in much deeper outcomes than do those expected of normal classroom processes, outcomes that produce a critical consciousness able to apprehend the problematics of everyday social and cultural common sense. Such learning may produce constructivist learning that deconstructs and reconstructs commonly accepted views. It is nonlinear and creative, involves asking questions as much as giving information, and results in the development of numerous skills and understandings.

Relevance

When teachers plan learning activities, they are often constrained by available time and energy. The seemingly endless demands on teacher and class time inhibit the possibility of envisaging any learning activity as anything more than a brick in the wall—a separate, unrelated skill or piece of knowledge that will become useful for some purpose at some time in the future. Our experience suggests, however, that learning activities related to the ongoing realities of individual, family, and community life become powerful tools of learning.

At their finest, such learning experiences ultimately pose questions of meaning and identity that are at the heart of human experience. Both the context and the processes of knowledge production provide the opportunity for people to confront fundamental issues such as who am I?, in a personal, professional, or social sense. The way that learning can become deeply personal was articulated in many of our discussions and is epitomized by "the realization that there was some purpose [in our activity] that was more than just about 'research' or 'school' " (Rhonda). The power of storytelling that provided the basis for our narratives did not just relate to the knowledge that people produced, but derived from the connections of these accounts to our everyday lives, connections that became evident in the stories that we constructed about ourselves.

As we strove to articulate the significance of our experience we became aware that, like all human experience, our attempts to represent teaching must always be incomplete; that there could never be one right way to describe teaching, or one truth that could explain how teaching must necessarily be enacted. We grew more sensitive to the notion that our definitions and interpretations of such constructs as *teaching* and *learning* enable us to make sense of our teaching in ways that are illuminative and productive only when they are relevant to a particular cultural and historical context.

As we talked and wrote, we also became increasingly sensitive to the metaphors embedded in the language that we used to describe teaching and learning. We characterized our learning experience in terms like *the journey* as we tried to express the experience of self-discovery that appeared to be inherent in the process. This fact enabled us to understand the relevance of what we were learning to our everyday professional, public, and personal lives in a deeply personal way. Learning, we discovered, was not just about arriving at knowledge or wisdom, but was part of a journey that allowed conflicts to emerge; part of learning was to find ways to resolve these interpersonal, intrapersonal, professional, and intellectual conflicts.

Crises, we also discovered, are part of the dynamics of change. They do not have to be traumatic or epiphanic, but nevertheless require us to re-envision parts of our world to accommodate the experience before us; to work through the crises and resolve them as part of the learning processes. This approach to teaching focused as much on providing the skills and opportunities to seek answers as on the acquisition of information. To the extent that our learning became relevant to real-life issues in our everyday life, therefore, we became engaged and committed to the processes of acquiring knowledge. Good teaching, we therefore maintain, requires learning activities that have direct links to the everyday life of learners and requires the development of skills that enable teachers to resolve conflicts that emerge in productive learning contexts.

Relevant learning situates activities in real life, relates activities to real-life concerns, reveals the meanings that support customary ways of understanding events or doing things. Relevant learning allows people to tell stories of their lives, reveals new ways of understanding events, issues, and concerns, and reveals new ways of understanding self. It allows conflict to emerge, provides ways to resolve conflicts, and presents learning as unfinished, incomplete, and tentative.

TEACHING: REFLECTION AND CHANGE

As we reflected on the events that contrasted so dramatically with our usual experience of classroom environments, we became sensitive to the ways that the highly stylized routines of customary teaching practices place severe limits on the human potential for learning. What, then, do these events reveal about moving past these limitations, breaking through the boundaries of customary practice, and establishing more productive approaches to teaching? How can we reach past the ritualized conventions that inhibit learning and explore the full range of educational possibilities open to us?

Our experience suggests that really dramatic or revolutionary transformations are not necessary. Rather, by modifying and adapting current techniques and strategies and reframing the way we use materials and resources already at our disposal, we can dramatically increase the educational potential of classrooms, schools, and community learning environments.

In so doing, we may also need to vary our emphases and take a different slant on practices and procedures to instill a different set of values. In our class, for instance, achievement and competence were highly valued, but they were not defined in competitive terms. Grades did not signal a general sense of worth or status, but provided clear signals about specific strengths or weaknesses in performance. They reflected levels of competence that were amenable to change so that participants could upgrade their work to desired levels of proficiency through multiple trial and feedback opportunities.

In these circumstances, learning became "the thing" (or in Texan parlance, "th' thang!"). This emphasis was not accomplished immediately, however, and some valuable lessons emerged in the initial stages of the course as participants adjusted their customary ways of responding to a classroom environment. As Vicky's account so clearly demonstrated, people tend to respond to new circumstances according to known patterns of behavior, even when conditions have changed rather dramatically. They initially resist change or fail to realize the necessity of changing their behavior, as they incorporate new learnings into their social repertoire.

In our own context, the ability to see and respond to the educational possibilities open to us was catalyzed by the quality of the teaching–learning environment in which we worked. As the instructor transferred some of his power and enabled other participants to make significant decisions about their learning, he facilitated safe, active, and relevant learning processes that cultivated a sense of community. In these circumstances we were able to engage in learning experiences that not only illuminated the topics we studied, but enabled us to acquire the understanding, skill, and motivation to explore them further.

One outcome of these conditions was that class participants were not only able to engage in recurrent reflection on the "subject" we were studying, but were also moved to explore and interrogate their own learning processes. We suspect that if we could arrange for versions of this approach to learning to permeate school systems, students would learn how to deconstruct and reconstruct learning experiences themselves, so that by the time they completed primary school they would have accomplished the equivalent of a diploma of education.

By reflecting on what we have learned and exploring learning's relation to the agendas and experiences of our professional lives, we have been able to re-vision teaching–learning. Our new understandings are relevant and meaningful, not just as a grade or course requirement that can be checked off and forgotten, but as an illuminating way of understanding our own experience. Reflection in a learning community, therefore, enables us to accomplish new meanings that are the necessary precursor to change.

TEACHING IN CONTEXT: THEORY
AND RESEARCH IN EDUCATION

The issues in this text have been the subject of debate among scholars and practitioners for many years. Our own experiences revealed how deeply ingrained, traditional practices of teaching and learning are so pervasive that they are often treated as unremarkable, even by those most vehemently critical of current educational arrangements. This is as true for university-based scholars that have traditionally critiqued educational life as for any other set of practitioners.

Consequently, a serious problem facing many university educators and other professional practitioners is the lack of congruence between their espoused philosophies and their professional practice. Although recent developments in postmodern, feminist, and critical theory have radically altered the philosophical and ideological landscape, teaching and research in schools and universities still embody very traditional philosophical and theoretical teaching–learning practices. The constructivist, interpretive, and relativist philosophies now advocated in many educational and professional circles are consistently undermined by traditional approaches to pedagogy and inquiry that implicitly promote transmission models of learning and positivistic methods of knowledge acquisition. There is a dearth of literature that demonstrates how these emerging theoretical and philosophical perspectives can be enacted in practice.

The major themes of this book seek to break the boundaries of traditional practice and to enrich the understanding of practitioners who wish to enact a constructivist pedagogy and an interpretive approach to learning and inquiry. A fundamental proposition embedded in both constructivist pedagogy and interpretive inquiry is that teachers and researchers relinquish their stance of superiority and objectivity to collaborate with students and other "subjects" to reconfigure the processes of learning and inquiry.

Our diverse accounts of a community-based, reflective, action-oriented approach to teaching and research show how we were able to confront many fundamental philosophical and practical issues as we challenged the assumptions embedded in our teaching and learning practices. We learned of the need to integrate formal learning requirements with the multiple demands of our intellectual, professional, and personal lives and to extend our understanding of teaching. In the process we were also able to explore many critical issues that confront people in their daily lives in any educational institution. The academic, we discovered, is not separate from the everyday, and we were often confounded by the ways that truly educational experiences were based on assumptions that continued to shape the consciousness of our educational life. Our private experiences in our research methods class revealed some deeply held and unacknowledged assumptions that still dominate the educational life of schools and other educational settings.

FOUNDATIONS OF TRADITIONAL PRACTICE

The following sections explore some of these major assumptions embedded in everyday perceptions of teaching and demonstrate how institutionally accepted procedures embody a set of presuppositions that work to maintain traditional teaching practices and reinscribe a system of meanings that is at odds with contemporary thought. The power of these assumptions may be seen in the routines and practices that still permeate all levels of institutional life.

Assumption 1: The Nature of Knowledge

When Lois said that "conventional instruction is based on the premise that knowledge can be transmitted," and Shelia said that "our system of schooling perpetuates [the view of] teacher as transmitter of knowledge," they signaled a pervasive view of knowledge. This rarely challenged perspective signifies that the purpose of schools is to teach a fixed body of knowledge representing truths to be learned by "the student." Knowledge is deemed to be fixed insofar as it represents the reality of the world, and learning is assumed to be a function of the ability and willingness of "the student" to acquire this knowledge.

None of these assumptions, however, holds up to close scrutiny. Even within the physical sciences the process of describing nature is now acknowledged to be affected by both the observer and the means of observation. When we observe something, we change it, and we structure our vision of the natural universe both according to predetermined definitions of this reality and to our methods of observation (Davies & Gribbin, 1991). Knowledge about the physical universe is based on constructs and understandings that have proven useful for describing its immense complexity. Newtonian "laws," based on constructs like *gravity* and force, are useful ways of describing the operation of the physical universe, so useful, in fact, that they are more than adequate to enable us to send a rocket to the moon. As precise descriptions of cosmic space or the microcosmic world of particle physics, however, Newton's laws are inadequate and have been superseded by modern formulations that include Einstein's theories of relativity and Bohr's and other physicists' versions of quantum mechanics.

In the social world, the notion of a fixed universe and neutral knowledge is even more difficult to sustain. In recent times scholars have become increasingly sensitive to the perspective that human beings create the universes in which they live according to perceptions and ways of responding that come from their own experiences in particular social and cultural contexts. Human beings create their social worlds in a general sense and construct and reconstruct these worlds in an ongoing way as they engage in their day-to-day activities and interactions.

What we *know* is not facts or descriptions of the way things really are; we know the ways of viewing the world or of interpreting a situation generally accepted by people in a particular social context. What is known is less a process of discovery than a process of agreement, whereby people come to learn or accept one definition, description, or interpretation of the situation or phenomenon as adequate or useful for the particular purpose and context in which they are engaged.

Even in the physical sciences, *discoveries*—definitions or interpretations that are firmly grounded in and consonant with rigorous observation—often take some time to be accepted as truth or reality by the scientific community; a new version of events or phenomena is not always immediately taken up. The notion of *oxygen* as an entity took some time to replace *phlogiston* as an explanation for the phenomenon now called oxidation. Darwin's ideas of evolution roused people to furor or ridicule when he published them and are rejected by some even today.

In the social world, it is even more difficult to have a particular way of viewing or describing the world accepted as truth. In the United States and Australia, history texts usually refer to these countries as having been settled rather than invaded, and the current debates in many U.S. school districts as to the rightness of evolutionary versus creationist theories have even entered the domain of the presidential elections. The production of knowledge is a more political event than people imagine.

The descriptions and explanations about what teaching is, or what constitutes good teaching practice cannot be seen as facts or truth; the facts chosen and the truth that is accepted only make sense to people who accept the veracity of the specific cultural context from which these truths are derived. People teach not truths or facts but curriculum content that has been selected as being relevant to particular educational purposes.

Assumption 2: How Knowledge is Acquired

The perspective in which teaching is seen as a process of transmitting knowledge about the real world leads directly to assumptions of the ways in which people can come to know about the world. Teaching becomes a process of transmitting that which is known—facts, truth, descriptions of reality—or a process of developing skills that enable people to acquire these facts and truths—reading, writing, math.

Although educational curricula include such objectives as critical thinking, analysis, and synthesis, most teachers place far more emphasis on the acquisition of knowledge—pre-existing formulations about reality—than to analytic, critical, or creative skills that enable students to critique, redefine, or deny the knowledge given to them. Education tends to evolve around processes that ensure that students learn the content of the curriculum, rather than around teaching–learning processes that enable students to work critically and creatively on content.

It is far easier to test a fixed content: Most tests are based on recall of material that is relatively easily presented in written form or on the application of formulas to problems of known form and structure. Both forms are comparatively easy to evaluate. When a teacher marks a test she or he usually has the correct answers on record, and student performance is judged by the extent to which answers are similar to those of the teacher. Not only is this focus on content or the application of formulas easy to evaluate, but it is also simple to justify. Students are either able to recall and record the information or apply the formulas, or they are not. Creative and analytic skills, on the other hand, are far more difficult to test and even more difficult to justify. Degrees of difficulty, creativity, and critique do not necessarily fit the precise formulations required by a school grading system.

Understanding that knowledge is not about ultimate truths or fixed reality changes the way people come to know about the physical and social universe. Teachers then take the stance that says, in effect, "Here is a way of describing the world that people including experts, agree is useful," rather than one that says, "Here is the way things are." The act of learning is less certain, when students acquire knowledge that is useful and that they are free to accept or reject, rather than knowledge that determines the way they or the world *must* be. In these conditions, students must be able to understand, or make sense of what they are learning; learning must be meaningful in terms that relate to people's current experiences and understandings.

The formulations of cognitive psychology are useful here. Psychology suggests that people learn best that which fits pre-existing knowledge. Difficulties occur where a person cannot make connections between what is to be learned and what is already known. This rather obvious feature of educational life is often ignored entirely in schools, despite well-established procedures for "starting where the child is," or in technical terms, for administering a pretest to identify the point of departure for a learning process or lesson. In practice, teachers skate past this requirement to move through the material prescribed in the curriculum. The imperative to "cover the content of the curriculum" impels them to continue presenting content with judicious speed, regardless of whether students are able to assimilate that material in any meaningful way.

> I can still remember the agony of the boring hours I spent in high school history classes learning about Germany in the 19th and early 20th centuries. I have flashes and glimpses of names, dates, and events that, I was told, were very significant in world history. The significance, however, along with most of the details of the information related to this period, eluded me. As I grew up in a post-World War II era, when many families were without fathers or uncles or when sepia-colored photographs on walls of rooms showed long lost friends and relatives, the significance of this period could easily have been linked to events that had an enormous impact on the lives of people in my neighborhood. These links were never made.

Ultimately, therefore, learning can be envisaged as making meaning: a process that takes that which is meaningful in a learner's life as the link to new knowledge. Teaching may also be envisaged as an art, craft, or process that provides the conditions or activities to enable new meaning to be incorporated into a person's "stock of knowledge." If teaching–learning is seen as meaning-making, the processes of education are transformed. No longer are they tied to a fixed body of knowledge to which students can attach little meaning and that therefore require increasingly virile external motivation—"You'll never get a decent job if you don't pass these exams!" Teaching is no longer bound by curriculum content that remains unconnected to students' experiences and life agendas. Rather, teaching is a process that requires teachers to enter the worlds of students; to understand the experiences, histories, and systems of meaning that make up their life worlds; and to formulate teaching–learning processes that use these experiences and meanings as the basis for new learning.

Teaching thus becomes more than just the mechanical transmission of predefined knowledge that requires teachers to know the truths and facts and the ways of communicating them. It becomes a creative and engaging profession that taps into the energy of people's lives. In these circumstances, teachers become learners and students become teachers. Teachers must learn, at least to some extent, about the life-worlds of students and learners must provide teachers with an understanding of the experiences, agendas, and meanings that makeup their life-world.

These ideas are not strange to experienced, successful practitioners, who recognize the importance of relationships and know the joy that comes with properly attuned associations with their students. Many, however, also recognize the difficulty of maintaining this quality in their teaching lives. The sheer number of people involved and the profusion of personal transactions required in any classroom are likely to overwhelm the capabilities of the most dedicated teacher, especially in situations where students have been damaged by the social environment. Previous sections of this book provide some indication of the practical ways that teachers can deal with these connections, interactions, and activities, through teaching–learning processes that make use of all the people-power available in the context. These ways of dealing with teaching may involve changing in the structure of classroom environments, reorganizing of the curriculum, and modifying power relationships in the class setting.

Assumption 3: What Is Worth Knowing?
The Politics of Knowledge

One event that was most remarked on by participants in this study was the way that the instructor gave up his power to define the content of the class syllabus. Few, if any, students had previous experience of a "negotiated curriculum" and were nonplussed, some to the point of distress, at the thought that they were responsible for helping to define what they were to learn. Kenneth noted that "when a professor decides that power in the classroom should be shared with other participants and not remain monopolized by the teacher, he creates a context few students have experienced in educational settings" and that "class members were amazed and pleasantly impressed when their wishes about course content were treated as if they were significant." In the boundaries prescribed by the various controlling bodies—school administrations, school boards, state departments—teachers have the authority and power to define what is taught and learned in their class. They represent, in other words, one level in a chain of authority and control that governs the knowledge to be taught and learned in the school. Knowledge in school contexts, we therefore discover, is politically defined.

In the last decade people have become increasingly sensitive to the ways that politics are embedded in almost all aspects of school life. I am not referring to party politics in this instance, but to the ways by which one person or group is able to control or dominate other people's lives by controlling the knowledge on which school life is based. These processes can be thought of in terms of the micropolitics of everyday life. Most social interactions entail power differentials that allow the version of one person or group to be accepted as correct or that allow one person's or group's events and activities to be acted out according to their wishes or desires. In modern industrial society, for instance, it is accepted that parents be able require their children to behave correctly; older siblings typically "boss" their younger brothers and sisters; children are usually expected to obey the wishes of adults.

In these instances, as in other parts of social life, the right to dominate another is not necessarily accepted by all parties; studies have shown that in all social situations some negotiation takes place to establish the "rules" of the particular interaction. Even in classrooms or prisons, where teachers or wardens have overriding powers of coercion, the day-to-day life of the institution cannot proceed without the acquiescence of students or prisoners. Though images of prisoner and student strikes may come to mind, the negotiation process in everyday interaction in these environments is much more subtle. Students may exhibit their independence by being slow to give the teacher their attention, by walking sluggishly to their assigned places, by refusing to look at the teacher when he or she speaks, or by engaging in any number of delaying or denying behaviors. Experienced teachers have no difficulty in recognizing the multitude of ways that students are able to resist the imposition of a teacher's power, and it is likely that much of the stress in teaching arises from the struggle to maintain the system of dominance.

In a variety of ways, those with authority or sanctioning powers can work to impose their will on others. This fact is especially obvious in hierarchical environments such as schools, where superintendents are superior to and have power over principals, who are superior to senior teachers or department heads, who in turn have authority over classroom teachers, who have extensive authority to order the lives of their students.

The result of this imposed system of authority is that certain groups of people can disproportionately influence the points of view, priorities, and agendas that determine school life. Though they pay homage to a democratic ideology, most school systems have evolved in ways that are intrinsically authoritarian. The structure and content of a school curriculum—what is to be learned and how it is to be learned—usually result from quite limited consultation among curriculum experts and people who are relatively senior in the established order. The same is true in classrooms, where teachers have the authority, within the boundaries of mandated curricula and school regulations, to determine almost all aspects of classroom life—who learns what, how, when, and where.

This phenomenon of those high in the educational hierarchy formulating rules, regulations, organization, and curricula imposed on those below them was discussed in general terms by Foucault (1972). Unlike conflict theorists who, in Marxist vein, tend to define power in macrosocial terms, Foucault urged rethinking the nature of power imposed on people. According to Harvey (1989), Foucault broke with the notion that power is located in macrosystems like the state, and emphasized an ascending analysis beginning with infinitesimal mechanisms of power and control implicit in day-to-day social and institutional lives. He suggested that the techniques and tactics through which power is imposed at the local level may be extended to ever more general mechanisms that are eventually manifested in general or global systems of domination. He proposed that: "close scrutiny of the micro-politics of power relations in different localities, contexts, and social situations shows how there is an intimate relationship between the systems of knowledge that codify techniques and practices within particular local contexts" (1989, p. 45) and the systems of social control that enable some groups to dominate the lives of others.

This formulation suggests that power, often described as "the system," with implications that it is out of reach or control, is created and recreated in the lives of people through their everyday interactions and the ordinary processes of organizational and institutional life. One the basis of Foucault's ideas, universities, and schools may be seen as sites where a dispersed and piecemeal organization of power is built up independent of any systematic strategy of class domination. What happens at each site cannot be understood by appeal to any systematic strategy of class domination, only by localized impositions of power and control.

To put it bluntly, school superintendents, principals, and teachers do not impose their power on people in ways that are dictated by the state. Though they are, to a greater or lesser extent, able to dominate people's lives through the power invested in them by the state, they do so according to inclinations and propensities that ultimately derive from their own social histories and experiences. Teachers may choose to be dramatically democratic or rigidly authoritarian in their own classrooms, and they are able to enact varying approaches to their professional life according to the micropolitics that operate in their particular school or community. Despite perceptions that they are often prisoners of the system, they have great flexibility to apply any policy or program they see fit. Teachers need not assume that the system or big brother has control over their professional lives. As Foucault suggested, teachers can eliminate the "fascism in our heads"—the notion that authority *must* be obeyed—by exploring and building upon the open qualities of human discourse, thereby intervening in the way that knowledge is produced or social life is organized in particular local sites.

Foucault is but one of a generation of writers and theorists who, in recent decades, have pointed out the politics inherent in the everyday professional and public world. These writers, rather than endorsing current organizational logic and accepted practices, maintain that all features of social life are open to critique. They highlight the micropolitics of everyday life and accentuate the ephemeral, transitory nature of social worlds.

Lyotard (1984) and Derrida (1976), for instance, have viewed social life as constructed from texts made up of language that can be manipulated, transformed, organized, and reconstructed. A text may be defined as any ideas that determine how social life is described or ordered. Lyotard suggested that social life cannot be described in any definite or deterministic way and pictured the social world as made up of an indeterminate number of flexible networks of language games, each relevant to a particular context. People, he proposed, resort to quite different codes—relevant, presumably, to a particular language game—according to the situation in which they find themselves.

In this dispersed heterogeneity of language games, people struggle to find meaning and order. Those in bureaucratic organizations tend to impose a hierarchical order and a set of meanings that specify what is and is not admissible in their realm of authority. As Fish (1980) pointed out, "interpretive communities" made up of producers and consumers of particular types of knowledge—texts—mutually control what they consider to be valid knowledge in their domain. Where the validity of this knowledge is not accepted by actors in the domain, struggle occurs. Teachers who have experienced troublesome classes or students who are difficult to control recognize the validity of this formulation. Students who do not accept the validity of the texts imposed on them—the authority of a particular teacher, the worth of some part of the curriculum—resist in a variety of ways.

The problem with texts, however, goes much deeper. Derrida presented a view of social life that reveals the problems in any attempt to impose one set of rules or regulations on professional activities. He suggested that social or cultural life is a series of texts that intersect with other texts. To speak or write about these texts—rules, regulations, organization, curricula, timetables—conveys unintended meanings. Those who read or hear these texts do so according to ways of interpreting phenomena which incorporate an infinite variety of meanings and associations related to their own experiences. Derrida wrote that neither "reader" nor "writer" of these social and cultural texts can master them; can understand precisely either what they say or what they mean. Each person has a unique set of lenses and filters that "color" his or her world.

From this perspective, negotiation in social life becomes even more important. Not only must people negotiate with others to ensure that everyone's interests are met, but they must negotiate the very set of meanings on which the activities are based. The inability or unwillingness to negotiate meaning, I believe, creates many problems in our school systems. Teachers and principals tend to operate on the basis of an assumed fixed body of knowledge and a fixed set of rules or understandings about the way things "should" work. When they meet students who do not operate according to these texts, teachers tend to look for ways to impose these texts, rather than to understand why and how the texts might have meaning in the lives of the students.

I have known many parents, whose children were in trouble or were not doing well scholastically, who refused to cooperate with school authorities to remedy the problem. Teachers and principals complain of parents who "aren't interested in their children's education"; who refuse "even to come to the school" or to participate in programs designed to help their children. What these teachers fail to appreciate is the long history of these parents' experiences with schools, whose teachers and principals often represent a distasteful, discomfiting, or threatening authority. I have seen such parents, uncomfortably dressed in clothing that is foreign to their everyday attire, sweating as they fought to interact with a teacher or principal, fear evident in both their voices and their nonverbal communication. The set of meanings inherent in their lack of participation in school life is quite evident to me, but eludes school staff who envision their schools as benign educational sites and their activity as helpful and concerned.

The power of teachers to define what is to be learned in a classroom and to define the rules and regulations that govern the way it is to be learned is strongly imbued, almost preordained, in the cultural ethos. As our study indicated, however, significant benefits can be acquired by sharing power. When students and other stakeholders realize that they have the right to govern aspects of their own learning, they are likely, if the process is handled sensitively, to realize the responsibility that goes with power. A focus on the politics of teaching and learning does not point only to the problems of power, but also to the potential rewards gained from acknowledging these dimensions of educational life. As Vicky pointed out, however, changes in power relations do not come easily and are not automatically translated into democratic processes. Existing structures—the commonly accepted "right ways" of doing things—may reinscribe themselves in different form. Reorientations in the use of power must be subjected to critical reflection and repair. Teaching is, ultimately, a political activity.

Assumption 4: Learning as a Technical Process: The Politics of Teaching

A corollary of the assumption that students learn a fixed body of truths in schools is the assumption that learning is essentially a technical process. When Kenneth and Patricia spoke of the efficacy of a "community of learners," they were challenging the common wisdom that learning is essentially an individual process. Vast sums have been spent on educational research in the last few decades to determine how humans learn, with the intent to find ways to ensure that all students in schools learn to the full extent of their abilities. Two driving forces behind this push to understand individual learning are the significant discrepancies in the educational performances of different racial, ethnic, and class groups and the desire to find the technical means to ensure that learning discrepancies are overcome.

This expenditure has failed to produce any significant teaching–learning techniques that make a perceptible difference to the educational performance of groups who have traditionally fared poorly in the scholastic arena. Special educational programs, projects and courses, innovative teaching and learning techniques, culturally appropriate curricula, and a whole range of interventions in classrooms and schools have failed to significantly change the overall school performance of children in these groups.

Views of teaching tend to be transmitted from generation to generation of teachers, so that those who have been successful in the school system reinscribe the practices they perceive as the source of their success. As Terresa wrote in her biographical account, experienced teachers often place great pressure on new teachers to enact forms of instruction that are consonant with their own practices:

> I became able to stand my ground when confronted by the bureaucrats who arrived at my door with the truth carved in curriculum documents of stone. My professional life fluctuated between the incredible power and excitement of my classroom … as I watched children learn in ways perceived to be blasphemous and incredible frustration and mounting anger at my professional peers, who believed they had discovered the truth about ways to teach children and were ordering me to be faithful to the canon.

The arguments made in the previous chapters help to clarify the reasons that teachers may refuse to change. The texts of school life—curricula, language, forms of organization, mores, rules, and regulations that make up the life-world of the school—are derived from the experiences of teachers, principals, school boards; people with radically different experiences encounter an alien educational context, especially when alienation from a socially dominant group is an ongoing part of learners' consciousness of everyday life.

Critical theorists have clearly described the forces at work in many schools in socially and culturally diverse contexts (e.g., Aronowitz & Giroux, 1987; McLaren, 1989). Their accounts of school life have shown the extent of divisions between social groups and the very real barriers that inhibit learning. Critical theory started from Focault's assumption that knowledge is not neutral but is socially constructed, culturally mediated, and historically situated. This perspective has no ultimate truth; what is accepted as truth results from the ability of one social group to determine what can be said and who can say it. Some truths have precedence over others because one group can privilege its own perspective over others, to allow what it considers meritorious or important to dominate the texts that govern the conduct and operation of school life. This group can impose its beliefs and values on a school systems—curricula, rules, regulations, pedagogical processes—so that the skills and understandings that emerge from its own social history dominate the operation of the school.

The discourses that govern school life can be understood as all the regulated statements that make up the minutia of school life. These statements govern what can be said or done and the status of any set of behaviors or knowledge. This process is insidiously maintained with the consent of those who are likely to benefit least. Hegemonic practices—those that make up the everyday, accepted processes and contents of school life—enable dominant groups to maintain the system as it is because these practices are accepted as legitimate, right, or good, even by those who find them alien. Children who either consciously or unconsciously resist the dictates of an alien culture are as likely to be critical of themselves or to be criticized by their friends and family as they are to be critical of the "rules" that they have broken.

Increasingly, however, parents of these children are criticizing the outcomes of their children's schooling and pointing to racism or ethnocentric bias as primary causes of school failure. What few can articulate, however, is the depth or extent of this bias. Teachers may have negative feelings toward children because of their race or ethnicity, but more important the children are resisting the culturally alien practices and content that are deeply embedded in the texture of classroom and school life. A focus on any one aspect of school tends to trivialize the complexity and multiplicity of interwoven threads of cultural life that are played out day by day as children interact with teachers, classes, the curriculum and the school in terms of their language, behavior, proxemics, dress, attitudes, beliefs, assumptions, perspectives, interpretations.

If learning is a technical process, learners do not carry out learning tasks in a social and cultural vacuum. The quality of the cultural air affects childrens' performances as surely as the air affects an athlete who practices at sea level and competes at high altitudes. Steps to bring school environments in harmony to students' cultural environments are likely to be inadequate without considerable cultural learning on the part of those who control the texts of school life. They must become acclimatized to the cultural air of their students, a process that requires them to experience an appropriate cultural atmosphere rather than to read books about the effects of atmosphere.

In other contexts I have written of ways in which schooling might be transformed by integrating the cultural texts that make up children's lifeworlds. Teachers and principals need not throw away all they have learned or deny the very real benefit of the knowledge and professional skills that they have acquired during their training and professional experience. Their experiences and professional skills, however, should become resources that are amenable to the cultures of the learners; and these cultures should play a significant role in determining the forms and contents of their school experience—curriculum content, learning strategies, school and classroom organization, rules and regulations.

Learning thus becomes not merely a technical process that entails manipulation of individual learners and the content being taught, but a social process that is always carried out in a cultural context deeply infused with cultural forms and meanings. The task for today's educators is to find the ways and means to use the resources embodied in learners cultural contexts, to enact the potentials in the social lives of all cultural groups that inhabit these contexts, and to formulate approaches that enact the joy of inquiry and discovery that are natural parts of truly educational experiences.

In my research classes, I have often told the story of Yiyili School. Tired of sending their children away at a very early age to attend school in a town hundreds of miles distant, parents at this small desert Aboriginal community combined their meager economic resources to hire a teacher and build a boughshed classroom for their children. For many months they planned and organized every aspect of the operation of the school with the teacher, then helped her on a day-to-day basis to teach their children. This school, despite the extreme poverty of its resources, was one of the most effective schools for Aboriginal students that I have seen. The exuberance and energy of the children, the extent to which they focused on their schoolwork, and the easy, Aboriginal-oriented atmosphere of the classroom were in stark contrast to the rigid, alien—from an Aboriginal perspective—environments typical of many schools in the region. Yiyili, the people knew, was their school. They owned it in many real ways. Not only did they legally own the school, but they owned it culturally insofar as the ongoing operation of the school was infused with the presence, demeanor, and etiquettes of Aboriginal life. The school made sense in terms of everyday cultural life, including these perspectives and orientations, purposes and processes that made up their life-worlds. They were at home in their school.

BREAKING THE BOUNDARIES: EXPLORING
TERRITORIES OF PRINCIPLE AND VALUE

Overemphasizing the use of science and technology to understand the nature of teaching or to explain its problems risks losing sight of cultural, value-laden aspects of human experience. Technical explanations are only effective as a means of understanding when integrated with human experience that might be called spiritual or cultural. As Persig (1974) wrote: "The Buddha, the Godhead, resides quite as comfortably in the circuits of a digital computer or the gears of a cycle transmission as he does in the top of the mountain or in the petals of a flower."

I use words like *spiritual* with hesitation; such words are often associated with institutionalized religion in ways that provide too narrow a frame of reference for current purposes. In previous works I have talked of "life-enhancing experience," but recent consultations with widely divergent groups of

Aboriginal people have led me to the word *spirituality* to describe the particular aspect of life that seems to relate to the human experience and to define the unique quality of our species. I recently wrote by email to the authors contributing to this book:

> I think about the work that I've done to put new graduate programs together, talking with Aboriginal people about the things they'd like, the things that they need to learn.
>
> For this group, as I first heard them, social justice loomed clearly an essential ingredient of a program of learning. "What can we, the most impoverished and marginalized people in Australia, learn that will enable us to gain social justice; to improve the conditions in which we live, including our health standards, our education, our housing, the way we are treated by the criminal justice system, and so on?" This message is not to be denied and is to be taken most seriously in any program that is meant to be educational for Aboriginal people.
>
> Then, as I listened further, they started to speak, first in hesitant words and phrases, then in increasingly clear and articulate voices, about the need to celebrate who they are and what they are. They spoke of identity and spirituality … in the context of the broad sweep of humanity that recognized the fundamental strength deeply embedded in their cultural experience.
>
> Spirituality! I started to think about the spirit in people; the force to stand up in the world in a strong and certain way; the vitality and energy to dance and sing, to let our spirits soar, to be with people in ways that celebrate our togetherness, our common unity.
>
> I know that the parts of my life that really mean something to me are those that enable me to work with people in ways that set our spirits free. There is something special, and yet so very ordinary, when the work that I do with people is personalized, rather than technical or mechanical; when I know that I am working with their spirit and their soul, so that they learn in ways that enhance their feelings of being alive. Really alive.
>
> So I ask myself, "What does that mean for you, as an educator, Ernie?" And I know that when I teach and people acquire skills and knowledge that will be useful in their lives, that the relationship that I have with them, and the relationship that they have with these knowledges and skills are central ingredients in the process. If I am out of sync with the people, if I have a damaged relationships with them, or if what I am teaching them or the way I am teaching damages their spirit, then what is the good of it?
>
> So, ultimately, I think to myself, teaching is an act of love. Not a romanticized love; not something that speaks of deeply intimate, emotional ties; but an attitude of caring and togetherness that, maybe, is about a community of souls. Education is spiritual work.

I am wary of using these words because they have often been cheapened and twisted, but they are, I think, a very ordinary part of life that brings me back to what I, as an educator, am about. If I focus merely on the technical and mechanical aspects of teaching and learning, I lose my self in the process. If I valorize the physical and material aspects of what I am teaching and what my students are learning, then I leave a central ingredient out of the process.

As people focus on the technical aspects of teaching they also need to be clear about these other dimensions of human activity that are necessarily part of lived experience—the philosophical principles and cultural values inherent in teaching–learning processes. To neglect these principles and values risks providing a soulless, disembodied education with little nourishment for the humanity of those we aspire to educate.

The reform of teaching practices is a central theme that permeates the literature on educational reform. Despite continuing and large-scale efforts to reform teaching and teacher training, however, Fuhrman (1995), commenting on an article by Kirst (1995), reported on the inability of categorical programs of reform to affect the deep structure of teaching and learning. Part of this deep structure lies in the domain of meaning—the ways that people conceptualize, theorize, or represent teaching and learning. This, we have suggested, explains why customary practices are continually reproduced in the profession and in schools and classrooms. The failure of reform efforts can also be attributed to the dominance of scientific-technical representations of teaching and learning that focus on relatively superficial aspects. We concur with Alexander, Murphy, and Woods (1996) that those responsible for innovation do not have a rich understanding of these innovations that lead to superficial solutions to complex problems.

Other conceptions of teaching are available. A recent genre of scholarship, emanating largely from postmodern, feminist, and critical theoretical traditions, but including other philosophically traditional perspectives, provides an impetus to broaden the way people conceptualize teaching and offers the necessary conceptual base for a change in teaching practices. Hicks (1995), for instance, suggested the need to take an interpretive stance in the exploration of teaching and learning, Acker (1995) spoke to a body of work that reclaims women's traditional qualities, and Casey (1995) described several strands of narrative research that "deliberately defies the forces of alienation, anomie, annihilation, authoritarianism, fragmentation, commodification, depreciation, and dispossession" (p. 213). Thus far, however, the literature appears to have little impact on the life of schools. Education, it seems, still operates according to traditional modes of teaching and learning and is still largely examined in frameworks that, responsive to issues of accountability and economic rationalism, emphasize technical, scientific, and bureaucratic perspectives.

In their book *Responsive Teaching*, Bowers and Flinders (1990) discussed the problem of relying solely on constructions of teaching that focus on its technical functions and operations. They suggested that teachers need to develop a balanced perspective that includes the empowering potential of the educational process; a classroom environment that facilitates educationally significant communication; and fidelity to students that involves caring for them as people as well as for the quality of relationships among class participants.

Quoting Noddings (1986), Bowers and Flinders (1990) proposed that when teachers act as models of caring they also "model a host of other desirable qualities: meticulous preparation, lively presentation, critical thinking, appreciative listening, constructive evaluation, genuine curiosity" (Noddings, 1986, p. 503).

Bowers and Flinders (1990) argued for an approach to teaching that looks past the narrow boundaries of competitive self-interest, the motivating force of many classroom activities, to a fuller vision that fosters richly educative learning processes. Their intent was to portray teaching in terms of outcomes providing learners with a full sense of their place in the social and physical order, a sense to help them transform their social environment. Our experience of a teaching–learning environment characterized by reflective, community-based learning processes suggested that such outcomes are possible. Levels of awareness that greatly enhanced our vision of the structures and practices of teaching at the center of our professional lives emerged in the class. As Rhonda said in her final interview:

> We're much more aware. We're not so definite or absolute anymore in who we are—in a productive, good way. We're able to absorb so much more when we don't deflect what comes our way. We went through a process of evolution … went in with preconceived notions of school, but became aware of different life perspectives [and] realities. We started from one point, became different people, and have continued to evolve as we tried to recreate the learning experience. We're different teachers for it.

Our new visions of teaching complement those presented by people like Aoki (1992) and Van Manen (Brown, 1992), who wrote of the need to engage ways of thinking about teaching that are not too closely directed by narrowly product-oriented outcomes such as scores or grades. We would likewise concur with Bowers and Flinders (1990) when they suggested the need to engage the full potential of an educational environment and cast the products of teaching in the context of the existential well-being of individuals and the broad ecology in which humans act out their lives. We agree with them when they suggested that educators like Hunter (1986) and Sprick (1986), who focused on the technical aspects of teaching, provided a vision that is by no means complete. As we have demonstrated, teaching encompasses a range of human experiences, attributes, responses, and purposes that need to be accommodated in teaching–learning contexts.

It is also necessary to accommodate an expanded vision of the outcomes that legitimately emerge from sound teaching–learning processes. Meaningful learning, we suggest, can sometimes be truly epiphanic and transform the lives of learners by giving them a greater awareness of their experiences and engaging their commitment in and ownership of the learning process. The terms that we used to characterize our own learning experiences included *evolution, transformation, change,* and *development* that "blew out [the] dimensions of the knowledge creation process." We were able to crystalize and clarify our thinking in ways that inspired us to keep working toward increasing clarity and crystallization.

We also became more sensitive to the different types of learning that were possible and to the multidimensional nature of the learning process. Where our previous experience enmeshed us in visions of learning that focused on the acquisition of a fixed body of knowledge, we came to see that learning could encompass processes that were nonlinear, ongoing, reflective, reflexive—turning back on themselves and spiralling outward. Meaning-making processes of learning and discovery that enabled us to formulate rigorous and complex explanations of the social world could not be encapsulated in mechanical, linear, technical approaches commonly advocated in much literature on teaching. The linear or technical is not wrong, merely more suited to some forms of learning than to others. By engaging a broad perspective of teaching and learning, we open up possibilities for the creation of rich educational processes that extend the learning process.

The experience has been more than a philosophical transformation, however. It enabled us to reinterpret our experiences to improve the match between our beliefs and our practices. Reflective, community-based, inquiry-oriented learning experiences not only provided an impetus for a strong change from within, a paradigm shift that provided a new view of our selves and the world; it also led to the desire to re-enact or reproduce what we had learned in our professional practice. All of us have, in some way, instituted changes in our practice that reflect our new visions of teaching and learning.

But the results of our experience go deeper; the depth and extent of our learning struck at the very heart of our experiences of our selves. In our final conversations, Vicky talked of the personal issues that emerged from the processes of reflection and dialogue. Terresa expressed corresponding ideas that suggested that our inquiry processes enabled people to pose questions and listen to others' questions and "helped us deconstruct our own thinking about who we *really* are; to question, in fact our very identity, … as we became able to see more clearly our selves as products of our socialization." As Lois suggested, the intimacy of the environment made it possible to share ourselves in ways that, for her, made the experience more human than usual.

Readers may question whether teaching–learning processes engaged by senior educators are suited to school classroom environments. There is, after all, a substantial difference between doctoral studies and the life of most school classrooms. Shelia's experience indicated that the teaching–learning processes we describe are productive at the high-school level. As students in her group engaged processes of reflective inquiry and became researchers in their own right, their views of their school and their communities were transformed. Discussions related to their own observations revealed penetrating insights into the close connections between community and school, a level of understanding that would be difficult to acquire through a disembodied learning process that provided objective knowledge. As one of them commented, "Involvement in the ethnography project helped me to realize the complex diversity in human relations."

On the basis of these and similar experiences elsewhere, we suspect that the teaching–learning processes revealed in our accounts would function successfully even with young children. Moreover, we believe that these processes are sufficiently powerful to sustain themselves over time. A synergism, described in our final discussions as an ongoing process, produced a ripple effect in people's lives that keeps spreading and suggests the evolution of life-long learning. The evolving dimensions of this process are evidenced by the subtitles that have appeared from time to time as each step in the journey has revealed other paths and directions—"Stringing Along with Stringer" and "The Never-Ending Story!"

There is also a political dimension to our reconstruction of teaching. The honesty and openness that became possible in this community-oriented learning environment was empowering at many levels. We were able to experience the feeling of energy generated when we all became involved in the processes of decision making, when nobody's voice was silenced, and when our collective voices were engaged in determining the nature and direction of our learning. We became aware of the power generated by a new set of ideas—a new paradigm—that not only revealed the nature, type, and context of cultural boundaries in our learning environment, but provided clear ideas about how these boundaries might be reconfigured: what change was needed and how the change might be accomplished. Not only were we able to retheorize our worlds but to engage the new ways of seeing as changes in our practice and, more broadly, in our professional and private lives. By seeing the world in new ways, we were also able to understand what changes to make in the way we acted. This praxis, the direct marriage between thought and action, was one of the most power-ful aspects of our experience.

COMMUNITY-BASED LEARNING: TOWARD
AN EXTENDED VISION OF EFFECTIVE TEACHING

The accounts that we have presented speak clearly, sometimes exuberantly, of the qualities of a teaching–learning experience that we experienced as personally and professionally enhancing. The following section draws the threads of these accounts together and weaves them into a conceptual scaffolding that provides, in summary form, a typification of the key features of an enhanced teaching–learning context. Professional practice might be enhanced if the characteristics and qualities that we delineate were incorporated into learning and research activities in classrooms, schools, organizations, and communities.

PRINCIPLES

Community—collaboration, cooperation, consensus.
Knowledge—open-ended, evolving, creative, critiquing.
Authenticity—relevant, contextualized (meaningful in learners' contexts).

STRUCTURES

Relationships—supportive, tolerant, cooperative.
Decision making—participatory, consensual.
Setting—safe, comfortable, flexible, distraction-free.

PROCESSES

Teaching—planned, facilitative, goal-directed, student-centered, modeling, responsive, spontaneous, open, supportive, collegial, participatory, trusting.

Learning Activities—diverse: talking (presenting), explaining, discussing, recounting, analyzing, deconstructing, constructing, reading, modeling, interviewing, role-playing, journaling, drawing, photographing, recording, videoing, enacting, simulating, practicing, trialing.

Quality of Learning Experiences—ongoing, integrated, active, authentic, collaborative, structured, revealing, trusting.

Curriculum—negotiated, emergent, relevant, diverse, exploratory.

Outcomes—type: knowledge, meaning, understanding, skills; quality: practical, relevant, multi-faceted (thinking, feeling, doing), success-oriented, revelatory, illuminatory.

How, then, can readers use these ideas and integrate them into their own professional repertoire, even though they do not provide step-by-step procedures that map out particular courses of action? These ideas can provide orientations, variations, or additions to be built into a teacher–researcher's professional routines and procedures. Readers might ask themselves the following questions as they explore ways to enhance the quality of their professional lives, their students' school experiences or the experience of investigating their research "subjects":

What am I trying to achieve? What are my goals and objectives? What content and activities have I planned?

How am I doing this? How can I organize myself to include others in making these decisions?

Who can help me set my goals and objectives, plan relevant teaching–learning strategies, and select appropriate content? Who will benefit from this process? In what ways?

When and where can we do this work together?

Why, ultimately, am I doing this?

REFERENCES

Acker, S. (1995). Gender and teachers work. In M. Apple (Ed.), *Review of research in education, No. 21* 1995–1996. Washington, DC: American Educational Research Association.
Alexander, P., Murphy, P. K., & Woods, B. (1996). Of squalls and fathoms: Navigating the seas of educational innovation. *Educational Researcher, 25*(3), 31–39.
Aoki, T. (1992). Layered voices of teaching: The uncannily correct and the elusively true. In W. Pinar & W. Reynolds (Eds.), *Understanding curriculum as phenomenological and deconstructed text* (pp. 17–23). New York: Teachers College Press.
Aronowitz, S., & Giroux, H. (1987). *Education under siege: The conservative, liberal, and radical debate over schooling.* London: Routledge & Kegan Paul.
Bowers, C., & Flinders, D. (1990). *Responsive teaching: An ecological approach to classroom patterns of language, culture and thought.* New York: Teachers College Press.
Brown, R. (1992). Max Van Manen and pedagogical human science research. In W. Pinar & W. Reynolds (Eds.), *Understanding curriculum as phenomenological and deconstructed text.* New York: Teachers College Press.
Casey, K. (1995). The new narrative research in education. In M. Apple (Ed.), *Review of research in education, No. 21*, 1995–1996. Washington, DC: American Educational Research Association.
Davies, P., & Gribbin, J. (1991). *The matter myth: Beyond chaos and complexity.* London: Penguin.
Derrida, J. (1976). *Of grammatology.* Baltimore: Johns Hopkins University Press.
Fish, S. (1980). *Is there a text in this class? The authority of interpretive communities.* Cambridge, MA: Harvard University Press.
Foucault, M. (1972). *The archeology of knowledge.* New York: Random House.
Fuhrman, S. (1995). Introduction: Recent research on education reform. *Educational Researcher, 24*(9), 4–5.
Harvey, D. (1989). *The condition of postmodernity.* London: Blackwell.
Hicks, D. (1995). Discourse, learning, and teaching. In M. Apple (Ed.), *Review of Research in Education, No. 21*, 1995–1996. Washington, DC: American Educational Research Association.
Hunter, M. (1986). *Mastery teaching.* El Segundo, CA: TIP.
Kirst, M. (1995). Recent research on intergovernmental relations in education policy. *Educational Researcher, 24*(9), 18–22.
Lyotard, J. F. (1984). *The postmodern condition: A report on knowledge.* Minneapolis: University of Minnesota Press.
McClaren, P. (1989). *Life in schools: An introduction to critical pedagogy in the foundations of education.* New York: Longman.
Noddings, N. (1986). Fidelity in teaching, teacher education, and research for teaching. *Harvard Educational Review, 56*, 496–510.
Persig, R. (1974). *Zen and the art of motorcycle maintenance.* New York: Bantam.
Sprick, R. (1986). *Discipline in the secondary classroom.* West Nyack, NY: Center for Applied Research in Education.

Appendix: Syllabus of Qualitative Research for Educators

DEPARTMENT OF EDUCATIONAL CURRICULUM AND INSTRUCTION

EDCI 689-110 SPECIAL TOPIC
QUALITATIVE RESEARCH FOR EDUCATORS

PRELIMINARY SYLLABUS

INTRODUCTION

Qualitative research methods provide the means to enable educators to enhance their understanding of a broad range of educational issues. This class is designed to furnish participants with the knowledge and skills required to implement qualitative research projects in educational settings.

The course will be relevant to those who intend to use qualitative methods for basic research, but will be particularly useful for educators who wish to apply qualitative research methods to the solution of specific problems in classrooms, schools, and other educational settings.

OBJECTIVES

To develop and extend an understanding of the rationale and methodology of qualitative research.

To develop and extend qualitative research skills.

To practice qualitative research processes in educational settings.

TEACHING/LEARNING PROCESSES

The class will participate in a diverse array of learning activities, including individual presentations, group projects, field work, role playing, skills development exercises, discussions, dialogue, monologue, writing, reacting, critiquing, analyzing, and synthesizing.

CONTENT

The assumptions and methodologies of qualitative research.

Qualitative research skills, including focusing, entry, observation, interviewing, documenting, recording, analyzing data, reporting.

Application of qualitative methods to educational settings.

REQUIREMENTS

Three projects, to be negotiated with the instructor according to the level of understanding and skills development required by individual student needs.

TEXTS

Basic Texts

Spradley, J. (1979). *The ethnographic interview.* New York: Holt, Rinehart & Winston.
Denzin, N. (1989). *Interpretive interaction.* Newbury Park, CA.: Sage.
Guba, E., & Lincoln, Y. (1989). *Fourth generation evaluation.* Newbury Park, CA: Sage.

Extension Texts

(For students who have completed a qualitative methods course.)

Whyte, W. (1984). *Learning from the field.* Newbury Park, CA: Sage.
Marcus, G., & Fischer, M. (1986). *Anthropology as cultural critique.* Chicago: University of Chicago Press.

COLLEGE OF EDUCATION

DEPARTMENT OF EDUCATIONAL CURRICULUM AND INSTRUCTION

EDCI 689-110 QUALITATIVE RESEARCH FOR EDUCATORS

SUPPLEMENTAL SYLLABUS

GOALS

The course will enable participants to acquire and extend their knowledge of the following:

The nature and purposes of qualitative research.
Characteristics of qualitative research.
Types of qualitative research.
Qualitative research processes.

Participants will develop skills that enable them to:

Plan and implement qualitative research projects.
Apply qualitative research processes to the solution of problems in educational and other settings.
Evaluate qualitative research.
Discuss the complex issues related to qualitative research methodologies.

CONTENT

Philosophic Issues

Purposes of qualitative research.
Scientific method and qualitative research.
The relationship between qualitative and quantitative research.
Objectivity and subjectivity.
Validity.
Reliability.
Rigor.
Ethics.

Ethnographic Method

Focus
Entry
Data collection
Data recording
Analysis and interpretation of data
Reporting
Applications

SCHEDULE

Timing of learning experiences will be flexible to ensure that participants learn at a rate consistent with their educational needs and objectives. The following schedule provides approximate goals for completion of learning activities.

WEEK ONE

Content

Orientation to qualitative research.
Data collection: interview.
Data recording.

Sources

Basic: Spradley.
Advanced: Whyte.

WEEK TWO

Content

Data collection and recording: interview and observation.
Thick description.
Planning and implementing group project.
Planning individual project.

Sources

Basic: Spradley; supplementary readings; Denzin.
Advanced: Whyte; supplementary readings.

WEEK THREE

Content

Interpretation.
Reporting.
Other applications.
Group project: interpretation and report.
Individual project: data collection and analysis.

Sources

Basic: Denzin; Guba and Lincoln; supplementary readings.
Advanced: Whyte, Marcus, and Fischer.

WEEK FOUR

Content

Reporting.
Evaluating.
Philosophical issues.
Group project: evaluation of individual project: Data collection and analysis.

Sources

Basic: Denzin; Guba and Lincoln; supplementary readings.
Advanced: Marcus and Fischer; supplementary readings.

WEEK FIVE

Content

Evaluating.
Philosophical issues.
Applications.
Individual project: analysis, interpretation, reporting, and evaluation.

Sources

Basic: Guba and Lincoln; supplementary readings.
Advanced: Marcus and Fischer; supplementary readings.

MAJOR LEARNING ACTIVITIES

Participants in this class will develop and complete three major projects during
this course:

1. Group project: an ethnographic study of a classroom environment.
2. Individual project: an ethnographic study of an educational setting.
3. Portfolio: an organized portfolio of information and materials that will
   act as a resource for future research activity.

Individuals may negotiate variations from these activities, according to their
educational, academic, or professional needs.

SUPPLEMENTARY READINGS

Supplementary readings will be drawn from the following:

E. Stringer,   *Socially responsive educational research.*

J. Spradley,   *Making ethnographic observations.*

G. Berreman, *Is anthropology alive?*

H. Varenne,   *Doing the anthropology of America.*

L. Dunne,   *Pearls, pith, and provocation.*

American Anthropological Association, *General principles of professional
      responsibility.*

B. Naidu et al., *Researching heterogeneity.*

C. Geertz,   *Deep play: Notes on a Balinese cock fight.*

R. Bogdan & S. Biklen, *Eight common questions about qualitative research.*

J. Stacey,   *Can there be a feminist ethnography?*

B. Tedlock,   *From participant observation to observation of participation.*

C. Geertz,   *Thick description: Toward an interpretive theory of culture.*

A. Nihlen,   *Schools as centers of reflection and inquiry.*

J. Lipka,   *A cautionary tale of curriculum development.*

C. Hartman,   *A task analysis of solution focused parent–teacher conferenc-
      ing.*

Contributors

Mary Frances Agnello   is a former classroom teacher of English and French. Her bachelor's degree is from the University of Texas at Austin, and her masters degree is from Texas A&M University. She teaches foundations of education at the University of Texas at San Antonio, and secondary methods in an associated professional development school. Her interests are democratic educational practices and effective student engagement through improved teacher–student relations.

Sheila Conant Baldwin   a high-school teacher with over 15 years' experience, has taught courses in language arts, reading, English as a second language, and American culture studies. She has a BA in sociology from the University of Mississippi, an MEd with an emphasis in reading, and a PhD in curriculum and instruction with an emphasis in multicultural education from Texas A&M University. Her interest is promoting collaboration between educators and students in the exploration and implementation of alternative instructional approaches in public-school classrooms.

Lois McFadyen Christensen   is an assistant professor in the Department of Curriculum and Instruction at the University of Alabama at Birmingham. Her research interests include the application of ethnographic methods to teachers-as-researchers in elementary preservice and inservice education and in social studies. She is currently engaged in a professional development school partnership between an urban middle school in Birmingham and the university.

Deana Lee Philbrook Henry   holds a BS in economics from the University of Illinois, an MS in community development from the University of Missouri, and a PhD in Adult and extension education from Texas A&M University. She is co-facilitator of leadership development and community research with the Frankford Group Ministry, a network of agencies begun by four inner-city United Methodist congregations to help develop their neighborhood and its people, spiritually, socially, and economically. With her husband, Kenneth, Deana has helped initiate a new program in participatory action research as an experiential form of leadership development. Her particular interests are community-based and experiential learning, research as learning, and the church and community development.

Kenneth Ivan Henry holds a BS in accounting from the University of Illinois, an MS in community development from the University of Missouri, and a PhD in urban and regional science from Texas A&M University. With Deana, he is co-facilitator of leadership development and community research with the Frankford Group Ministry. For many years Kenneth and Deana, as staff members of the Ecumenical Institute-Institute of Cultural Affairs, worked at village and urban community development. Kenneth's particular interests are the use of community-based ethnographic research in social planning, using the Internet and distance education to enable participatory research among dispersed communities, and improving systems that incorporate the voices of community residents in local organizational planning.

Terresa Payne Katt is a doctoral candidate in the College of Education at Texas A&M University. She has extensive experience in elementary schools as a classroom teacher, teacher-as-researcher, and curriculum coordinator, with particular interests in language and literacy development. She has taught in a university teacher preparation program and is currently principal of South Knoll Elementary School in College Station, Texas.

Patricia Gathman Nason is assistant professor at the University of North Carolina at Charlotte where she teaches graduate and undergraduate science methods, analysis of teaching, and computer technology. She is facilitator of a professional development school, co-principal investigator and project coordinator of Technology Tools for Mathematics and Science Learning, co-leader of the North Carolina Rainforest Workshop in Peru, and is engaged with faculty in designing and implementing a vision of excellence for the Middle Grades Program at University of North Carolina, Charlotte. Her research interests focus on how pre- and in-service teachers construct understanding of their own learning as well as of their students'.

Vicky Newman is assistant research professor at the Institute for Families in Society at the University of South Carolina in Columbia, South Carolina. Before to her appointment at the institute, she was a lecturer in the Department of English at Texas A&M University and a visiting lecturer in the Department of Educational Psychology at the University of South Carolina. In addition to her work in community development, she is engaged in a cultural studies project about representations of teachers in the cinema. Her other research interests include the significance of landscape, sense of place in community, and cultural constructions of silence.

Rhonda Petty is a doctoral candidate at Texas A&M University. She teaches at an elementary school in a small rural town in Texas.

Ernie Stringer has a BA and a BEd from the University of Western Australia and an MA and a PhD from the University of Illinois at Champaign-Urbana. His early work as primary teacher and school principal in West Australia and Britain was complemented by work in teacher education programs at Curtin University of Technology in West Australia. Since 1983 he has worked in the Centre for Aboriginal Studies at Curtin University where, in conjunction with Aboriginal staff and community people, he has participated in the development of various education and community development programs and services. He engages his interests in sociology, anthropology and philosophy through explorations of postmodern social theory and qualitative and interpretative research methods. He is currently engaged in the development of postgraduate programs in the Centre for Aboriginal Studies at Curtin University.

Patsy S. Tinsley-Batson is a pioneer in the emerging distance learning industry. She has worked in the development and implementation of interactive-instructional television networks for more than 20 years and in the mid 1980s founded the first private satellite network in the United States to serve public schools. Her research interests are primarily action based and focus on how to ensure user satisfaction in emerging paradigms of distance learning, how to develop and support technology-based communities, and how to support wider diffusion of successful innovations in distance education. She serves as president of Satellite Learning Systems Corporation, a Texas-based research and consulting firm.

Index